Advance praise for

# *Voice Applications with Alexa and Google Assistant*

*Dustin Coates's book is not just a grounded, comprehensive how-to guide to voice app development. As a lead developer, what separates his approach from others is the conceptual sensitivity he has toward the hardest problems in multimodal interface and voice-activated AI: for example, building for the changing physical contexts in which users talk to their computers. These problems sometimes exist outside of the code lines but are central to getting the experience right for humans. His book is a great place to start on that quest.*

—Lin Nie, Research Scientist
in Psychology/HCI, Dataminr

Voice Applications for Alexa and Google Assistant *is an indispensable reference for voice practitioners, whether new to the field or a grizzled veteran. The book provides a concise, helpful overview of state-of-the-art voice design practices, as well as detailed, hands-on guidance on how to build for these platforms. It covers the essential topics voice developers need to understand—entity resolution, dialog management, SSML, even design best practices. I highly recommended it to anyone looking to better understand building for voice—they will come away with a stronger conceptual* and *practical grasp of how to do it.*

—John Kelvie, Cofounder and CEO, Bespoken

*I find Dustin's writing so valuable because it weaves together high-level concepts with super pragmatic, in-the-trenches explanations at the SDK level with code samples. There are so many moving parts to these ecosystems, and trying to piece them all together without some guidance can be really daunting. I wish this book had existed when I started out.*

—John Gillilan, Creator, Chop Chop Alexa Skill;
and Founder, bondad.fm

*Every few years an entirely new technology opens up a gold rush for entrepreneurial developers. Back in 2007, it was mobile apps. Now, it's voice applications powered by Alexa and Google Assistant. This book walks developers through all the steps required to build professional-grade voice applications. It's one of the few books that teach development on both the Alexa and Google Assistant platforms. The author has done a wonderful job of walking the reader through the steps of building robust, intuitive voice applications and getting them published.*

—Conor Redmond, Manager of Software
Infrastructure, InComm Product Control

# Voice Applications
## for Alexa and
## Google Assistant

DUSTIN COATES

Foreword by Max Amordeluso

MANNING
SHELTER ISLAND

Manning Publications Co.
20 Baldwin Road
PO Box 761
Shelter Island, NY 11964

| | |
|---|---|
| Development editor: | Kristen Watterson |
| Technical development editor: | Mike Jensen |
| Review editor: | Ivan Martinović |
| Production editor: | Lori Weidert |
| Copy editor: | Andy Carroll |
| Proofreader: | Keri Hales |
| Technical proofreader: | David Cabrero |
| Typesetter: | Happenstance Type-O-Rama |
| Cover designer: | Marija Tudor |

ISBN 9781617295317
Printed in the United States of America

# brief contents

# contents

# *foreword*

As an Alexa Evangelist, I work hand-in-hand with developers and brands from around the world in creating delightful voice user interfaces (VUIs), and I get to meet a lot of interesting and creative people. They range from novice developers curious about this new trend to seasoned pros with experience in creating Alexa skills. Dustin is not only a pro, he went a step beyond by writing this book. So when he asked me to write a foreword, I happily accepted, as I knew the quality of his work. This is a practical book, and one that you can use to quickly get up to speed on one of the defining technologies of our time. "Defining technologies of our time? Slow down, Max!" you might be thinking—but hear me out.

I grew up surrounded by the marvels of science fiction. My younger years were filled with talking cars and computers that were accessible from anywhere and seemed to know everything. Today, these entertaining fantasies of the past have become reality.

Cloud-based voice services, such as Alexa, are now able to understand us and our endless variety of voices and accents. Now our cars are able to converse with us. We can ask our living rooms to be warmer and our headsets when the next bus is coming. We are living the beginning of an era in which ambient computing will give us easier access to technology from wherever we are.

Periodically, something arrives that dramatically changes how we use technology. In just the last 20 years, we already have gone through two of these pivotal moments: both the World Wide Web (soon we'll forget it was called that) and smart phones, with their ubiquity, are now integral parts of the lives of billions of people. Both technologies have changed how we access information and how we get the things that matter to us done. Some of the largest companies in the world today were born out of these innovations. The innovation opportunities represented by voice are comparable. Voice is redefining how we talk to computers—literally. Today we are living in the initial phases of this technological era. A new wave of occasions has arrived.

If you feel like you have missed the boat on the web and mobile revolutions, this is your chance to enter a new industry early. It's day one for voice, and you can be a pioneer of this new technology. Embrace the voice revolution, and start building delightful Alexa skills using this book today.

Thank you, Dustin, for bringing voice forward.

—Max Amordeluso, EU Lead Evangelist Alexa

# *preface*

I remember a discussion I had with my coworkers not long after I got my Amazon Echo. I had been lucky and bought one on a whim when Amazon first announced the device, and I didn't have to wait months like many of my colleagues did. I told them it was pretty great, but it wasn't perfect. "You're used to waiting for a computer to start listening to you. With the Echo, you almost have to train yourself to speak naturally." That's right. Amazingly, the problem was that it worked too well. I, of course, wanted to extend this thing and bring my own spin to it. I had to wait a few months, but eventually Amazon brought "skills" to Alexa. I dove right in, at that time building exclusively for my own benefit.

Google's announcement of the Google Home device was welcome news, too. I rely on so many Google products day-to-day. My music provider of choice is Google Play Music, my wife and I chat during the day on Hangouts, I use Google Calendar, and more. My interest was strong enough that I flew to the United States just to pick up a device. (Well, that and to see my then girlfriend, now wife, who was still living in Brooklyn.) Of course I was going to start building Actions for the Assistant, too.

When Manning reached out to me to ask if I wanted to write this book, I thought, "Yeah, let's do it!" I've had absurd amounts of fun building for these platforms throughout the years. But there was some frustration, too. I made a lot of mistakes and had to learn from a lot of different sources. There were great books out there, but none that I felt really targeted developers. That's what I set out to write—a book for professional or amateur developers who want to code voice applications for Alexa and Google Assistant while learning the principles of what makes a good voice experience. Along the way, the team at Manning and I saw the book evolve due to changes in the ecosystem as well as reader feedback. And midway, both Amazon and Google decided to rewrite their SDKs, which led to a rewrite of this book.

Broad voice applications are still new, and I don't believe we've yet seen the height of what developers can build. I hope that working through this book gets you on the way to creating voice applications that will blow us all away. Or, at the very least, I hope you have fun and learn. Thank you for reading.

# acknowledgments

I never imagined how many people would work to put together this book when I first started writing it. While the words came from me, this book wouldn't have come together had it been me alone. The whole team at Manning has been great and deserves all the thanks in the world, but I want to highlight Kristen Watterson and Brian Sawyer especially. Kristen, thank you for helping me get to the finish line, providing practical feedback on my chapters and being an all-around useful sounding board. Brian, thank you for selling me on the idea of writing a book on voice applications and getting me excited that this was possible! Thank you as well to Richard Watternbarger for the guidance you provided during the first half of the writing process. And special thanks to Max Amordeluso for graciously agreeing to write the foreword and endorsing my book.

I would also like to thank all of the reviewers, who provided valuable feedback: Asif Karedia, Brian Tarbox, Conor Redmond, Dan Kacenjar, David Cabrero, Ferit Topcu, Jacopo Biscella, James Matlock, James Nyika, Jasba Simpson, Markus Breuer, Michael Jensen, Ozgur Ozturk, Patrick Regan, Prabhuti Prakash, Raffaella Ventaglio, Richard Meinsen, Sambasiva Andaluri, and Thomas Peklak.

A special thank-you, of course, to my wife Kate: thank you for your support and advice. It's true: I couldn't have done this without you.

# *about this book*

## Who should read this book

By the end of this book, I want you to be able to build voice applications for both Alexa and the Google Assistant platforms. I want you to understand the code necessary, and I want you to understand how information moves through a request between human and computer. Finally, I want you to understand the principles that provide a strong voice user experience.

To learn all of this, we'll build a number of voice applications. Therefore, this book is ideal for anyone who wants to learn by doing and who has at least a basic understanding of programming. We'll use JavaScript as our language of choice, although you don't need to understand advanced JavaScript to follow along. I want you to focus on what we are doing to build the *voice* applications, so sometimes, I'll explain portions of the JavaScript code that might be unfamiliar to those who don't use the language regularly. Nonetheless, this book does not try to teach JavaScript.

## How this book is organized: A roadmap

There are 12 chapters in *Voice Applications for Alexa and Google Assistant*. Because I strongly believe that building voice applications is as much about understanding the opportunities and limitations of voice, I have included these lessons throughout the chapters and I use code to illustrate the lessons. Still, there are several chapters that focus almost exclusively on the voice user experience. Altogether, there are four chapters that focus on voice UIs, four that focus on Alexa, and four that focus on Google Assistant.

- *Chapter 1*—What a voice UI is, and how speech becomes a request
- *Chapter 2*—How to build an Alexa skill and deploy it

- *Chapter 3*—How to build for voice user interfaces and how they differ from graphical user interfaces
- *Chapter 4*—How the Alexa Skills Kit CLI and entity resolution allow you to build skills faster and build skills that are more robust
- *Chapter 5*—How to use state and information storage to remember a user's progress through a skill
- *Chapter 6*—How to use context and favorites to introduce conversational best practices
- *Chapter 7*—How to make voice applications sound more human through discourse markers and SSML
- *Chapter 8*—How to direct the flow of a conversation through questions and dialogs, as well as handling errors
- *Chapter 9*—How to understand the differences between Actions SDK and Dialogflow actions, and build your first application for Google Assistant
- *Chapter 10*—How to unite screen and voice in a multimodal Google Assistant application
- *Chapter 11*—How to add push interactions to the Google Assistant application
- *Chapter 12*—How to build applications with the Actions SDK

If you are completely new to building on the Alexa and Google Assistant platforms, I recommend that you read this book in the order presented. Some projects continue in subsequent chapters, so you will need the code from the previous chapter to fully follow along in the next one. There is much less overlap between the Alexa and Google Assistant chapters, although you learn some voice user experience best practices in writing your code as well. You could, however, jump immediately to chapters 9 or 12 if you wanted to start with the Assistant platform.

## About the code

This book contains many examples of source code both in numbered listings and in line with normal text. In both cases, source code is formatted in a `fixed-width font like this` to separate it from ordinary text. Sometimes code is also **in bold** to highlight code that has changed from previous steps in the chapter, such as when a new feature adds to an existing line of code.

In many cases, the original source code has been reformatted; we've added line breaks and reworked indentation to accommodate the available page space in the book. In rare cases, even this was not enough, and listings include line-continuation markers (➥). Additionally, comments in the source code have often been removed from the listings when the code is described in the text. Code annotations accompany many of the listings, highlighting important concepts.

I've uploaded all of the code to a GitHub repository, which you can find at https://github.com/dustincoates/voice-applications. It's organized by chapter, which gives you the ability to jump immediately to a chapter or verify that your code is correct from a previous chapter.

## liveBook discussion forum

Purchase of *Voice Applications for Alexa and Google Assistant* includes free access to a private web forum run by Manning Publications where you can make comments about the book, ask technical questions, and receive help from the author and from other users. To access the forum, go to https://livebook.manning.com/#!/book/voice-applications -for-alexa-and-google-assistant/discussion. You can learn more about Manning's forums and the rules of conduct at https://livebook.manning.com/#!/discussion.

Manning's commitment to our readers is to provide a venue where a meaningful dialog between individual readers and between readers and the author can take place. It is not a commitment to any specific amount of participation on the part of the author, whose contribution to the forum remains voluntary (and unpaid). We suggest you try asking the author some challenging questions lest his interest stray! The forum and the archives of previous discussions will be accessible from the publisher's website as long as the book is in print.

## about the author

**Dustin A. Coates** is a web developer and web development instructor. He has taught hundreds of students online and offline at General Assembly. Dustin also developed popular courses for OneMonth.com and the European nonprofit Konexio, which teaches refugees how to code.

## about the cover illustration

The figure on the cover of *Voice Applications for Alexa and Google Assistant* is captioned "Woman from Dalmatia." This illustration is taken from a recent reprint of Balthasar Hacquet's *Images and Descriptions of Southwestern and Eastern Wends, Illyrians, and Slavs*, published by the Ethnographic Museum in Split, Croatia, in 2008. Hacquet (1739–1815) was an Austrian physician and scientist who spent many years studying the botany, geology, and ethnography of many parts of the Austrian Empire, as well as the Veneto, the Julian Alps, and the western Balkans, inhabited in the past by peoples of many different tribes and nationalities. Hand-drawn illustrations accompany the many scientific papers and books that Hacquet published.

Morlachs were a rural population that lived in the Dinaric Alps in the western Balkans hundreds of years ago. Many of them were shepherds who migrated in search of better pastures for their flocks, alternating between the mountains in the summer and the seashore in the winter. They were also called "Vlachs" in Serbian and Croatian. The rich diversity of the drawings in Hacquet's publications speaks vividly of the uniqueness and individuality of Alpine and Balkan regions just 200 years ago. This was a time when the dress codes of two villages separated by a few miles identified people uniquely as belonging to one or the other, and when members of an ethnic tribe, social class, or trade could be easily distinguished by what they were wearing.

Dress codes have changed since the nineteenth century, and the diversity by region, so rich at the time, has faded away. It is now hard to tell apart the inhabitants of different continents, let alone different towns or regions. Perhaps we have traded cultural diversity for a more varied personal life—certainly for a more varied and fast-paced technological life.

At a time when it's hard to tell one computer book from another, Manning celebrates the inventiveness and initiative of the computer business with book covers based on the rich diversity of regional life of two centuries ago, brought back to life by illustrations from collections such as this one.

# Introduction to voice first

The best technologies come to our lives in two ways: gradually, and then suddenly. This is how it went with voice. For decades we dreamed of computers with whom we could speak. We gradually got some of that, though it was particularly domain-specific and not something most people interacted with daily. Then, all of a sudden, a product came from Amazon that has millions of people wondering how they ever got by without it. The Echo brought voice-first computing to our daily lives.

If you're reading this book, you're probably already aware of the draw of voice-first platforms. Perhaps you even have a voice-first device, like an Amazon Echo or Google Home, in your living room. Because of this, it can be difficult to remember just how out-there the idea of voice first was when Amazon announced the Echo a few years back. If you were to look at articles commenting on the announcement and count the number of paragraphs before you saw a variation on the phrase "no one saw this coming," you wouldn't be counting for long.

1

Building on voice-first platforms means focusing on the big players in voice first today: Amazon, Google, and Microsoft. These are the companies that have opened their platforms to developer-driven extensions and allowed us to build with voice what we want to see. There are other tools, as you'll see, but these are the ones that most developers look to first.

> **NOTE** You have probably already noticed that Apple is not listed here. Although Siri is a globally popular digital assistant, and HomePod is sure to be a successful product, Apple has not decided to open it up to third-party developers.

Voice control is far from a new idea. Not only have we seen it for as long as there have been computers in pop culture (see *The Jetsons, Star Trek,* and *2001: A Space Odyssey*), but most of us have been interacting with it for years. Don't believe me? Call your bank or favorite airline and ask yourself what's on the other side.

Voice applications exist to help users complete their goals more efficiently by passing data between conversational actors and using conversational best practices that have evolved over millennia. In this book we'll use JavaScript and Node.js to design voice interfaces that users will enjoy using. You'll learn about the conceptual underpinnings of building for voice, and how to develop these voice-first experiences.

Voice-first platforms are still in their nascent days, but they're growing quickly. Think back to the first apps on iOS and Android, and compare those to what's on the App Store and Play Store today. Voice has the same opportunity, and the growth in the number of homes that have a voice-first device shows that people are eager for a new way to interact with their computers.

## 1.1    What is voice first?

Voice-first platforms have two defining characteristics. First, they are interacted with primarily through voice. Second, they are open for extension by third-party developers.

Compare your bank's phone-tree system to what a user can do on the Amazon Echo. The options on the Echo are, quite literally, limitless. Instead of the rigid structure we saw before, we now can have a more natural conversation:

> USER: *Alexa, ask Mega Bank to give me my balance.*
>
> ALEXA: *You currently have one thousand and four dollars in your checking account and two hundred sixteen in savings. Would you like to make a transfer?*
>
> USER: *No, thank you.*
>
> ALEXA: *Alright, have a great day!*

### Voice first isn't what you remember from your bank's phone system

There's a difference between the interactive voice response (IVR) systems of the past—like the one you interact with when calling your bank—and the voice-first platforms of today. Those automated IVR systems are constrained compared to what we're now working with. You know how it is:

"Thank you for calling Mega Bank. Please say balance to check your balance, please say pay bill to pay a bill, or say representative to speak with a representative."

IVR systems are designed for a tiny pool of choices and responses. Their ultimate goal is to get the caller to follow a decision tree to the desired outcome.

Not only can voice-first devices perform built-in functions, they can also search the web or take advantage of apps created specifically for the platform—"skills" in Alexa and Cortana parlance. This is the big difference between classical IVR systems and voice-first: voice first brings the web to voice.

Voice assistants were around before the Amazon Echo. Siri has been on iOS devices since 2011, Google Assistant has been on Android phones in one form or another since 2016, and Cortana has been bundled with the Xbox and Windows since 2015. This book will teach you how to code for Alexa and Google Assistant, but it will also change how you think about interactions. You will likely have come from platforms that rely on visual representations, which are secondary or absent on voice-first platforms.

A useful way to think about it is that voice first shifts the burden away from users and onto developers and designers. Think about all of the ways we "help" users on the web, and consider how we can do the same thing with voice first, as in figure 1.1.

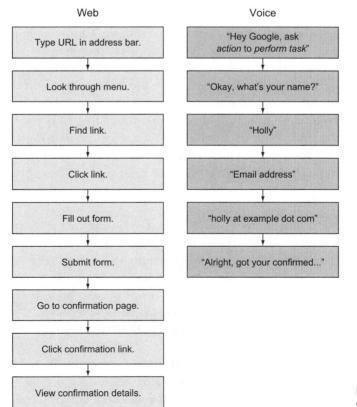

**Figure 1.1 Web flow compared to voice flow**

With voice first, we can't provide as much guidance, so getting it right the first time is even more important. An example is search results. On the web, you generally see a list of results—the famous "10 blue links"—on Google. With voice, no one wants to listen through 10 results to get the right one. There's a higher standard for skill builders to reach. As you can see in table 1.1, with voice the platform takes on more responsibility.

**Table 1.1    Shifting the responsibility from user to platform**

| Problem | Web solution | Voice-first solution |
|---------|-------------|---------------------|
| Pages with a large number of navigation options | Hide them behind drop-downs or hamburger menus. This says, in essence, "We couldn't decide what's most important, so here, you figure out what you want." | Make the options discoverable and intuitive. |
| Forms to fill out | Ask users to fill out information in exactly the right order, in exactly the right places, in exactly the right formats. | Handle input in a natural way, considering that what is "natural" can vary from person to person. |
| Information retrieval | Provide users with different options and ask them to decide which is most relevant to their needs. | Significantly limit the number of results that come back, often limiting them to only one result. That result needs to be relevant too. |

To be clear, voice first is not voice only. With the Echo Show, the addition of Alexa to televisions, and Google's connection of Google Home with the Chromecast, voice first is increasingly becoming *multimodal*—using multiple forms of interaction such as voice and display. This addition opens up opportunities for developers who want to bring new functionality to users while still retaining voice as the main interaction model.

Because this new world of voice-first platforms brings the web to voice, it has also brought along web developers. Owing to our expertise in building APIs and graphical user interfaces, creating voice interactions often doesn't come naturally. We can't simply take our web pages or apps and put them in a voice context. How can we design for voice in a way that uses the platform's strengths?

## 1.2    Designing for voice UIs

Voice user interface (VUI) design is how users interact with voice-first platforms. Voice is both something where most developers have little experience and something where they have the most experience. We have conversations every day, from nearly the moment we wake up to when we go to bed. We've been conversing with others since we were tiny, and we've been learning from conversations since we were in the womb. Because of this, we often take for granted what makes a good conversation. Thankfully, there are guidelines that outline what makes a natural, flowing conversation and what leads to misunderstanding and frustration.

It's good to remember that voice is the most natural interaction mechanism we have for interacting with our computers. Think about it: How often do you swipe with your finger when not using a smartphone or tablet? Did our ancestors regularly perform movements that are similar to typing on a keyboard? We all know how to use our voice, however.

To build a good VUI, you want to consider what makes for a good conversation partner outside of a VUI setting. Then factor in the limitations posed by half of the conversation being handled through code. Think about the best people you've interacted with in a public setting, like a hotel concierge or a fast-food clerk. They likely had personalities that were appropriate for the setting. You'd expect a bartender to be outgoing and energetic, but bring that same personality to a nurse in an ICU, and something would seem amiss.

These people gave you the right amount of information for your inquiry, asked follow-up questions if something wasn't clear, and considered the context around you in the conversation. Asking for the restrooms doesn't require an answer that tells you there are restrooms on the first, third, fifth, and sixth floors, and that there used to be restrooms on the second floor but they are closed for the next month.

These conversational savants also helped you out if you got in a jam. Maybe you answered a question in an unexpected way. If you didn't know what to do, the person was ready with advice or worked with you to formulate your question. You've probably experienced the awkwardness of someone who stood there, unhelpfully looking at you while you fumbled through your thoughts. Don't let your VUI imitate that person.

A good VUI would look like this:

> ALEXA: *Hello! Welcome to Mega Bank. What do you want to do today?*
>
> USER: *Check my balance.*
>
> ALEXA: *Okay, your balance is one thousand, five hundred dollars.*

The list of possibilities is long, but the user doesn't know what can be done. This opens up the possibility that a user might want to do something that isn't supported. The VUI can handle it at that point by providing options explicitly:

> ALEXA: *Hello! Welcome to Mega Bank. What do you want to do today?*
>
> USER: *Buy stocks.*
>
> ALEXA: *Sorry, buying stocks by voice isn't supported. You can check your balance, hear recent transactions, or find out more about your branch. Which would you like to do?*

VUI is about anticipating and understanding users' intentions, guiding them through the process, and giving them the right information and no more. In later chapters, we'll take a deep look at how we can use conversational qualities that we've learned from birth to make VUIs that users want to come back to. The first thing to do, though, is to understand the user. To do that, we need to see how voice-first platforms work.

## 1.3 *Anatomy of a voice command*

How do voice-first platforms work? After all, it's not simply a matter of speaking to the device and hearing the response. There's a flow of sound to information to code to text and back to sound. This flow only has a few steps, but understanding each step will help us understand why certain workarounds are necessary, avoid possible traps, and enable a fuller use of the platforms.

There are small differences in implementation and flow between the different platforms, but there are even more commonalities. The voice-first device streams the user's speech to the platform, which in turn performs the natural language understanding (NLU). After the platform completes the NLU step, it passes the now-structured data to the fulfillment, which is developer-created code that contains skill-specific logic. The fulfillment builds the response into a structured format, and reverses the process. The response goes back to the platform, and the platform transforms the text to speech. Finally, that speech is streamed back to the user. Speech to data, and then data to speech again. As you can see, voice-first development involves several pieces, each handling a single step of the flow, passing data to the next piece, and combining to build a voice experience.

Take sports-fan Molly, who is a perpetual believer in her local team's chances to win the World Series. Molly has an Echo in her living room. Sitting on the couch, she wonders aloud, "I wonder if Houston won the game last night?" No one's around to answer. Then Molly remembers something and says, "Alexa…" Immediately her Echo lights up and begins streaming audio to the Amazon servers. "Ask Houston Baseball to tell me who won the game last night."

The flow is illustrated in figure 1.2. Over on Amazon's servers, the Alexa platform begins to transform Molly's speech into text. Because she said "ask" after "Alexa," the platform can guess that she wants to use a skill. The platform looks at Molly's account and the skills she has enabled, trying to find one with the invocation name "Houston Baseball." Molly enabled one, so the platform starts to compare the phrases the developer of the skill has provided to what Molly actually spoke. This list of utterances maps to what the developer expects users will want to do, or their *intents*. In the utterances, the platform finds `ResultsIntent I wonder if Houston won the game {time}`. Alexa has found a close enough match belonging to the `ResultsIntent`, and it's a match with a slot.

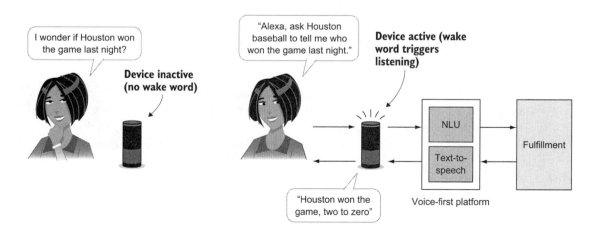

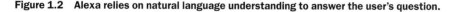
**Figure 1.2   Alexa relies on natural language understanding to answer the user's question.**

A *slot* is like a matching group inside a regular expression. The Alexa platform looks at the values the skill developer has provided as those that *should* show up in this space. Sports fan Molly's phrase doesn't match up with "yesterday" or "last week" or "the other day," but there it is: "last night." We've got a match. Alexa has all the information it needs from what Molly said: the intent (ResultsIntent) and the slot value (last night). It passes these, and information about the session, to the code that the skill developer has written to handle requests.

This code is known as the *fulfillment*, and the developer has placed the code on AWS Lambda using the Alexa Skills Kit Node.js SDK (ASK SDK). Because Lambda is built to handle one-off, short-lived requests, it's perfect for Alexa skills. The developer's code looks at the incoming request, sees that it's coming for the ResultsIntent, and emits an event for that intent. The developer wrote a handler for this intent, which listens for the event and matches the slot value "last night" to a time range in order to reach out to another API that will grab the score of the game.

Houston has won! The fulfillment puts together a string that will say "Houston won the game, two to zero," and sends that as JSON back to the Alexa platform. The platform takes the text, transforms it into audio, and streams it back to Molly, who is happy to hear that the march to October continues strong.

Let's look at what that would look like in a generalized manner.

### 1.3.1 *Waking the voice-first device*

When we talk about voice first, we are often talking about stand-alone devices like the Amazon Echo, Google Home, and others. These platforms are also on other devices—for example, Google Assistant is loaded on most Android phones—but stand-alone devices make the interactions different. It's easy to shout out to your Echo, "Alexa, what is the weather going to be tomorrow?" before you go to bed. You're unlikely to do that with your phone sitting on the other side of the room. You'll be less sure that it can hear you, and the speaker may not be loud enough for you to hear the response.

To wake these stand-alone devices, a *wake word* is used. On the Amazon Echo, you can change it, but it comes with "Alexa" as the default ("Echo," "Amazon," and "Computer" are the other choices). Google uses *wake phrases*, with "Hey Google" or "OK Google" waking the device. Siri is similar, with "Hey Siri." What sets apart the wake word is that it is recognized locally. By doing the recognition locally, the devices can wake up quickly, and potential privacy concerns can be (partially) abated.

The device maintains a buffer of speech and reviews it, looking for the wake word. This sounds scary to a lot of people at first, but without constantly listening, the device wouldn't be able to wake when the wake word was said. You could say "Alexa," but you could alternatively say "alive," "Allegheny," or "Alex is my friend." The device keeps these sounds in the buffer and constantly reviews the words and phrases for recognition.

Once the wake word is invoked, the device starts streaming speech over the web for processing, and each platform uses different tooling for this process. Amazon has released its as a stand-alone product called AWS Lex, Google Assistant uses Dialogflow, and Cortana uses LUIS. These tools are forms of what's called natural language processing (NLP). Let's look at how this works.

### 1.3.2   *Introducing natural language processing*

First we should define the term: *NLP* is the process through which a computer can interact with natural language—natural language being what people speak, write, or read, such as English, French, or Hindi.

A large part of NLP is natural language understanding (NLU), which is how the computer takes a free-flowing conversation and extracts meaning. Thankfully we don't need to implement the technology that powers NLU in order to build our skills. That's one of the boons of the rise of voice first. We can use these technologies and plug in our functionality, just as we don't need to be experts in network stacks to build a website.

For Alexa, the NLU technology is chosen for us and goes directly through Amazon. For Google Assistant, we can bring our own, but the one most developers new to the platform will use is Google's Dialogflow.

Knowing how to implement NLU isn't necessary, but it is helpful to understand the general principles of NLU and what you can control.[1]

> **NOTE**   We are using the terms that the Alexa Skills Kit uses, but the principles are universal.

### 1.3.3   *How speech becomes text*

The most fundamental thing that these platforms need to know is how to transform what the user says into text. This is a difficult problem. Before you put the book away, rest assured that you won't need to implement speech-to-text yourself. But I'm a big believer that having a general understanding of what is happening under the hood will help you once you start to code.

To understand why this is such a difficult problem, let's first look at what goes into a conversation. This may seem far too theoretical, but let's follow this thread a bit.

A spoken conversation is made up of

- Multiple participants
- Nonverbal signals
- Context
- Sounds

In a conversation with a voice-first device, one of the participants will be the voice-first device itself. Beyond that, each participant in a conversation expects a certain set of behaviors, which we'll examine in chapter 2, and a computer is not exempted from these. The computer won't have access to the nonverbal signals, which provide valuable information in human-to-human conversations.[2] That makes the developer's job of understanding precisely what the user wants more difficult.

---

[1] For an examination of natural language understanding, you can start with *Natural Language Processing in Action* from Manning Publications (2019).

[2] Nick Morgan, *Power Cues: The Subtle Science of Leading Groups, Persuading Others, and Maximizing Your Personal Impact* (Harvard Business Review Press, 2014).

Every conversation has a context. Context allows for richer conversations and for things to go unsaid. When your boss says "This is fine," does he mean "This is good" because he's laconic? Or does he mean "I'm disappointed" because he's not someone to express negative emotions directly? Likewise, when a guest arrives to a wedding with a box in her hand asking "Where can I put this?" one might say "Just on the table over there" instead of "What would you like to put somewhere? A gift? Are you bride's side or groom's side? Please answer by first saying how many items you have" or even, "What is the box in your hand?" Because the participants are at a wedding, we can assume that the box is a gift. Sometimes context has explicit components (that table is the one for the gifts) and it always has implicit components (we all understand that we're at an event where people bring gifts).

The sounds are what most people think about when they think of communication, so part of the computer's job is separating sound that represents speech from other sounds. Humans do this as well. In fact, babies can tell the difference between speech sounds and other sounds starting from their very first day.[3]

Ultimately, what people in a conversation care about are not so much *sounds* as *words*. But what are words? (We're getting deeper into the theoretical world, I know!) For most of human existence, words have been groups of sounds that represented something, as writing (representing sound with symbols) is relatively recent. A certain group of sounds would represent "the large body of water over there," whereas another group of sounds would represent "that smaller body of water." The sound groupings that represent words are, in fact, approximations. Someone from Boston will make different sounds for "the green car" than someone from New Zealand. An old man with a deep, gravelly voice will make different sounds than a teenage girl. The computer needs to take these different sound groupings and transform them to text— in effect, *speech to text.*

With each word being made up of smaller sounds, the first task is to separate them into the smallest components—*phonemes.* There are about 44 phonemes in the English language depending on regional differences. With the sounds broken down into phonemes, the software compares the phonemes to what it already knows and groups those together to form words. The implication is that speech recognition software needs a lot of training data.

Even with significant training, transforming speech to text can be difficult. Background sounds, mumbled speech, and other factors can influence how much is ultimately understood. As a simple example, say out loud "I want it to go away" and "I wanted to go away." In normal speech, these sound practically identical, and with background noise it is even more difficult to distinguish between them. Most NLU software attempts to solve this problem by using statistical models. People are generally predictable and will say some combinations of words more than others. As an extreme example, the phrase "this towel is wet" will be more common than "this towel is debt." For a more nuanced example, "this towel is wetter than this one" may be more likely than "this towel is better than this one."

---

[3] Clifford Nass and Scott Brave, *Wired for Speech: How Voice Activates and Advances the Human-Computer Relationship* (MIT Press, 2007).

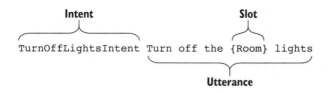

**Figure 1.3   The overall user goal (the intent), the intent-specific variable information (the slot), and how it's invoked (the utterance)**

Once the software understands *what* is being said, the next step is to understand what is desired from that speech, using intents, sample utterances, and slots, as in figure 1.3.

**NOTE**  We'll cover slots, intents, and sample utterances in more depth in chapter 2.

### 1.3.4   *Intents are the functions of a skill*

When you say to your spouse, "Will you please turn off the lights in the kitchen when you go to bed?" what do you want to happen? To us it's obvious: we've trained all our lives to derive meaning from conversations, and we can tell that you want your spouse to turn off some lights. Computers need to be told ahead of time, however, what certain words grouped together mean.

One way to give voice-first devices the ability to understand is through "skills" or "actions." These can be thought of as "apps" that extend the device. Written by third-party developers, skills provide capabilities that weren't previously in the device by connecting to external code or services.

For example, your device might have a smart-home skill that is connected to your lights, so you can stop bugging your spouse. This could be a simple skill that does only one thing: turn off the lights. That is, shutting off the lights is its only *intent*.

In reality, most skills will have multiple intents. Perhaps you have beefed up your smart-home skill so you can now

- Turn off the lights (`TurnOffLightsIntent`)
- Turn on the lights (`TurnOnLightsIntent`)
- Dim the lights (`DimLightsIntent`)

Your skill now has three distinct things it can do. It has three different intents. One way to visualize intents is to think of them as being similar to functions in your code.

Of course, conversing with a computer wouldn't be much fun if we had to say, "Alexa, trigger TurnOffLightsIntent" every time we wanted it done. The platforms need to learn how to know which intent we want. It does this by learning from sample utterances.

### 1.3.5   *Training the NLU with sample utterances*

One of the beautiful things about human language is how many different ways there are to say the same thing (even if, as we saw, some phrases are more statistically likely than others). A novel turn of phrase, or even a different word order, makes our conversations lively and prevents monotony from setting in. As is often the case, though, what's good for humans makes life more challenging for voice-first developers.

If there was only one way to say everything imaginable, we wouldn't need intents or sample utterances. We would say, "When a user says 'Turn out the lights,' then do this." Speech isn't this limited, so we need to provide the system with possible ways that a user might request an intent—sample utterances.

Sample utterances are possible phrases that a user might use to perform an action with Alexa. These utterances are then used to train the Alexa platform by building a statistical model that takes what the user says and matches it against what you said users might say. For example, if you have the utterances "turn up the volume" and "turn up the sound," it's unlikely that the speaker is discussing famed children's party performer Turnip the Clown. As anyone who has had to give an impromptu speech or toast can attest, speaking off the cuff can be difficult, and there are a lot of starts, stops, and filler words. The sample utterances are useful for providing an idea of what might be in there.

Sample utterances are mapped to intents. An intent will often have multiple sample utterances, but each phrase should be tied to a single intent. (Even humans have difficulties picking up on unspoken subtleties.) For the `TurnOffLightsIntent`, you might have the following sample utterances:

- "Turn off the lights"
- "Turn out the lights"
- "Turn off my lights"
- "Turn out my lights"
- "Shut out the lights"
- "Shut out my lights"
- "Flip the switch down for the lights"
- "Make the room pitch black"
- "I don't want the light on any more"
- "I don't want any more lights on"

There are undoubtedly more ways that a user could ask for this. In chapter 2, we'll discuss how to come up with sample utterances. The more utterances you provide to the system, the better it will understand the user and route their intents. Thankfully, you don't need to figure out in advance everything that could possibly be said: that would be the mark of a weak NLU. These systems will take the sample utterances and extrapolate from there.

Sample utterances are like incredibly lax conditionals whose job is to call the correct functions. You are telling the system, "If something *like* this is said, then invoke this specific intent."

Your skill is coming along, but it still falls short of your original request to your spouse: "Will you please turn off the lights in the kitchen when you go to bed?" You could create intents for every possible room, or you can use slots.

### 1.3.6   *Plucking pertinent information from spoken text*

If *intents* are *functions*, then *slots* are the *arguments* passed to a function. When you ask your spouse to turn off the lights in the kitchen on the way to bed, "turn off lights" is the intent—the general action the user wants to accomplish. The slots are pieces of information that can vary within a single action.

Slots must be tied to utterances so that the platform knows which parts of what's being said are the relevant parts that need to be plucked out and handled. Because utterances are always tied to intents, that means that slots are tied to intents as well. For example, the "turn off the lights" intent will have a slot for specifying which lights should be turned off.

Slots will generally be connected to a certain corpus of words (if it's helpful, you can think of slots as being "typed") that act as the training set for the NLU. For example, if your slots are in the domain of musicians, it's safe to guess that the user is referring to the "Beatles drummer" and not the "little drummer." You'll train the NLU in this by providing a list of expected values. A music skill could have an artists slot seeded with the top 5,000 artists, whereas a New York City subway skill would have a slot for subway stops seeded with all of the stop names.

These slots will appear in specific places in the sample utterances. It's generally easy for humans to pluck the relevant details from a conversation, but computers need some help. You want your spouse to not only turn off the lights, but the lights in a specific room. How does the computer know which room? Remember, the computer doesn't even know you're talking about rooms. You could as easily be talking about the white lights, the old lights, or the annoying lights. Providing guidance as to where the slot will likely appear when someone speaks, and combining it with the list of slot samples we discussed earlier, improves the chances of a successful match.

With the Alexa Skills Kit, you combine your slots with sample utterances like so:

- `TurnOffLightsIntent Turn off the {Room} lights`
- `TurnOffLightsIntent Turn off the lights in {Room}`
- `TurnOffLightsIntent In the {Room} turn off the lights`

Here `Room` refers to a specific slot type that has been defined and seeded with sample values, such as "kitchen," "living room," "dining room," "den." Using the slot and sample utterances together, the NLU can extrapolate to match these phrases and more:

- "Turn off the kitchen lights"
- "Turn off the living room lights"
- "Turn off the dining room lights"
- "Turn off the den lights"
- "Turn off the lights in the kitchen"
- "Turn off the lights in the living room"
- "Turn off the lights in the dining room"
- "Turn off the lights in the den"

Using this knowledge of *where* the pertinent information could be and *what* it could be, the Alexa platform can grab that information from the user's speech and send it back your way: the user wants to turn off the *kitchen* lights. You can then use that information in your fulfillment.

## 1.4 The fulfillment code that ties it all together

The *fulfillment* is the code that fulfills the user's request. This code can run on your own server, but most commonly it runs on a *serverless* platform. These platforms run code on demand, based on certain triggers. For voice first, two of the most common platforms are AWS Lambda and Google Cloud Functions.

In the fulfillment, you run all of the code necessary for the specific request. If you come from the web world, you can think of this as being like a controller. Most of this book is about fulfillment, so we'll discuss this in depth in later chapters.

A common slice of the fulfillment might look like the following. Notice that this code is tied to a particular intent and uses a slot that is defined elsewhere. This example fulfillment is nothing more than a glorified "Hello World" program that says how many letters are in a word.

Listing 1.1 Handling a request

```
const WordInfoIntent = {
  ...
  handle(handlerInput) {
    const word = this.event.request.intent.slots.word.value;
    const length = word.length;
    const firstLetter = word[0];
    const response = 'The word ' + word + ' is ' + length +
      ' letters long and begins with the letter ' + firstLetter;

    return handlerInput.responseBuilder
      .speak(response)
      .getResponse();
  }
}
```

The value of the word slot for the current intent for the current user interaction (request)

In the next chapter, you'll learn how to implement your own skill. What you need to know for now is that there is a *handler* (`WordInfoIntent` here) that maps to an intent with the same name. The handler is a function that assembles what the voice assistant is going to say (in this example, by combining the length and first letter of the word with explanatory text), and then emits that for the assistant to share with the user.

## 1.5 Telling the device what to say

After you run your code, you will generally need to send information back to the user. As mentioned before, this can be a multimodal experience—turning off the lights is also information—but it usually involves speaking back to the user. Most of the time, it is your responsibility to tell the device what to say.

The Alexa and Google Assistant platforms use something called Speech Synthesis Markup Language (SSML). It was created by the World Wide Web Consortium (W3C), it's based on XML, and it's used to differing degrees on Alexa, Google Assistant, and Cortana.

The simplest way to use SSML is to provide the speech inside the `<speak>` tag:

```
<speak>I'm going to turn off the lights now.</speak>
```

Wrapping the text inside `speak` tags is so fundamental to using SSML that inside the Alexa Skills Kit and Google Assistant tooling it's hidden away, and developers never need to worry about it. SSML gives developers the ability to change the prosody, or the manner of speaking. With SSML, you can make Alexa whisper, shout, speak slowly, specify the pronunciation of words, and more. Google Assistant can do many of these same functions, but it also adds its own, such as layering audio and responses. We'll look at SSML in chapter 7.

Put this all together, and the computer uses the text and the SSML guidance to respond to the user. The cycle has come full circle—the computer is now responding to the user, starting a conversation.

## Summary

- Voice interfaces require developers and designers to assume the burden of conforming to the users to help them complete actions, rather than the reverse.
- Data in a conversation flows back and forth between partners to complete an action.
- Building a voice application involves reliably directing this data between systems.
- Begin to think of requests in terms of intents, slots, and utterances.

# Building a call-and-response
# skill on Alexa

### This chapter covers

- Building with the Alexa Skills Kit SDK for Node.js
- Becoming acquainted with serverless platforms, including AWS Lambda
- Building a call-and-response skill
- Handling intents
- Communicating with voice

The magic of being a coder is that you are able to create something from nothing—a web page to click on, an app to swipe, an algorithm to sort with. By the end of this chapter, you'll be able to make an app that talks. And not just talk, but *respond*. That's enough to shout, "It's alive! It's alive!"

Making Alexa talk involves two steps:

1. *The interaction model*—Teaching Alexa how to understand what's said
2. *The fulfillment*—Directing Alexa in how to respond

The skill you'll build in this chapter is a call-and-response skill; your user will say something and Alexa will respond. End of interaction. In future chapters, you'll build on top of the skill to make it even more interactive, but this will be sufficient to ease us into Alexa skill development.

We're trying to develop a skill that will be useful, so it should be one that doesn't require a lot of forethought by users. They shouldn't need to remember a bunch of complicated commands and steps. Indeed, one of the big themes of designing voice interfaces is guiding users, leading them to grasp intuitively what they can do. The skill will also need to provide useful information, ideally in a manner that's just as well suited, if not better suited, to voice as to mobile or the web.

If you're like me, one of your recurring goals is to wake up earlier. Yet I'm constantly bumping up against getting enough sleep. I put off thinking about this conflict until the morning, and half-awake Dustin is awful at making decisions. I would much prefer to have something that helps me understand if I'm going to be well rested the next day. Alexa is perfect for this. I can ask, no matter what I'm doing, and I'm always near my Echo when it's approaching bedtime.

By the end of this chapter, you'll have a skill that allows users to ask if they will be well rested in the morning, depending on how many hours of sleep they plan on getting and how well they slept the previous night.

> **NOTE**  A physical device is helpful, but not necessary, for testing your skills (and the same goes for Google Assistant apps later in the book). Simulators are also available for testing. The Amazon Developer Console that you'll use in this chapter has its own testing dashboard where you can interact with your skill, and Echosim.io is an in-browser Alexa simulator. You can additionally use Alexa on iPhone or Android through the Alexa app.

To build the sleep-tracker skill, there are three primary pieces that you'll need to connect: your skill's metadata and interaction model, which both live in the Amazon Developer Console, and your fulfillment, which is the code that will run in response to Alexa.

## 2.1  Skill metadata

To start building an Alexa skill, begin with the metadata. We'll fill this in from within the Amazon Developer Console, located at https://developer.amazon.com/alexa/console/ask. To test this on your Alexa device without any additional setup, you'll need to create the skill while logged in under the same account on which you use Alexa.

Once you've logged in, you should see where the list of skills you're creating will live, along with all of their top-level data, such as title, description, and status.

> **NOTE**  You may have also noticed inside the Developer Console the option for the Alexa Voice Service. This service gives developers of physical objects, like cars, smart speakers, or even washing machines, the tools to add Alexa to their products. For the amateur, Alexa can be added to a Raspberry Pi. Once installed, Alexa works similarly to any Echo device. Amazon's goal is to make Alexa a *platform*, rather than a *product*.

Start the skill-creation process by clicking the Create Skill button, as in figure 2.1. This leads to the first page for metadata, shown in figure 2.2. You'll need to give your new skill a name, which is what will be displayed to users in the Alexa app and in the Alexa skill store on the website. We'll use the name Sleep Tracker. The name doesn't affect how the skill functions, but it's incredibly important for skill discovery. Right now, the primary way for users to discover new skills for Alexa is by searching the skill store, and the name plays an important role in the results ranking—along with ratings, category, description, and skill developer name.

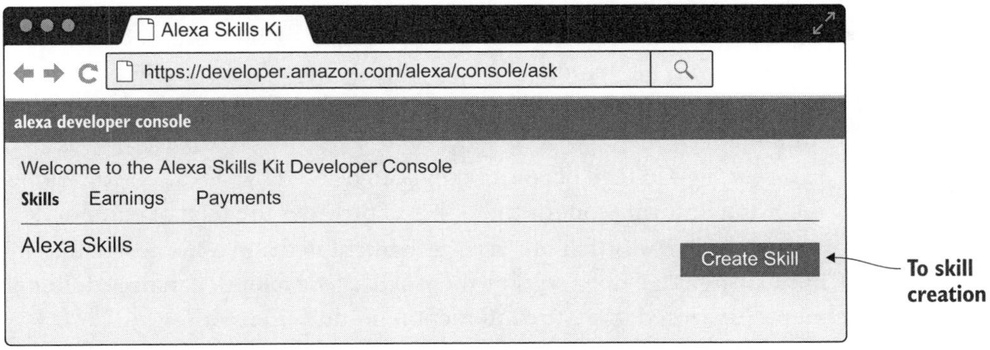

**Figure 2.1** Where to start creating a skill

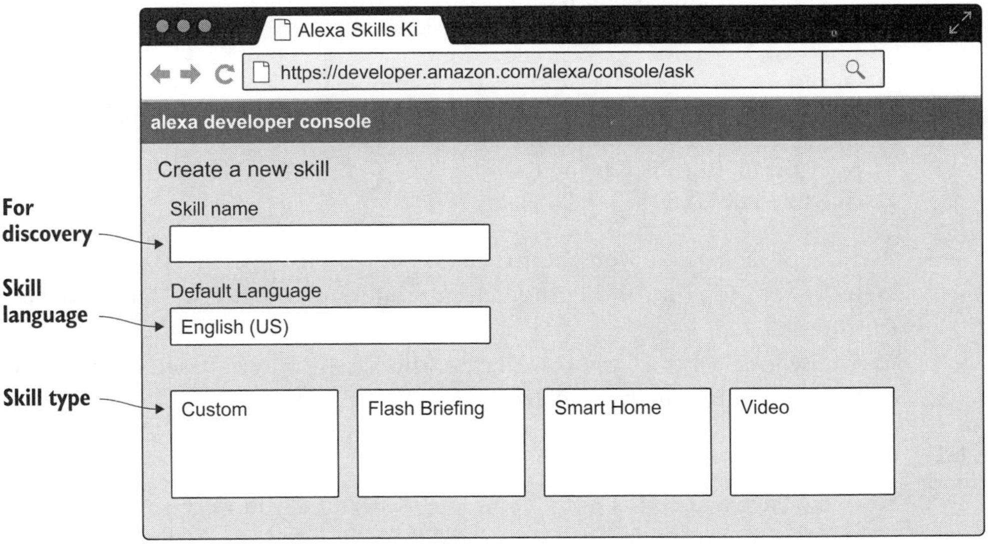

**Figure 2.2** Setting up the new skill

The next field is where you specify the default skill language. The language affects which utterances Alexa expects for built-in intents, such as the stop intent, as well as details for the local skill stores in which the skill is found. There is a big difference, of course, between English and German, but there are also differences between locales of the same language. For example, *speechcons* are exclamations you can add to a response to give it a more natural sound, such as "woohoo!" or "uh oh." They differ between locales, with some appearing only in one and not others. You can have skills across multiple languages use the same fulfillment, but for now we'll start with only an English variant.

Next up is the kind of skill type you're using:

- *Custom*—A skill in which the developer defines how the skill is invoked, which requests will be handled (the intents), how it's handled (the interaction model, including slots and sample utterances), and how Alexa responds (the fulfillment).
- *Flash briefing*—A feed of content that can be read by Alexa. The developer defines the listing information for the skill and provides the feed of content.
- *Smart home*—Skills that are used to control items in a home, such as lightbulbs, blinds, or garage openers. For these skills, a developer can only define the fulfillment. Amazon defines the interaction model and intents.
- *Music*—A skill for playing music. It comes with a prebuilt model for common interactions, such as playing, pausing, or shuffling music.
- *Video*—A skill that can display television and movie content. Amazon defines the intents and interaction model for this one as well, leaving the developer to create the fulfillment for handling requests.

**NOTE**   There's one more type of skill—the list skill. This skill will react to a user changing their Alexa to-do and shopping lists and is most often used by third-party list platforms to bring their services to the Alexa Skills Kit. It is not available from the Developer Console.

Our sleep-tracker skill won't control a home, read from a feed, or play music or video. We also want to control the interaction model in its entirety. That leaves us with the Custom skill type.

After you select the Custom skill type, choose the option to self-host your fulfillment code. Now we'll create the skill from scratch.

### 2.1.1   *Interaction model*

You now have a skill. It's not a complete skill, but if you were to leave the Developer Console and return later, you would see the skill listed. Accordingly, you have a dashboard where you can configure all of the details supporting the skill, the foremost being the interaction model.

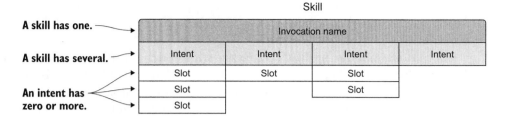

**Figure 2.3  The interaction model**

There are three top-level components for the interaction model: the invocation name, the intents, and the slots, all of which you saw in chapter 1. You can see the relationship between them in figure 2.3.

The invocation name serves as a skill identifier, the intents show what the user wants to do with a skill, and the slots are variable data points that are provided to the code that handles each intent. All three are defined by the developer and affect what Alexa understands when users speak to the skill.

### 2.1.2  *Invocation name*

The first part of the interaction model that a user interacts with, and the only part where users must be trained exactly what to say, is the *invocation name*. For a skill called My Skill, this is where a user says "Alexa, ask My Skill to…" or "Alexa, tell My Skill that I want…" The invocation name can be considered analogous to a domain name, with users including the invocation name in requests much as they would type a domain name into the browser's URL bar.

> **NOTE**  The comparison between invocation names and domain names isn't perfect because Alexa allows multiple skills to have the same invocation name, giving preference to the skill a user has enabled. Google Assistant follows the domain name analogy more closely, requiring unique invocation names.

Beyond the official rules that invocation names are to be two or more words in the same language as the skill, a good invocation name is short, easy to pronounce, and memorable. "Short" and "easy to pronounce" are related in that you want there to be as little friction as possible when launching your skill. If users have to say, "Alexa, ask Peter Piper Picked a Peck of Pickled Peppers to tell me how many pickled peppers were picked," they may do it once for the novelty, but they won't do it twice. When thinking about length, think as much about syllables as you do the number of words. Earplay and Yes, Sire—two of the first breakout Alexa games—are each just two syllables in length.

For memorability, you should balance generic and esoteric unless you already have a strong brand behind you. If you go too generic, your skill may end up as a "commodity," with nothing to set it apart from all of the other skills that do a similar thing, even if the functionality is superior. Make it too unique and remembering the invocation name is more difficult. Remember, users need to get it right the first time or they will get frustrated. This isn't like the web where a search engine will provide a "Did you mean?" prompt.

For our invocation name, we'll go the generic-but-descriptive route and select Sleep Tracker, which is also the name of the skill. In general, having this overlap is a best practice, although you can add more to your skill name. For example, we could have named our skill Sleep Tracker to Wake Rested or something else similarly descriptive to aid in skill store discovery. Amazon will automatically set the invocation name to match the skill name, but you can always change it.

> **NOTE**   After every change, you can choose to *save* or *build* your model. Saving will keep the changes local to the dashboard, whereas building will assemble the NLU that is then available to the Alexa platform. In this book, I won't always direct you to save or build your skills, so remember to save regularly and to build before testing a skill.

Once you've selected an invocation name, the Developer Console will present options for configuring the interaction model. In this section you'll train Alexa to better understand the ways you expect a user will interact with your skill, beginning with the intents.

### 2.1.3   *Intents*

If the invocation name is considered analogous to a domain name, intents are similar to paths. They map what a user wants to do with a specific action. Imagine the simplest possible skill that can only do one thing: say hello to the user when the user says hello to it. This skill has a single intent. It can be called nearly anything you want, but it might commonly be named something like `HelloIntent`.

Intents express to the code what the user wants to do. This is necessary because Alexa does not provide developers with the raw text of what a user said. Intent detection is a tricky discipline and is often better performed at the platform level, where developers can take advantage of Amazon's wealth of software brainpower and experience detecting intents across the entire Alexa platform.

Thanks to this experience, Amazon has noticed that certain intents come up across a swath of skills. To aid in creating skills that perform these actions, the Alexa platform has a number of built-in intents. These intents can perform actions, like adding an event to a calendar, or search for commonly needed information, such as movie showtimes or weather. These built-in intents can save you time figuring out what a user wants.

How can we know what the user wants? We compare what they say to a list of possible phrases we've assembled ahead of time—the sample utterances.

### 2.1.4   *Sample utterances*

Key to intents is understanding how a user might ask for them. Users are never going to say, "Give me the current time intent, please," because they likely don't—and shouldn't need to—know a skill's internals to the level of knowing intent names.

They will instead say, "What time is it right now?" or "What's the time?" or even just "Tell me the time." For each custom intent, you provide the Alexa platform with a list of phrases that you imagine a user might say to express their interests—the *sample utterances*. Alexa uses this list to train its NLU and provide the fulfillment code with an intent on each request. You can see in figure 2.4 how utterances fit into the entire interaction model.

For example, the `HelloIntent` for a skill called My Skill might have "to say hello" as a sample utterance. The user could say "Ask My Skill to say hello" or "Tell My Skill to say hello." Alexa would consider each a request for `HelloIntent`.

> **NOTE** Voice-first concepts often have different names on different platforms. I'll use the name appropriate for the platform I'm discussing, but I'll often point out the names on other platforms. For example, sample utterances are called *training phrases* in Dialogflow, the primary NLU for Google Assistant applications.

Each utterance needs to be paired with only one intent, although that intent will nearly always have multiple utterances. For example, here are three ways to trigger `HelloIntent`:

```
to say hello
to say ahoy
if it can greet me
```

Each time a user says "Alexa, tell My Skill to say hello" or "Alexa, ask My Skill if it can greet me," the Alexa platform will know that the goal is to invoke `HelloIntent`. We've seen in figure 2.4 a top-down view of the different parts that create an interaction

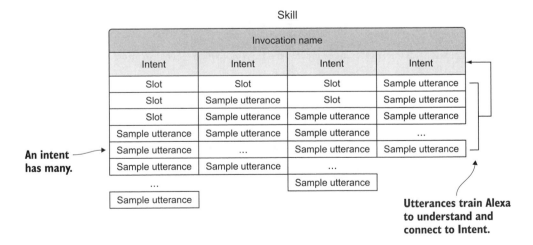

Figure 2.4 **The interaction model with utterances**

**Figure 2.5   An intent will have many sample utterances.**

model, but we can start to see a different view in figure 2.5. We can again see that intents will have many sample utterances.

Users don't have to say an utterance exactly. They could say "to say… umm… hello" or even "if it can say hello to me," and Alexa would still recognize that what they're saying aligns with `HelloIntent`. This means that developers don't need to write out every possible thing that a user might say. Instead they need to capture the gist and provide enough possibilities that Alexa can figure out which intent should handle the request. In figure 2.6, Alexa would determine that "to tell me the time" maps to the `GetTimeIntent`, whereas "to say hello" references the `HelloIntent` instead.

For a rich user experience, a skill should do more than just perform a single action. Think about it from a software perspective again: if you wanted to create a method that adds two numbers together, you wouldn't create one that adds 0 and 1, another for 0 and 2, another for 0 and 3, all the way down the line. You'd create, instead, a method that accepts variable pieces of information that can be specified by the user. You'd accept arguments. In the world of Alexa, we call those *slots*.

| | | |
|---|---|---|
| "Alexa, ask Custom Skill to say hello." ---► | to say hello | `HelloIntent` |
| | to say ahoy | `HelloIntent` |
| | what time is it now? | `GetTimeIntent` |
| "Alexa, ask Custom Skill if it can say hello to me." ---► | if it can greet me | `HelloIntent` |
| "Alexa, tell Custom Skill to tell me the time." ---► | tell me the time | `GetTimeIntent` |

**Figure 2.6   Sample utterances provide the training to map request to intent.**

### 2.1.5   *Slots*

Continuing the URI analogy, slots are like query parameters. They are variable pieces of information that might impact the behavior of the request, but that don't affect the routing. For `HelloIntent` we may want to greet someone by the name they provide us.

> *"Hi, my name is Kate."*
>
> *"Oh, hi, Kate."*

We *could* create an intent for each name we expect to encounter, but that would be a lot of work and might leave us saying, "I've got a `HelloJackIntent` and a `Hello-JillIntent`, and the rest of you are on your own."

Instead, we can use slots. Slots are placeholders inside sample utterances, and when a user says a matching phrase, the value in that slot can be plucked out. In figure 2.7,

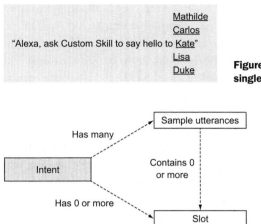
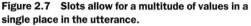

**Figure 2.7 Slots allow for a multitude of values in a single place in the utterance.**

**Figure 2.8 We use slots to capture variable information in utterances.**

different names are available for the slot, whether the name is Kate, Lisa, Duke, or something else. Those slots belong to both intents and sample utterances (see figure 2.8).

You could also think of slots as being like matching groups inside a regular expression. One of our sample utterances might be

```
say hello to {name}
```

The curly braces wrap the slot. When the user says, "say hello to Kate," the value of the name slot will be Kate. "Say hello to Carlos" will match up with Carlos. And, thanks to Alexa's fuzzy matching, "say a hello *greeting* to Lisa" will return a value of Lisa for name.

Slots have three parts: a name, a location inside the sample utterances, and a type, as shown in figure 2.9. The name is how slots are referred to both inside the sample utterances and in the data that's later provided to the fulfillment. The fulfillment code receives a JSON object for each request, and nestled deep within, accessible via this.event.request.intent.slots.name.value, is the value: Kate, Carlos, or Lisa, in this example.

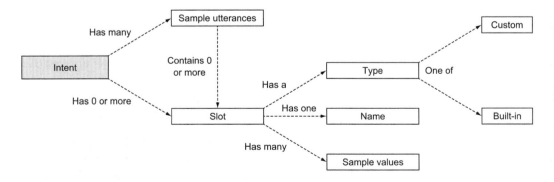

**Figure 2.9 Relationship between slots and the interaction models**

The location inside the sample utterance is where the NLU will expect to see the value to pluck out. For the `say hello to {NAME}` sample utterance, Alexa will expect that a name will come at the end of what the user says, after "say hello to." "Say hello to Kate" will map to a slot value of `Kate`, whereas "say hello to Kate tonight" might lead to a value of `Kate tonight` instead. You won't need to worry about the location of the slot in the sample utterance in your code—in fact, you won't even have access to it. It's relevant only in understanding how people will speak to the skill and what its effect will be on the NLU.

Sample utterances represent what the developer expects a user to say for an intent. Similarly, the slot type represents what the developer expects the user to say for a slot. There are two kinds of slot types: custom and built-in. *Custom* slot types are those where you specify as many values as possible to train Alexa in what you expect to hear from the user. If a skill called for a user to specify a day of the week, there would be a custom `DAY_OF_THE_WEEK` type, with values of "Sunday," "Monday," and each day through "Saturday." These values bias Alexa's NLU. Maybe one user dresses up one day of the week, and he insists on calling it "Tie Day." It's likely that Alexa will hear that as "Friday," which may be just as well, because who has ever heard of Tie Day falling on a Thursday?

That's not to say that values *must* fall within the values you provide. If someone says "hump day," the Alexa NLU will do its best to match it to one of your values. If it can't, you'll receive what Alexa heard instead. There are no validation errors with Alexa, and slot types are not enums.

Creating a `DAY_OF_THE_WEEK` custom type is something that you wouldn't actually do. Amazon provides dozens of built-in types, and days of the week is one of them. Where possible, Amazon recommends using built-in slot types, since they will provide the best recognition with the least work. You don't need to worry about seeding a far-reaching slot with hundreds of values, as Amazon has already done it for you.

These are a few noteworthy built-in slot types:

- `AMAZON.Book`, `AMAZON.Movie`, `AMAZON.MusicAlbum`—You wouldn't expect any less from Amazon, and these are just a few that can be used to match creative works.
- `AMAZON.US_FIRST_NAME`, `AMAZON.DE_FIRST_NAME`, `AMAZON.GB_FIRST_NAME`— First names popular in different locales.
- `AMAZON.Room`—Values like living room, lobby, or nursery are useful for smart home skills.
- `AMAZON.PostalAddress`—You can only imagine the example values you would have to provide to get good matching on *2016 Hillcrest* or *609 W Avenue B.*

*Slots* are variable values that act like parameters, and they belong to *intents*, which act like paths. Intents are invoked by comparing user speech to *sample utterances* that are mapped to those intents. Putting them all together, your skill has an *interaction model*, which is a good place to start when building a skill.

## 2.2   *The interaction model*

The skill we're building in this chapter is a call-and-response skill. The user will say something to Alexa, Alexa will say something back, and the interaction will be complete. In future chapters we'll build larger, more complex skills upon this base.

In this skill, users will ask Alexa how well rested they should expect to be depending on the hours of sleep they'll get. Users can also tell Alexa how well they slept the night before.

You can start to see what you'll need for the interaction model.

- *Intent*—A single intent that takes the number of hours until the user wakes up, plus the quality of sleep from the night before, and uses those to determine how well rested the user can expect to be. We'll name this `WellRestedIntent`.
- *Slots*—Two slots will be needed: one for the wake-up time and one for quality of the previous night's sleep.
- *Sample utterances*—The user can express an action in a number of different ways. "How well rested will I be…?" "Will I be tired if…?" and more.

A useful, and often skipped, step when building a skill is to spend some initial time thinking about the skill's functionality and how users will interact with it. One way to do this is by pairing with someone else, instructing your new conversation partner in general terms what the skill is meant to do, and making it clear that you'll pretend to be Alexa. Write down what is asked of you, respond in a way that you think appropriate, and pay attention to any follow-up interactions. This is a version of *Wizard of Oz testing*, which takes its name from the titular wizard who was in fact a "man behind the curtain." It's a way to test an interface before the logic powering it is built, using a human in place of the code.

This approach to voice applications is most useful for those who have never built for voice before. Creating intents, utterances, or fulfillment without exploring the human side directly can lead to a skill that takes too much guidance from how things are done on the web or mobile. Voice first has its own paradigms and considerations that are best experienced through advance user interaction. This can even be without a partner, with the developer playing both sides. In this case, requests and responses should still be spoken aloud, to catch what might look natural on the page but not sound natural when spoken.

### 2.2.1   *Building the intent*

Once you've settled on an invocation name and done some user research, the next step is generally setting up the intents. The skill dashboard navigation allows you to add intents individually or all at once through a JSON editor. In chapter 4 you'll see how to build the interaction model through JSON locally, but for now we'll build the various pieces one at a time, to get a good understanding of how everything works together. Start by adding a custom intent in the console and naming it `WellRestedIntent`.

The `WellRestedIntent` configuration page has a place to add sample utterances. To put together your sample utterance list, dig deep into your empathy and understanding of human nature. How might someone ask Alexa for your action? Think back to your earlier testing, ask people around you, or say aloud what you think people might say and ask yourself if it sounds right. Take these utterances and think of them as a combination of constituent parts.

> **NOTE** Users will often not be saying the utterance on its own. They will use invocation names, launch phrases ("launch," "ask," "search," and others), and connecting words ("to," "about," and more) with the utterances. Because the utterances don't have these accoutrements when we enter them, they will look unnatural, even if they are perfectly normal when combined with the full request.

A descriptive phrase would make sense here—something like "how well." Take into account the different ways you might refer to "sleep." You can sleep, snooze, rest, and so on. And then you'll need phrasing to indicate the passage of time, such as "if I sleep for six hours" or "if six hours pass." Finally, there's the indication of how last night's sleep was. These are the different parts involved, though not necessarily in that order. Put it all together and you'll have a few phrases, including those in the following listing.

**Listing 2.1    Sample utterances**

```
How rested will I be
How rested will I be if I get {NumberOfHours} hours of sleep
How rested will I be if I get {NumberOfHours} hours of rest
How rested will I be if I sleep for {NumberOfHours} hours
How rested will I be if I rest for {NumberOfHours} hours
How well rested will I be after {NumberOfHours} hours
How well rested will I be after {NumberOfHours} hours if I slept
    {SleepQuality} last night
How well rested will I be if I slept {SleepQuality} last night
How well rested will I be if I slept {SleepQuality} last night and I get
    {NumberOfHours} of sleep tonight
How tired will I be
How tired will I be if I get {NumberOfHours} hours of sleep
How tired will I be if I get {NumberOfHours} hours of sleep and I slept
    {SleepQuality} last night
How tired will I be if I get {NumberOfHours} hours of sleep and I got
    {SleepQuality} sleep last night
How tired will I be if I get {NumberOfHours} hours of rest
How tired will I be if I get {NumberOfHours} hours of rest and I slept
    {SleepQuality} last night
How tired will I be if I get {NumberOfHours} hours of rest and I got
    {SleepQuality} sleep last night
How tired will I be if I sleep for {NumberOfHours} hours
How tired will I be if I sleep for {NumberOfHours} hours tonight
How tired will I be if I rest for {NumberOfHours} hours tonight
How tired will I be after {NumberOfHours} hours
Will I be rested sleeping for {NumberOfHours} hours
Will I be rested sleeping for {NumberOfHours} hours after a night of
    {SleepQuality} sleep
```

```
Will I be rested if I sleep for {NumberOfHours} hours
Will I be rested if I sleep for {NumberOfHours} hours if I slept
    {SleepQuality} yesterday
Will I be rested if I sleep for {NumberOfHours} hours if I slept
    {SleepQuality} last night
Will I be rested if I rest for {NumberOfHours} hours
Will I be tired sleeping for {NumberOfHours} hours
Will I be tired sleeping for {NumberOfHours} hours tonight
Will I be tired if I sleep for {NumberOfHours} hours
I will sleep for {NumberOfHours} hours
I will sleep for {NumberOfHours} hours tonight
I will sleep for {NumberOfHours} hours and I got {SleepQuality} sleep last
    night
I will sleep for {NumberOfHours} hours and I slept {SleepQuality} last night
{NumberOfHours} hours of sleep
{NumberOfHours} hours of sleep and {SleepQuality} sleep last night
{NumberOfHours} hours {SleepQuality} last night
{NumberOfHours} hours tonight {SleepQuality} last night
{NumberOfHours} hours tonight {SleepQuality} sleep last night
```

The more variations you provide, the better the speech recognition will be, to a point. Each new utterance adds less of an impact than the one before it, so the idea of diminishing returns applies here. Nonetheless, you want to err on the side of over-delivering sample utterances. You can, however, hurt the speech recognition if you provide sample utterances that a user is very unlikely to say. For example, you could have added, "Doze until bell how much at {NumberOfHours}." It *is* possible that someone might say this, but it's very unlikely.

Some utterances in the list are incredibly short. It's easy to think in full sentences while writing sample utterances, but don't forget that users sometimes bark out single-word requests to their voice-first devices. Account for those as well.

Most of the utterances we created have at least one slot within them. Lower on the intent configuration page is space to define the type of each slot, biasing the NLU's interpretation of the values. We expect that people will say numbers for the Number-OfHours slot, and numbers are a common slot type across many skills. Thus, that type is built directly into the Alexa platform: the AMAZON.NUMBER type. That's what we should select for the NumberOfHours slot. SleepQuality is a statement of quality, such as "good," "bad," or "restful," and is more specific to our skill, so we should create our own custom slot type for it.

### 2.2.2 Slots

The first thing to keep in mind about slots is the difference between a *slot* and a *slot type*. A slot is the representation of a slot type inside a sample utterance and intent. The slot type includes all of the values expected within a slot of that type.

Our custom slot type for the SleepQuality slot will represent a quality, so add a slot type in the left navigation and name it Quality. Because this slot type is tied closely to the utterances that describe sleep quality, consider how a user might finish the sentence, "I slept __ last night."

**NOTE** This might be a good time to dust off your thesaurus. The Wordnik site (www.wordnik.com) is a good resource for English words, as it provides synonyms as well as words that are equivalent or often used in the same context.

Giving it some thought, I came up with the following values:

```
bad
poorly
little
very little
not at all
good
well
wonderfully
a lot
amazing
fantastic
great
not bad
```

Beyond using your understanding of user behavior and thumbing through a well-worn thesaurus, the best place to get slot type values is from user data for your existing website or application. Like in utterances, people might use different terms when speaking than when writing, and your current search or customer interaction data will show which words people currently use. Absent existing interaction data, look at the data set you're basing the skill on. If a skill is about the Beatles, BandMember slot values would be "George," "Paul," "John," and "Ringo"—but also "the drummer," "the bassist," and others.

Keep in mind that you are limited to 50,000 values across all of your different slots, and the more you add, the less power each subsequent value holds. Use the things that people say most often, and take a good representation of utterance lengths and forms. If the values are only ever single words, don't include five-word values. Likewise, consider all the variety people use in speaking, which might lead you to include formal utterances along with all of the informal ones.

After you've added the different sleep qualities, you can go back to the WellRested-Intent, set the SleepQuality slot to the Quality slot type, and build the model.

Next up is the fulfillment that will take the request shaped by the interaction model.

## 2.3 *Fulfillment*

Amazon provides two different options for the fulfillment:

- Host your own endpoint on a secure server.
- Use the serverless platform AWS Lambda.

There are positives and negatives to each approach, outlined in table 2.1.

**Table 2.1  Pros and cons of self-hosted skills versus Lambda-hosted skills**

|  | Pros | Cons |
|---|---|---|
| Self-hosted | You own the server | Have to maintain your own servers |
|  | Can more easily tie your existing database and services into your skill | Extra verification of incoming requests |
|  | More control over how requests are handled |  |
| Lambda | Auto scaling | More difficult to connect to existing database or services (although not impossible) |
|  | Automatically certified for PCI |  |
|  | Automatic security baseline | Less control over how requests are handled |
|  | Free for nearly all skills |  |
|  | No extra SSL/TSL configuration |  |
|  | No server management |  |

### 2.3.1   *Hosted endpoint*

Hosting an endpoint yourself comes with benefits and disadvantages, as you can see in the table. The primary benefit is that you own the server. You can more easily tie the skill into your database and any other services that you use for your website. Owning the server also offers you more control over how requests are handled; for example, you could increase the length of time that information is stored in memory.

Some of the downsides are that the fulfillment must be served via HTTPS (although by now, most websites are), and Amazon requires extra verification of incoming requests. Perhaps the biggest downside is that you have to provide and maintain your own servers—whether through physical hardware or by using a third-party platform-as-a-service like Heroku. For many skill developers, all of that might not be necessary, as Lambda is the best option.

### 2.3.2   *AWS Lambda*

For most skills and nearly all first skills, the best option is to use AWS Lambda. Lambda is a serverless architecture platform hosted by Amazon on AWS.

The term *serverless* often refers to an architecture where backend code is run on demand inside containers that are live for only a short period of time. Another term for this is *function-as-a-service*, reiterating the idea that serverless generally runs a small bit of code at a time. This architecture was initially popularized for single–web page applications and mobile apps. We'll use it to build voice applications.

### 2.3.3 Coding the fulfillment

Previously, if you wanted to use Lambda to create a skill, it was necessary to go into the depths of AWS. It's not a place that's friendly for those who aren't already accustomed to it. Amazon knew this, and it added *hosted skills*, where Amazon provisions the necessary AWS services and provides an input for the code directly within the Developer Console. You can still write the code in your favorite text editor (and we will work there exclusively in future chapters), but the code will end up inside the Code tab of the Alexa skill configuration in the Developer Console. Amazon will then send it to Lambda on your behalf, where it will handle requests after they go through the Alexa platform and its attendant NLU.

The directory structure for a skill like the one we're building is quite simple. Inside a lambda directory is an index.js file. The name of this file is important, because Lambda with its default settings will be looking for that filename.

Remember that a voice application works by sending information from the user to the device, through the platform and fulfillment, and then back in reverse order. Each step adds or transforms the data that goes to the next step, and the fulfillment is no different. The fulfillment performs the biggest change, as it reverses the flow and turns request into response. The ASK SDK facilitates this transformation by taking the request and directing it to a handler that can build the response.

The following listing shows the base of the sleep-quality skill. It's a step beyond a "Hello World" application and lays the foundation for everything that will come later. Inside the skill, we'll use the Alexa Skills Kit Node.js SDK package, which is tooling that builds the JSON that will be sent back to the Alexa platform. It provides the Alexa skill builder, which takes the added request handlers (just one in this code), and checks whether the `canHandle` method for the handler returns `true`. If it does, the `handle` method puts together and returns the response.

> **Listing 2.2  Handling a request (index.js)**

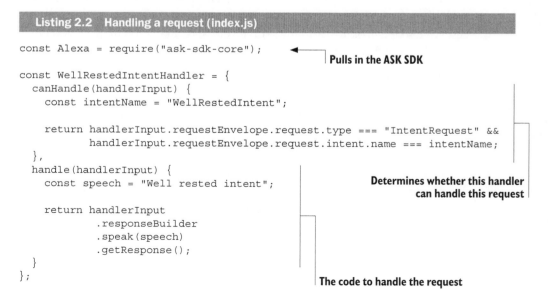

```
const Alexa = require("ask-sdk-core");        ◄──── Pulls in the ASK SDK

const WellRestedIntentHandler = {
  canHandle(handlerInput) {
    const intentName = "WellRestedIntent";

    return handlerInput.requestEnvelope.request.type === "IntentRequest" &&
           handlerInput.requestEnvelope.request.intent.name === intentName;
  },
  handle(handlerInput) {
    const speech = "Well rested intent";

    return handlerInput
            .responseBuilder
            .speak(speech)
            .getResponse();
  }
};
```

Determines whether this handler can handle this request

The code to handle the request

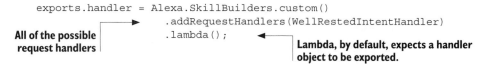

```
exports.handler = Alexa.SkillBuilders.custom()
                    .addRequestHandlers(WellRestedIntentHandler)
                    .lambda();
```

**All of the possible
request handlers**

**Lambda, by default, expects a handler
object to be exported.**

Here, `WellRestedIntentHandler` is the only request handler, but the SDK still calls its `canHandle` method to see if it returns `true`. Only in that case does it call its `handle` method. The flow of information is shown in figure 2.10.

Inside the `handle` method, helper methods from a `responseBuilder` object take the speech and return an object that's then sent back to the Alexa service. The `handle` method abstracts a lot away, and in those four lines creates an object in the correct format.

**Listing 2.3  The output of the `handle` method**

```
{
  outputSpeech: {
    type: "SSML",
    ssml: "<speak>Well rested intent</speak>"
  }
}
```

**SSML is a type of speech markup
we'll examine in chapter 7.**

This output speech object is further wrapped in another object before the skill builder sends it back to the Alexa service, where it's transformed through the speech-to-text engine and streamed to the user's device. For the developer, the technology underpinnings are interesting and exciting, but a voice application is ultimately based on data being manipulated and passed from one service to the next. You can save and deploy this skill, and just like that, you're ready to interact with it.

Testing the skill on an Echo is exciting but cumbersome to repeat, particularly if you're in a shared space. Amazon provides a testing service you can find through the top menu. From there you can enable testing on your skill, which allows for testing in the testing console and on your devices. In the console, you can talk to the skill through

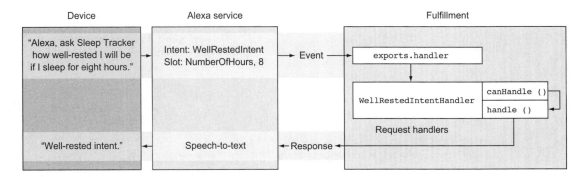

**Figure 2.10   Information flows from user through device and Alexa to the fulfillment and back.**

voice, text, or manually added JSON and see what request is going to the fulfillment. Give it a try—say "Ask sleep tracker how well rested I'll be if I sleep for 10 hours."

On the left side of the testing console is the information that was sent to the fulfillment—the event object that came in as the first argument. You'll see information about the session (Is it new? What is the user's ID?), the request (What intent is the user requesting, and what are the slot values?), and the context (Does the user's device have a display?).

On the right is the response that the fulfillment sends back to the Alexa platform. This is much simpler. There is output speech, the user agent, and the version, but that's all there is of note for this response. Currently the response is drab and not very useful. After all, who only wants to know which handler they triggered?

### WELLRESTEDINTENT

We'll take the code that we've already created and send a better response back to the user. As a refresher, `WellRestedIntent` will take the number of hours users plan to sleep, and the description of how well they slept the night before, and tell them if they'll be well rested in the morning. What do we need to do?

- Take the number of hours and the sleep quality from the slot values.
- Check to see if they correlate to being refreshed in the morning.
- Handle the situation where the user doesn't fill in a slot, or provide an invalid value.
- Provide Alexa with what it should say for each amount of sleep.

The error case is an important one for conversational interfaces, and it's one that developers often overlook. Nothing takes a user out of the moment more than Alexa saying, "There was a problem with the requested skill's response." (We'll examine how to handle errors in chapter 8.)

Taking these requirements into account, we end up with a `WellRestedIntent` handler that starts by taking the slot value and checking for validity.

#### Listing 2.4   Confirming slot value validity (index.js)

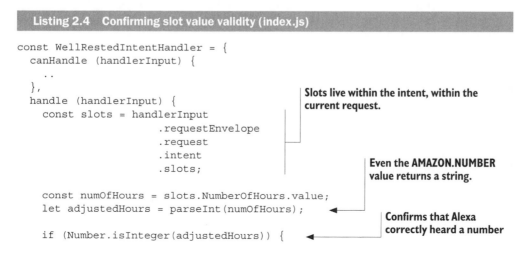

```
const WellRestedIntentHandler = {
  canHandle (handlerInput) {
    ..
  },
  handle (handlerInput) {
    const slots = handlerInput
                    .requestEnvelope
                    .request
                    .intent
                    .slots;

    const numOfHours = slots.NumberOfHours.value;
    let adjustedHours = parseInt(numOfHours);

    if (Number.isInteger(adjustedHours)) {
```

**Slots live within the intent, within the current request.**

**Even the AMAZON.NUMBER value returns a string.**

**Confirms that Alexa correctly heard a number**

```
      ...
  } else {
    console.log("Slot values ", slots);          ◄─── Logs the slot values to catch and correct
                                                       for responses without a number

    const speech = "Oh, I don't know what happened. Tell me again. " +
                "How many hours will you sleep tonight?";
    const reprompt = "How many hours are you going to sleep tonight?";

    return handlerInput                                 Gives the user a chance
          .responseBuilder                              to correct the error
          .speak(speech)
          .reprompt(reprompt)
          .getResponse();        ◄───
  }                                      Leaves the session open for a follow-up
 }
};
```

We grab the slot value first, before confirming that both the user gave and Alexa heard a number. Amazon will convert "ten" to 10 but will return a question mark for "a couple of" and nothing for "a dog."

If Alexa hasn't heard a number, we'll want to know what happened. This code logs the value to see what came through. (In the current case, the logs go to Amazon Cloud-Watch.) By looking through the logs periodically, you can alter the interaction model or how you direct users, to improve the skill experience.

There will also be times when your code doesn't work. Unlike improperly configured web servers, Alexa will never tell you (or the user) what went wrong. One way to figure it out is to look at the logs. With hosted skills, Amazon also connects the code and Lambda function to Amazon CloudWatch.

You can find a link to the logs in the Code tab of the console. You'll see a list of log streams sorted by recency. Click through, and you'll see the code invocations. If there are any logs to the console or errors logged out, you'll see them here.

The use of reprompt in listing 2.4 is necessary to keep the microphone open. This method sets a flag in the response that lets Alexa continue listening for the user to speak again without again saying "Alexa, tell Sleep Tracker…" The reprompt string we provide is what Alexa says if the user doesn't say anything, or if the device doesn't pick it up. The user has about eight seconds to speak before Alexa returns with the follow-up. Eight seconds isn't generally very long, but it is in the context of a conversation. The average response time for a conversation turn differs between languages, but in English the average is 236 milliseconds for a response to a question with an expected "yes" or "no" answer. (Japanese has a rapid 7 millisecond average between turns.) Sociologist Gail Jefferson determined that one second of silence is the longest amount of time people will generally let a conversation stay silent.[1] Eight seconds will be plenty of time to give the user a chance to respond.

---

[1]  N.J. Enfield, *How We Talk: The Inner Workings of Conversation* (Basic Books, 2017).

Finally, we want to allow the user to make a correction if Alexa misheard or if the user misunderstood what to do. The goal is to get them to return a number so the skill can provide the correct response.

**Listing 2.5  Responding to the user (index.js)**

```
const WellRestedIntentHandler = {
  canHandle (handlerInput) {
    ..
  },
  handle (handlerInput) {
    ...

    if (Number.isInteger(adjustedHours)) {
      let speech = "";

      if(adjustedHours > 12) {
        speech = "I think you may sleep too much and swing back to tired.";
      } else if(adjustedHours > 8) {
        speech = "You should wake up refreshed.";
      } else if(adjustedHours > 6) {
        speech = "You may get by, but watch out for a mid-day crash.";
      } else {
        speech = "You'll be dragging. Get the coffee ready!";
      }

      return handlerInput
              .responseBuilder
              .speak(speech)
              .getResponse();
    } else {
      ...
    }
  }
};
```

> Returns different responses based on hours of expected sleep

`WellRestedIntent` is long, but it's not doing anything particularly unusual. For simplicity, I've included all of the logic that chooses what to say to the user directly in the method, but in most cases you'll want to move it out.

There are a couple of reasons for this. Code maintenance is certainly one. Another reason to break out the response-building logic is a reflection of wanting to make a skill that users enjoy coming back to. Users expect some level of personality with voice assistants, and personality generally implies "like a person." Do you know anyone who says the same thing every single time? Maybe there's your friend Chuck who says "Could be worse" when you ask him how it's going. But that's Chuck and he's got a weird sense of humor and anyway you go way back so it's sort of an inside joke by now. Your users don't have inside jokes with Alexa, so you want to mix up what she says. This is much easier when the logic of deciding how to randomize or move through responses doesn't live with the rest of the intent handler logic. We'll see a way to do this in a later chapter. In the meantime, we are ready to add the last part of the skill for this chapter.

#### SLEEPQUALITY

The final step for this portion of the skill is handling the `SleepQuality` slot. This slot, even more than `NumberOfHours`, shows the power and peril of voice applications. The power is on the side of the users, as there are no formal constraints, and whatever they think, they can say. The peril is the developer's. All the wide-ranging possibilities must be handled properly. A VUI should guide a user's understanding of what's necessary preemptively, so that constraints don't come as a surprise after the request.

The Sleep Tracker skill will take the stated sleep quality and assume that the previous night's sleep has an impact of one hour in either direction. For example, a poor night's sleep means an extra hour must be slept the next night to make up for it, and an hour can be missed if the user slept well the night before. It's a crude measure, but it works for the purpose of illustrating slot handling.

**Listing 2.6    Categorizing incoming slot values (index.js)**

```
handle(handlerInput) {
  ...
  let adjustedHours = parseInt(numOfHours);          Guards against the case where
                                                      SleepQuality is undefined
  const quality = slots.SleepQuality && slots.SleepQuality.value;  ◄

  const good = ["good", "well", "wonderfully", "a lot", "amazing",
               "fantastic", "great", "not bad"];
  const bad = ["bad", "poorly", "little", "very little", "not at all"];
                                                      Lists all good and bad
  if (Number.isInteger(adjustedHours)) {              expected slot values
    let speech = "";

    if(good.includes(quality)) {
      adjustedHours += 1;
      speech = "You slept well last night, and ";
    }

    if(bad.includes(quality)) {
      adjustedHours -= 1;
      speech = "You slept poorly last night, and ";
    }
    ...
  } else {          For any quality that's noted as good, credit an
    ...             hour. If the quality is bad, debit it.
  }
}
```

We start out by comparing the inbound slot value with expected values that we've categorized into either "good" or "bad." Then we either credit or debit one hour from what the user has provided and build the beginning of the response. In forming this response, we're telling the user what we know about the request.

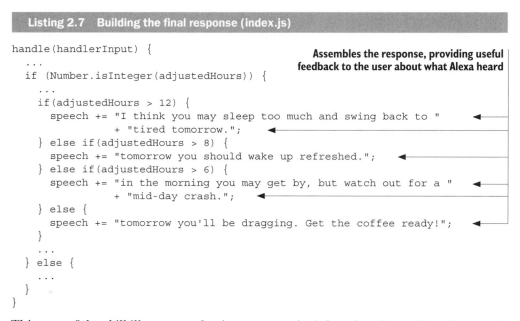

```
handle(handlerInput) {
  ...
  if (Number.isInteger(adjustedHours)) {
    ...
    if(adjustedHours > 12) {
      speech += "I think you may sleep too much and swing back to "
              + "tired tomorrow.";
    } else if(adjustedHours > 8) {
      speech += "tomorrow you should wake up refreshed.";
    } else if(adjustedHours > 6) {
      speech += "in the morning you may get by, but watch out for a "
              + "mid-day crash.";
    } else {
      speech += "tomorrow you'll be dragging. Get the coffee ready!";
    }
    ...
  } else {
    ...
  }
}
```

**Listing 2.7  Building the final response (index.js)**

**Assembles the response, providing useful feedback to the user about what Alexa heard**

This part of the skill illustrates a few important principles of crafting a friendly experience in voice. In short, handle what you know, be clear about what you know, and don't use what you don't know. The new addition to the code here lists the values that we expect for both "good" and "bad" sleep qualities. Sleep qualities aren't like numbers in that there isn't a well-defined understanding of what makes a quality and what doesn't. Because of this, the best way to handle it is to scope it to what you do know and can gather (again, through user testing, existing data, or a thesaurus). That way you only "handle what you know."

Because the skill only has a limited understanding of which qualities are good or bad, the second principle is to "be clear about what you know." This is also important because speech-to-text still is not perfect. Anecdotally, speech-to-text on a voice-first platform has between a 90% and 95% success rate. With potentially 1 in 10 slot values misheard, a skill VUI should be defensive. Not defensive in the sense of "It wasn't my fault, it was Alexa's fault!" but defensive in being aware of and guarding against the possibility of a mistake. One approach is to be clear with users. Users understand that speech-to-text isn't perfect and that there may be mistakes. They even tend to be more forgiving to computers.[2] Letting users know what information the skill is using is important, because it will let them determine whether the mistake was from speech-to-text or in the skill logic. If it was a speech-to-text mistake, the user can try again. If it was poor logic, there isn't much that can be done—which also implies that the skill logic must be intuitive.

Finally, the skill doesn't attempt to use everything that comes in—it "doesn't use what it doesn't know." In this skill, we ignore anything that is out of bounds. Another

---

[2]  See the preface in Cathy Pearl, *Designing Voice User Interfaces: Principles of Conversational Experiences* (O'Reilly, 2016).

option, especially in situations where the value is important, is to be explicit about not understanding the user. That's what the skill does for the number of hours. The skill can't function without knowing how long the user plans to sleep, so it doesn't attempt to provide an answer. For values that are this important, make it a point to tell the user. The worst possible situation is a skill that continually says "I don't understand" without giving an indication of what the problem is.

> **NOTE** The way that we've handled good and bad values through creating an array of possible matches in the code is useful for understanding VUI principles and perhaps for situations where a skill handles most of the NLU-type processing, but it isn't without drawbacks. For example, adding new values is cumbersome and requires updating both the code and the interaction model. In chapter 4 we'll examine another, better way to do this for Alexa.

With that, you've built a completely functional Alexa skill that can handle intents and slot values. But there's a lot more that you can do with it. We'll cover that next.

## Summary

- Craft *intents* to represent what users want to do, *slots* for variable information, and *sample utterances* for what users might say.
- Do not consider a slot as an enum, but as a biasing toward specific values.
- Use the Alexa Skills Kit (ASK) Node.js SDK to handle and respond to Alexa requests.
- Design skills defensively to handle unexpected user requests.

# Designing a voice user interface

## This chapter covers

- Understanding the voice user interface

- Seeing how a VUI differs from graphical user interfaces

- Learning how to use Grice's maxims to shape a VUI

The early use of each new technology tends to mimic older mediums. Early radio programs were like plays you could listen to at home. Early websites tried to take cues from the computer desktop, which itself was based on the physical desktop. This stage is never the pinnacle of the platform. It's the same with voice first. Early efforts on voice first may take guidance from the web, but learning how voice user interface (VUI) best practices are different will help drive the conversation forward.

A VUI is the combination of the words, the back-and-forth, and the ways of speaking that come together in voice applications to empower a user to efficiently complete a goal. Think of it as the "script" of a human speaking with a computer.

In this chapter, we'll look at the assumptions that sit behind every human-to-human conversation, and we'll look at how we can apply them to human-to-computer interactions. We won't forget the computer side of the family tree, either—we'll look at how a VUI compares to the interfaces you're likely familiar with: the graphical user interfaces (GUIs) of the web and mobile applications, plus everyday conversations between people. Finally, we'll look at the VUI of the sleep-tracker skill from the previous chapter and determine how it fits these assumptions and how it can be improved.

## 3.1 VUI fundamentals

The base of a VUI is a conversational interface, and a conversation has multiple participants. In a voice application, there are two sides to focus on: the device, or computer, side, and the human side. (There aren't yet any voice devices that will interject into cross talk between two humans, so you can think of all humans as being on one side of the conversation.)

As the application developer, you will have complete control over what the computer says. You won't have complete control over what the user says, but you must anticipate what might come into the application in order to understand how the application should respond.

> **TIP** You can't *control* how a user will respond, but you can shape their response. You'll see some methods for doing this in chapter 8.

I want to correct a common misunderstanding right here: a VUI is a conversational interface, but not all conversational interfaces are the same. Just as we would never say that desktop and mobile applications should have the same GUI, voice applications and chat applications won't have the same interface, even if they're both handled through conversation and both become popular around the same time. There are important differences between the two that destroy the dream of "one bot, any platform, no changes."

Let's start with the most obvious difference: a person chats with a chatbot through text, whereas they speak with Alexa, Cortana, Siri, and others through voice. The medium (voice or text) shapes what each partner in the conversation says. The words chosen, the rate of response, and the depth of the response are all impacted by the choice of using text versus voice.

Consider planning a camping trip with a friend through text:

> *ALEX: Okay, so we can go to Yellowstone, Yosemite, or Big Bend. If we go to Big Bend, we should go in October because it will be too hot in the summer.*
> *SOFIA: How about Big Bend?*

Now consider using voice:

> *ALEX: Okay, so we have a few choices.*
> *SOFIA: What are they?*
> *ALEX: Yellowstone, Yosemite, or Big Bend.*
> *SOFIA: How about Big Bend?*
> *ALEX: Alright, but we'll have to go in October because it's too hot before then.*

The difference between the first (text) and the second (voice) is clear. When information arrives through text, the other participant can scan the message for the relevant information, and there's less need to "share" the conversation. Both participants—within reason—can say something at any time.

The voice example downplays the true contrast because you're reading it. You can nonetheless see a rhythm: this, then that, then this, then that, then this. The text-based example is one long stream; voice-based is multiple beats dribbling out the relevant details.

These examples diverge from what often happens. They are formatted as you'd expect to see in a book—which is unsurprising, because you're reading them in a book. But people don't often type or talk like that. They diverge from meticulously formed sentences in ways that differ between voice and text.

In text-based conversations, people use abbreviations, misspell words, or leave out entire parts of sentences. The previous text example might actually look like this:

> ALEX: *yellowstone, yosmeite, or big bend?*
>
> ALEX: *big bend only in october. its hot in summer*
>
> SOFIA: *big bend*

Voice deviates in its own ways. There are no abbreviations or misspellings, but there are contractions, unexpected pauses, filler words ("uh" and "um," but also "like," "you see," or "well…"), swallowed words, and mispronunciations. These are all standard items that people know how to account for:

> ALEX: *We've Yellowstone or… um… Yosemite or Big Bend. Big Bend is [unintelligible] good for October 'cause ummm… it's really hot before.*

Many of these differences occur in the input—in what the user is saying to the computer. Although you're welcome to include pauses or other "disfluencies" in your application's voice response, I advise you not to, because you can easily slip into a situation where the application's response is just a bit off and ends up distracting from the experience.

That's not to say that any responses you build are unaffected by the medium. A good way to see how is to step away from the comparison with chatbots, and look at how voice differs from GUI, while using something called the *cooperative principle*.

## 3.2    *The cooperative principle*

The *cooperative principle* describes the features that contribute to an efficient conversation. It was first described by linguistic philosopher Paul Grice as he discussed the assumptions we bring to conversations that allow them to flow without much trouble. He outlined this principle as involving the four maxims of quantity, quality, relation, and manner:

- *Quantity*—Say enough, but not too much.
- *Quality*—Say the truth.
- *Relation*—Say something relevant to the conversation.
- *Manner*—Say it clearly.

If your skills are liberal in the utterances they accept, these principles offer a guide to being conservative in what your skills say. Remember, a voice-first platform mimics human interactions in a way that no other technology does. Alexa is a conversation partner to the person on the couch asking for music. Even if the devices is a computer, it's often treated like a person. Because people assume that their conversation partners will follow the four maxims, you'll find that the maxims can help your voice applications say more by saying less.[1]

### 3.2.1 Quantity

The maxim of *quantity* assumes that a good conversation partner will say enough information to complete a turn, with no less and no more.

Imagine asking a friend, "How did the presentation to your boss go?" A reply that broke down every minute of the presentation would be too much information, and you'd be likely to stop listening by the time she says, "And then the HDMI cable wouldn't work, so I had to…" On the other hand, a reply of "It went" isn't enough. (Unless you assume your friend is following the maxims, in which case those two words might be all you need to know that she isn't going to get that sought-after promotion.) "It went well, I think," addresses the question at hand, without going overboard.

> **NOTE** You could easily construct a response that seemingly fits the maxim of quantity that is longer or shorter than the preceding one. This maxim—like the rest—is not a precise formula, but of the class where you'll know it when you see it.

This maxim shows a clear difference between creating a GUI and a VUI. Even on a mobile display, a GUI can contain information that doesn't directly relate to the task at hand, such as advertisements, social sharing buttons, and menu options. Some of this extra information is due to the navigation methods of a GUI, where a user who doesn't see a link will likely not continue navigating. It's also largely a result of the dimensions in which a GUI exists.

A GUI exists in two dimensions—width and height—that combine to create the area where all of the information lives. The area is nearly always larger than the space necessary for the user request. In this extra space, the designer can provide information adjacent to the core response. Additionally, excepting UI flourishes like sliders or automatically updating timelines, a user can look away from the screen, or change focus, and the information will be the same when the user looks back. Users can dart their eyes around the page until they settle on what they want next.

A VUI, in contrast, exists in a single dimension—time. There's no location where a developer can store extra information that might be necessary for a small subset of listeners. Instead, the response needs to provide the right amount of information for

---

[1] James Giangola gave a good talk at Google I/O 2017 on this topic and its relation to voice applications, titled "Applying Built-in Hacks of Conversation to Your Voice UI." You can view it at https://youtu.be/wuDP_eygsvs.

the current listener, for the current request. The time dimension always moves forward, and if a response has too much information, the user will have to remember what seems most relevant or wait for what's coming up. Either situation adds more work for the user, when instead, the VUI should be taking on that responsibility.

Even without using a voice application, you've likely encountered a flouting of this maxim when calling a bank, airline, or other customer service line. "If you'd like to buy a ticket, please press 1. If you want to find our your miles balance, please…" This level of detail is rarely necessary. The key is to understand when it is. We'll look at several examples in this book, including solving the customer service problem of teaching callers what they can do.

Because most voice developers come from working with GUIs, the maxim of quantity is often ignored in the direction of *too much*. Developers can avoid this pattern by removing information piece by piece, asking on each turn whether the response still meets the maxim of quantity, as well as the others. The stopping point reveals itself when, to borrow from Saint-Exupéry, there is no longer anything to take away. If the user asks, "What is the weather tomorrow?" does the application need to respond, "The weather tomorrow is 88 degrees and sunny?" No, "Tomorrow it will be 88 degrees and sunny" is sufficient. Maybe you can even remove "degrees" and cut it down some more.

You will sometimes find creative options for reaching the most efficient quantity. For example, an application that reads out messages could drop all last names except where multiple people in an address book share a first name.[2] In a later chapter, we will look at this further, and discuss using context to *elide* implied information to get users even closer to their desired outcomes.

No matter how long or short your voice application's response is, it still must say what is true. That is the maxim of *quality*.

### 3.2.2 Quality

The maxim of *quality* says that speakers should avoid saying anything that they know to be false, and anything for which they don't have proper backing. These work in concert to prevent outright lies as well as lies of omission and innuendo. That's why we expect our conversation partners to hedge their statements when they don't know something for sure. "I think Tom is 35" follows the maxim of quality even if Tom is 52. The speaker *thinks* the statement to be true, and it's the thinking that's the focus in that statement. In a person-to-person conversation, the benefits of this maxim are obvious. No one wants to contend with a fabulist.

You might have a difficult time imagining how the maxim of quality plays into user interfaces. Because user interfaces don't have agency, they can't lie. But interfaces lie regularly! In a GUI, this lie happens when a link points to an incorrect URL, or with dark patterns that trick users. A website lies to users when it implies it's an official government website, and puts a disclaimer stating otherwise in fine print.

---

[2]  See "Conversational Pragmatics," in chapter 4 of Randy Allen Harris, *Voice Interaction Design: Crafting the New Conversational Speech Systems* (Morgan Kaufmann, 2004).

There will certainly be dark patterns in voice applications. No one who is so upstanding as to read this book would knowingly implement them, but your skills might still break the maxim if they imply that some functionality is possible but the skill doesn't support it, or if the skill doesn't understand the request for it. This is like a broken link, but significantly more likely to occur. You could crawl your website to find broken links, but you can only anticipate what your users might ask for, and how. Later in this chapter you'll learn how to foretell how a user will interact with your application.

If your application can understand a user's request, it needs to map that request to what the user wants to do and respond accordingly. It needs to follow the maxim of *relation*.

### 3.2.3 *Relation*

The maxim of *relation* requires any response to be relevant to what came before it. Having a conversation with a partner who continually changes the topic is frustrating, because we normally assume that a conversation's back-and-forth volleys build upon each previous point. When they don't, we feel unheard and unwelcome. The maxim of relation is strong enough that when people flout it, that itself is a message:

> ANNA: *I heard there might be layoffs soon.*
>
> LILY: *Wow, it sure is hot in here.*

Perhaps Lily wasn't listening to Anna and didn't catch what she said, but Anna's expectations are that Lily is saying something. There *are* layoffs coming, but Lily can't say that she knows anything about it, so she hints at it.

In a GUI, the maxim of relation doesn't come into play much. GUI interactions are designed such that the response to a user's request inherently has a relationship. Nonetheless, GUI designers can break this maxim by hiding content among unrelated details that are good for the business but bad for the user. Newsletter pop-up requests, ad overlays, and clickbait "related articles" all go against the maxim of relation, because that content is not related to what the user requested.

A VUI has a similar user-driven mechanism, and thus a response must be related to the request. Application builders following the maxim of quantity similarly shouldn't put unrelated information in the response. Where a VUI is most likely to run afoul of the maxim of relation is when the user's request is misunderstood.

You will guard against misunderstandings by anticipating how the user will speak to the application. You might also find that you need to change the application's functionality to work around current shortcomings of speech-to-text and intent detection. Eric Olson, whom Amazon named an official "Alexa Champion" and who built the popular Complibot and Insultibot Alexa skills, says that he had to remove secondary functionality when Alexa was routing too much primary functionality to the less important intents.

The maxim of relation is a gift to you, the voice developer, as well. Just as users expect the application to be relevant, you can expect your users to give relevant replies. By carefully considering what the voice application is saying, you can lead users' responses to utterances that the voice platforms best understand and functionality your applications can handle. For example, "Do you want to continue?" leads a user to respond "Yes" or "No." In chapter 9, we'll look at applying these implicit constraints.

Violations of the maxims of quantity, quality, and relation in voice applications are easily caught in text. But there's one maxim that requires you to speak out loud: the maxim of *manner*.

### 3.2.4   *Manner*

The maxim of *manner* directs conversationalists to be clear, specific, and orderly. When people use acronyms and jargon with people outside of their in-group (and sometimes even within), they are violating the maxim of manner through obscurity. The same goes for young children who struggle to tell a story: "And then I went to school, and… no… I actually went to the zoo and you were there. No, you and mommy…." Get to the point, little one!

Designers try to follow this maxim with GUIs by building interactions that are orderly and using language that is clear. An example of these efforts is seen in error messages. A 500 status code means nothing to a nontechnical visitor. A message such as "Something went wrong. It's on our end. Try again or send us an email," says what's actually happening, or how to progress, in the manner the user would prefer. Beyond error messages, GUIs must also make it clear to users how they can achieve their desired outcomes, by using hierarchies within pages, clear calls to action, and even color or design patterns.

A VUI has the same maxim-of-manner concerns, but they are heightened compared to a GUI. Errors can continue to befuddle listeners, and the problem is more difficult with a VUI because the source of the error isn't always obvious on the application side. Did the user really mean to say "Turn off the lights in the bread room" or did the speech-to-text make a mistake? If the former, you should respond that the user has no "bread room" registered. If the latter, you'll need to instruct the user to try again and speak slowly. Making an assumption about which of these happened breaks the maxim of relation, so the best approach is often to give a noncommittal answer stating that something went wrong. In chapter 8 we'll look at how to handle errors in a clearer way.

Unclear error messages are probably not even the most common way that voice applications violate the maxim of manner. That generally results from developers and designers writing responses without considering how they sound. Written and spoken language are different. The written word pulls from a grander corpus, uses a higher vernacular, and relies on complex formulations. Speech has a smaller vocabulary. It uses slang and other words "inappropriate" for writing. It has simpler sentences with fewer clauses. When a formulation that's appropriate in writing is spoken, users have more difficulty following it. Partly this is because the language is out of place, and people flinch at that (imagine a Valentine's Day card in business speak: "Memo: Opportunities for synergies and cross-functional collaboration between our two parties on 02.14"). A larger part of the struggle arises from written language being more complex. Spoken conversations move forward in time at a constant march. Whereas readers can go back over what they've read or jump forward over irrelevant information, listeners don't have those options.

Problems arise when speaking language that started out as written, and the solution is to go "spoken first." Speak aloud the application's responses as—or before—you write them. You'll discover issues that you wouldn't otherwise. Even better than speaking the responses aloud yourself is to run them through the voice platform voices (Alexa or one of the Google Assistant voices, for example). Unless you're hiring voice talent or recording all of the responses yourself, using the platform voices will get you close to how the user will experience your application. Computer-generated speech is not the same as human speech, and a phrase that sounds great in your voice might not land the same way when Alexa says it.

> **TIP** In chapter 7 we'll look at using Speech Synthesis Markup Language (SSML) to manipulate how Alexa and the others say what you want, but voices in applications are not yet good enough to be mistaken for human voices. Our goal when developing voice applications is to imitate the human qualities that make conversations more effective and efficient, but we should never try to fool users. We wouldn't be successful anyway.

To catch problems with the maxims of quality and relation, you'll need to start early, before you write any code or create any sample utterances.

## 3.3 *VUI planning*

When we have an idea for a new application—voice or otherwise—the excitement pulls us to our text editors, because we're eager to have something to play with and to show to others. I get that! Let me tell you, though, about a different approach that will lead to a better result.

You will get to test your assumptions about the user interactions. How will you do this? You are going to play the part of the application.

Start off with your primary intent for your application—the core functionality. What might people say to your voice application to get the information or complete the action? Don't spend much time on this—you'll soon refine it.

This exercise is intended to help you understand what requests you might want to support, or tell the user that you don't support. If a user can ask for last night's baseball scores, can they ask for scores from a specific date? Maybe you aren't willing to give that much granularity, but the application will need to respond appropriately. Or perhaps the behavior you want to support is not something that voice handles well. Data input is one example—you might start out wanting to ask for your user's phone number, but you may realize that providing 10 digits through voice is too cumbersome, and you may look for other options or drop that functionality altogether.

Once you know how a user might speak to your application, come up with some responses that you could send in return. If those involve asking questions of the user, think about how the user could respond in turn, and continue until the conversation comes to an end.

> **TIP** There are services online that can help you put together this interaction flow, but a spreadsheet or even a sheet of paper is enough to keep track at this stage.

Once you have your rough outline, it's time to get some better feedback. The problem now is that you know exactly what you want to build, and you have an idea of how you will build it. You know too much about the application to assess it with a neutral eye. Plus, you're only one person, and each of us has our specific way of talking, with phrases that we use repeatedly and others that we avoid entirely.

Instead, you can unlock a fuller understanding of how users will speak to the application by speaking to a potential user. That they will be using an application without any code or any configuration yet doesn't matter. What you're trying to learn is, if there *were* an application, how would they talk to it and what would be appropriate for the application to say back. Ideally, this proto-user will be similar to your target users, and it should be someone who doesn't know anything about the application before speaking with you.

Before meeting with the user, write out the information that you think might eventually appear on the application's directory listing page (if you're building something like an Alexa skill or Google Action) or marketing page. Include the name of the application, the description of the general functionality, and some sample phrases. Then ask your new user to start interacting with the application, speaking to *you* as if you were the voice-first device.

Note what you get as input. What kind of formulations do you get, and how do they differ from what you expected? Whatever you hear, add it to the list of phrases you'll later send to the NLU for training. For each request, you should respond back, continuing until the conversation ends, and then starting over with a new request. Feel free to use your rough draft, but what you'll likely find is that you didn't account for some of what users ask, and you'll find more natural responses on the spot than you originally wrote down. Because a VUI doesn't have the same bumpers that a GUI does with its well-defined interaction points and built-in limits, these surprises are going to come at some point in the lifecycle of the application. It's better for it to happen when you can ask questions of someone sitting across from you, and you don't have the risk of losing users you've worked hard to acquire.

**NOTE**   This method of testing is often called *Wizard of Oz testing*, because you're taking the place of the "man behind the curtain."

If you run through this exercise often, you'll probably find yourself using different responses, even after you've come up with one that meets all the maxims. That's because people enjoy variety in their conversation, including your users.

## 3.4   *Variety*

Voice applications should always complete the same action or give the same information for the same request, but the packaging doesn't need to be the same each time. This is another area in which a VUI diverges from a GUI. Whereas a GUI should present the same structure on each action, a VUI benefits from variety. Users find a VUI without variety to be "wearying and aggravating."[3]

---

[3]   See chapter 12 in Randy Allen Harris, *Voice Interaction Design: Crafting the New Conversational Speech Systems* (Morgan Kaufmann, 2004).

We can add some variability to the Alexa skill we put together in chapter 2. In truth, we already are responding with varied phrases, but each phrase maps to an input. A good night's sleep is always greeted with "Let's keep the great sleep going!" There are surely different ways to answer. Replying the same way each time sounds wooden and stilted. By creating a list of responses for each input and choosing randomly, we can make our VUI sound more fluid and even human.

**Listing 3.1  Choosing random responses for different inputs (index.js)**

```javascript
function pluck (arr) {
  const randIndex = Math.floor(Math.random() * arr.length);
  return arr[randIndex];
}
```

*A helper function to return a random value from an array*

```javascript
const WellRestedPhrases = {
  tooMuch: [
    "I think you may sleep too much and swing back to tired.",
    "whoa, that's a lot of sleep. You'll wake up rested for sure."
  ],
  justRight: [
    "you should wake up refreshed.",
    "it's clear you know rest is important. Good job, you.",
    "with that much sleep, you're ready to face the world.",
    "you'll wake up invigorated."
  ],
  ...
};
```

*All of the possible responses organized in a single object, with those for just under and too little omitted*

```javascript
const WellRestedIntentHandler = {
  canHandle(handlerInput) {
    ...
  },
  handle(handlerInput) {
    ...

    if (Number.isInteger(adjustedHours)) {
      let speech = "";
```

*Grabs a random value, based on the number of hours slept*

```javascript
      ...

      if(adjustedHours > 12) {
        speech += pluck(WellRestedPhrases.tooMuch);
      } else if(adjustedHours > 8) {
        speech += pluck(WellRestedPhrases.justRight);
      } else if(adjustedHours > 6) {
        speech += pluck(WellRestedPhrases.justUnder);
      } else {
        speech += pluck(WellRestedPhrases.tooLittle);
      }

      ...
    } else {
      ...
    }
  }
};
```

In this code, responses are set as arrays inside an object. It's not necessary to have the same number of phrases for each contingency; more common occurrences should naturally have more responses. There are more options for between 6 and 12 hours, as these are the lengths most people sleep during the night. A function (`pluck`) takes a random response on each go.

Randomly picking out responses might seem simple, but it can go a long way toward making your skill more enjoyable to use. Users will focus less on the fact that they are speaking to a computer, and more on how useful your skill is.

Beyond adding variety, you will want to tailor your responses to the context and the mood. Go ahead, give Alexa some irreverence for a skill that's reporting baseball scores. Baseball's just a game; no one will get too upset (but do me a favor and be sensitive if the Astros lose a close playoff game). If someone is checking their bank account balance, you may want to lean toward being more sedate. Possibly your user has discovered a surprise extra hundred, but it's just as likely that the number isn't as high as hoped, and a light mood won't go over well.

A VUI differs from a GUI in a number of ways. Because conversation in a voice application is always moving forward in time, and because conversations predate computers by thousands of years, voice developers should rely on the assumptions that everyone has about how a conversation will progress. They should make their application reply following the maxims of quantity, quality, relation, and manner. This is not an easy task when working on the application and writing responses in text, and it isn't any easier when you consider that the humans on the other side will have their own various ways of speaking to voice applications. We'll cover how to handle that in chapter 4.

## Summary

- A VUI is its own brand of conversational interface, distinct from chatbots and GUIs, with a reliance on brief, spoken information.
- A VUI should be liberal in what it accepts and account for the different manners in which a user will speak to a skill, from the fluid to the terse.
- Interfaces relying on voice must provide the most relevant information related to the user's requests, in the right quantity and with the appropriate manner.
- Playing the part of the computer with a user new to your application provides information about how your future users will speak to the application, how it should respond, and which functionality it should include.
- People crave variety in their conversations, including with voice applications.

# Using entity resolution and
# built-in intents in Alexa skills

**This chapter covers**

- Using the Alexa Skills Kit (ASK) CLI

- Handling synonyms and errors with entity resolution

- Handling built-in intents and the `LaunchRequest`

- Invoking a skill locally

Before we go on to make more complex skills, let's revisit how we created our first skill. We went to the Amazon Developer Console and we went to the AWS console; in short, we did a lot of work in the browser. Developers generally prefer to avoid going into the browser for configuration unless necessary. Thankfully, the Alexa Skills Kit Command Line Interface (ASK CLI) allows us to develop our skills locally, without heading out to the Developer Console, which permits a more efficient development cycle.

In this chapter, we'll improve on the Sleep Tracker skill we created in chapter 2 by better handling synonyms and using built-in intents, all while integrating the CLI into our workflow and testing our skill locally.

## 4.1   *Alexa Skills Kit CLI*

The Alexa Skills Kit (ASK) CLI is a command-line tool that provides an easier way to manage Alexa skills. Ultimately, it provides a wrapper for the Alexa Skills Management API (SMAPI), which itself can be used to develop skill-building and -testing automation tools. You can see this relationship in figure 4.1. Developers can use the ASK CLI to create, deploy, or manage skills without having to go to the browser. Developers can even submit their skills to the Alexa Skills Store using the CLI.

Think about all the work you did in the browser to create the Sleep Tracker skill. Here's a partial list:

- Specify the skill name.
- Go to another page and provide an invocation name.
- Go to another page and create a new intent.
- Go to another page and provide sample utterances for the new intent.
- Go to another page and create a new custom slot type.
- Go to another page and provide values for the new slot type.
- Go to another page and set the slot inside an utterance to the new custom slot type.
- Go to another page and add the code.
- Save and build the skill.

I don't mean to ridicule the Alexa team for this process. For developers starting out, or for those uncomfortable with the terminal, this works well. It's why we started there instead of going directly to the ASK CLI.

However, the ASK CLI and the organization it offers shortens that process into the following:

- Specify the skill name inside the skill manifest.
- Specify the invocation name, intents, sample utterances, slot types, and slot type values in the invocation model configuration file.
- Deploy the code using a single command in the terminal.

The SMAPI powers the ASK CLI in conjunction with the *skill manifest*. This is a JSON object that contains all of the skill configuration. In fact, you can do more through the skill manifest than you can through the Amazon Developer Console. Certain features, such as listening for events triggered on skill enablement or disablement, are constructed only in this file. By using the skill manifest, even if you don't use these new features, you gain the efficiency that comes with composing a skill in a single, local location.

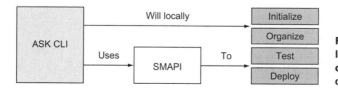

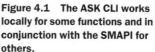

Figure 4.1   **The ASK CLI works locally for some functions and in conjunction with the SMAPI for others.**

**NOTE** This book was written using version[1] 1.3.0 of the ASK CLI. The commands you'll need to use for the ASK CLI and their output might be different if you use a later version of the package. If you want to ensure that your commands and results match this book, use version 1.3.0. It contains everything you need to create the skills we'll discuss.

Building a skill locally is easier and requires less context switching, but that's not the only benefit. There is also the conceptual benefit of seeing that a skill consists of configuring the NLU and creating the code that handles requests—a notion that can be obscured when working in the Developer Console, which splits the code and NLU configuration into separate workflows.

**NOTE** If you haven't already, you will need to sign up for AWS to continue. Amazon will ask for a credit card, but any situation where you have to pay to run your Alexa skill will be a cause for celebration: the free tier will handle all but the most wildly successful skills. Nonetheless, if you don't want to sign up for AWS, you can follow along with the examples in the book using two tools from Bespoken—proxy and LambdaServer— that allow for local development. You can find information in the Bespoken documentation: http://docs.bespoken .io/en/latest/tutorials/tutorial_lambda_local/.

The ASK CLI comes as an NPM package that must be installed globally so that it can create the files you need for organizing your skills. You may need to run this command with sudo:

```
$ npm install ask-cli@1.3.0 -g
```

**NOTE** If you're going to use the ASK CLI on Windows, you'll need the windows-build-tools package (www.npmjs.com/package/windows-build-tools).

Next, you'll need to create an AWS IAM profile in order to be able to push code directly to AWS Lambda. These credentials are separate from what you use to log in to AWS, and they buttress security by allowing for quick revocation in the case of a lost computer. This procedure can be tedious, but you only need to do it once, and it provides the ASK CLI with permission to work with Lambda, IAM, and cloud logs to deploy the fulfillment and set up logging. There are detailed instructions on how to do this in appendix A.

Once you've got your AWS profile set up and the ASK CLI installed, you are good to go. You're ready to initialize the CLI:

```
$ ask init
```

This command will ask you to choose an AWS profile for deploying the skill fulfillment on Lambda. (You probably only have one, in which case the choice is simple.) Then the CLI will open a browser window.[1]

---

[1] If you use the --no-browser flag, you will be given a URL to visit and then an authorization code to paste into the terminal.

NOTE  If you've run the `ask init` command before, the first question will be whether you want to create a new profile or overwrite the existing one. If you are only developing skills for yourself, you can overwrite the profile. Multiple profiles are useful for developers who build skills for multiple accounts, such as those building personal and professional skills, or those in an agency with multiple clients.

### 4.1.1  Creating an Alexa skill project

Now we'll create an Alexa skill project with the CLI. If you've ever used Rails or Meteor, you're familiar with what's about to happen. A CLI command will create the files necessary to structure a new Alexa skill.

This time our skill will be called Super Sleeper. This will allow you to keep the existing Sleep Tracker code inside Lambda and as an Alexa skill you can reference. When you enable two skills with the same name, Alexa chooses which one to go with, which can cause problems when developing and troubleshooting code.

In a different directory than the one you used in chapter 2, run the following commands to create and name the new skill project and install the dependencies:

```
$ ask new --skill-name super-sleeper
New project for Alexa skill created.

$ cd super-sleeper
$ npm install ask-sdk --save --prefix ./lambda/custom
```

In the current working directory, you'll have a new directory (super-sleeper) containing its own subdirectories and files. These new creations contain the interaction model, the skill configuration, the fulfillment code, and a not-to-be-touched internal project configuration. By default, this new skill is a "Hello World" example that we will replace in short order. You can see in figure 4.2 and table 4.1 that each directory or file in the top level performs a different task, and they are also grouped by where they'll go on deployment.

NOTE  By default, ASK CLI will install ask-sdk-core, which is a pared-down version of ask-sdk. The preceding code snippet shows you how to install the ask-sdk package. We will later connect our skill with DynamoDB, a data store on AWS where we can store information about the skill users. The easiest way to make the connection is through the full ask-sdk package, which includes an adapter to persist data to DynamoDB.

```
.ask/        ──────▸ Local
lambda/      ──────▸ AWS Lambda, or other host
models/      ──────▸ Alexa NLP training
skill.json   ──────▸ Skill store
```

**Figure 4.2   Each part of the directory corresponds to a location on deployment.**

**Table 4.1   What each part of an ASK CLI-created Alexa project does**

| Directory or file | Purpose |
| --- | --- |
| .ask | Local project configuration |
| lambda | Fulfillment |
| models | Interaction models, with each locale in a different file |
| skill.json | Skill configuration |

All of the interaction models live in the models directory, including the US English model, en-US.json. The interaction model for the first version of the Sleep Tracker skill contained the invocation name, intents, sample utterances, and slot definitions, and we added it to Alexa by entering everything in the browser. This interaction model file similarly holds all of that information. Your skill can have multiple interaction model files, each for a different locale, following the same naming convention as *en-US*.

If we start with the Sleep Tracker skill's interaction model and add the expected intents for Super Sleeper, we end up with the interaction model that follows. These files end up becoming quite large, but the good news is that they are structured in an easy-to-understand manner. You could easily scan a new interaction model and grasp the skill's interface. We'll replace the default interaction model with our own.

**Listing 4.1   Interaction model defining the user interaction (./models/en-US.json)**

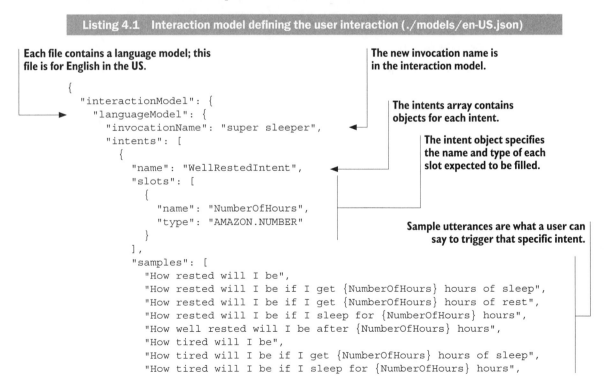

Each file contains a language model; this file is for English in the US.

The new invocation name is in the interaction model.

The intents array contains objects for each intent.

The intent object specifies the name and type of each slot expected to be filled.

Sample utterances are what a user can say to trigger that specific intent.

```
{
  "interactionModel": {
    "languageModel": {
      "invocationName": "super sleeper",
      "intents": [
        {
          "name": "WellRestedIntent",
          "slots": [
            {
              "name": "NumberOfHours",
              "type": "AMAZON.NUMBER"
            }
          ],
          "samples": [
            "How rested will I be",
            "How rested will I be if I get {NumberOfHours} hours of sleep",
            "How rested will I be if I get {NumberOfHours} hours of rest",
            "How rested will I be if I sleep for {NumberOfHours} hours",
            "How well rested will I be after {NumberOfHours} hours",
            "How tired will I be",
            "How tired will I be if I get {NumberOfHours} hours of sleep",
            "How tired will I be if I sleep for {NumberOfHours} hours",
```

```
          "How tired will I be after {NumberOfHours} hours",
          "Will I be rested sleeping for {NumberOfHours} hours",
          "Will I be rested if I rest for {NumberOfHours} hours",
          "Will I be tired sleeping for {NumberOfHours} hours",
          "I will sleep for {NumberOfHours} hours",
          "{NumberOfHours} hours of sleep"
        ]
      }
    ]
  }
}
}
```

**Sample utterances are what a user can say to trigger that specific intent.**

The interaction model file clearly demonstrates the move away from in-browser GUI configuration to local configuration. When we move from the browser to files, we gain the ability to work offline, to build tooling that can create configurations for us, and to track changes through version control. Within this single file, you can see how a user will invoke the skill (`invocationName`) and which intents that skill will handle (`intents`). For each intent, the file specifies the name that Alexa will send to the fulfillment (`name`), the slots that a user might fill when triggering that intent (`slots`), and how a user can trigger the intent (`samples`). This list of sample utterances is far from complete. How else might users trigger this intent?

In the previous version of the Sleep Tracker skill, we also considered how well the user slept the previous night. To do this, we created a custom slot type. We'll do that again in this configuration, but we'll use *entity resolution*.

## 4.2    *Entity resolution*

Much of the interaction model file is familiar: it's what you saw before, but configured in a different format. The intents, sample utterances, and custom slots are still there. The custom slots, however, will change.

Previously the slots consisted of a simple set of values. Now the slots also have IDs and synonyms. The best way to consider slot types now is to think of them as *entities*. An entity has an ID, a standard (or canonical) value, and a list of synonyms.

> **Listing 4.2    A custom slot with values having IDs and synonyms (./models/en-US.json)**

```
{
  "interactionModel": {
    "languageModel": {
      ...
      "intents": [
        {
          "name": "WellRestedIntent",
          "slots": [
            ...
            {
              "name": "SleepQuality",
              "type": "Quality"
            }
```

**A slot with a custom type**

```
        ],
        "samples": [
            ...
            "How well rested will I be after {NumberOfHours} hours if I slept
    {SleepQuality} last night",
            "How tired will I be if I get {NumberOfHours} hours of sleep and
    I slept {SleepQuality} last night",
            "{NumberOfHours} hours of sleep and {SleepQuality} sleep last
    night",
            "{NumberOfHours} hours {SleepQuality} last night"
        ]
    }
    ],
    "types": [                    ◄── The types array holds objects      The name the slots use
        {                             defining the custom types.           to reference the type
            "name": "Quality",   ◄────────────────────────┐
            "values": [
                {
                    "id": "good",
                    "name": {
                        "value": "good",
                        "synonyms": [
                            "well", "wonderfully",  "a lot", "amazing", "fantastic",
                            "great", "not bad"
                        ]
                    }
                },
                {
                    "id": "bad",                          A value object contains an ID
                    "name": {                             and an object defining which
                        "value": "bad",                   values a user might speak.
                        "synonyms": [
                            "poorly", "little", "very little", "not at all"
                        ]
                    }
                }
            ]
        }
    ]
    }
}
```

With this new format for custom types, we can still include all of the values we listed before, but now the values that are effectively similar are grouped together as a list of synonyms, along with an ID and a canonical value. In this example, the ID is the same as the canonical value, but that isn't necessary. You can see how this works in figure 4.3.

Entity resolution need not only be used for classical synonyms, like "bad" and "terrible." It can also envelop the wide number of ways people can communicate and devices can understand. For example, it's true that "awful" is another way to say "bad." But so is "I tossed and turned all night." When you include these similar statements as entity synonyms, you get two benefits: you train the NLU to recognize the phrase, and the fulfillment receives both the canonical and original values.

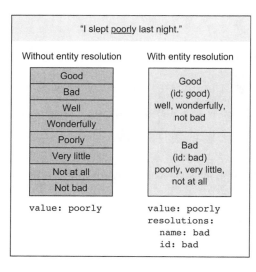

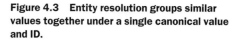

**Figure 4.3   Entity resolution groups similar values together under a single canonical value and ID.**

Phonetic "typos" can also be fixed with entity resolution. While you're testing, or as users interact with a skill, slot values will come in that don't match an existing entity and don't make sense in the context of the skill either. Perhaps Alexa hears "middle" instead of "little." Setting these misheard values as synonyms will return an expected canonical entity value that you can match inside the fulfillment. That will head off a class of errors that would otherwise derail the user experience.

Entity resolution has a few implications for the fulfillment. You'll recall that in our previous code, we checked a slot value against an array of good or bad sleep qualities.

**Listing 4.3   Checking for whether slot values are good or bad in Sleep Tracker**

```
handle(handlerInput) {
  ...

  const quality = slots.SleepQuality.value;

  const good = ["good", "well", "wonderfully", "a lot", "amazing",
               "fantastic", "great", "not bad"];
  const bad = ["bad", "poorly", "little", "very little", "not at all"];

  ...

  if(good.includes(quality)) {
    adjustedHours += 1;
    speech = "You slept well last night, and "
  }

  if(bad.includes(quality)) {
    adjustedHours -= 1;
    speech = "You slept poorly last night, and "
  }

  ...
}
```

Be thankful, because that nonsense is over: all you need to do now is check the entity ID. This will make the code easier to understand and make the skill easier to extend. Now there's no need to update both the slot values *and* the code when making an addition. Everything concerning the interaction model lives in a single location.

Let's move on from the language model configuration to the fulfillment, and see how we can improve on the synonym matching.

### 4.2.1 Fulfillment

The first thing we need to look is at where the ASK CLI expects the code will live. When you deploy the skill through the CLI, the CLI will look inside lambda/custom for code that it will then send to AWS Lambda to handle skill requests. That's where we need to place the fulfillment.

Take the code from last chapter's Sleep Tracker skill and paste it without changes into lambda/custom/index.js, replacing everything that was in that file.

Once that's done, you'll need to make two small changes. First, import ask-sdk instead of ask-sdk-core. Second, use the `standard` skill builder rather than the `custom` one. These changes are both shown in the following listing.

---

**Listing 4.4   Using the `custom` skill builder (./lambda/custom/index.js)**

```
const Alexa = require("ask-sdk");          ◄──┐ Imports the heftier SDK

...

exports.handler = Alexa.SkillBuilders.standard()   ◄──┐ Uses the standard skill builder
...
```

**NOTE** Future listings will show additions or changes to the existing code. Although it could be useful to see the code reprinted in its entirety, it would also make for a book that's more difficult to read. I'll explain where the changes should be made. You can also see the code at each step through the commits available in the code repository at www.manning.com/books/voice-applications-for-alexa-and-google-assistant and also at github.com/dustincoates/voice-applications.

We will build up this skill so that it interacts with DynamoDB to store information. Using the `standard` skill builder will make that easier, and it will be easiest of all if we start using the `standard` builder now, instead of the `custom` one we used in the past, which requires more work to connect to a data store.

To move away from checking the slot value against a list of synonyms, we need to take a different approach and check instead against a single, unchanging value that represents the group of synonyms. This is the entity ID.

**Listing 4.5    Responding based on the sleep quality ID (./lambda/custom/index.js)**

**Grabs the value without entity resolution**

```
handle(handlerInput) {
  const slots = handlerInput.requestEnvelope.request.intent.slots;
  ...
  // const quality = slots.SleepQuality && slots.SleepQuality.value;
  // const good = ["good", "well", "wonderfully", "a lot", "amazing",
  //                "fantastic", "great", "not bad"];
  // const bad = ["bad", "poorly", "little", "very little", "not at all"];

  if (Number.isInteger(adjustedHours)) {
    let speech = "";

    const resolutionValues = slots.SleepQuality &&
      slots.SleepQuality.resolutions &&
      slots.SleepQuality.resolutions.resolutionsPerAuthority[0] &&
      slots.SleepQuality.resolutions.resolutionsPerAuthority[0].values;

    if (resolutionValues) {
      const quality = resolutionValues[0].value.id;

      if (quality === "good") {
        adjustedHours += 1;
        speech = "You slept well last night, and ";
      }

      if (quality === "bad") {
        adjustedHours -= 1;
        speech = "You slept poorly last night, and ";
      }
    }
    ...
  }
  ...
}
...
```

**There could potentially be more than one value if you add the same synonym to multiple canonical values.**

**Grabs the ID of the entity**

As in most software, as power increases so does complexity, and the added complexity is evident in the fulfillment as well. We could continue to use the value from the sleep quality slot, but that value represents what Alexa heard. Instead, we just need to determine if last night's sleep was *good* or *bad*. Because the entity ID is the representation of the grouping of synonyms, we can grab that value and use it inside the conditionals to begin building the response.

> **NOTE**  We only assume a single value in `resolutionsPerAuthority`. For a very long time, this was a safe assumption. Amazon, however, has released dynamic entities, where developers can specify entity values at runtime. This feature is also available inside of Dialogflow for use with Actions on Google Assistant, and developers can use it to specify entity values that a user might provide that can be user-specific or context-specific. Members of a user's family, "soups of the day," or guided quiz responses where the answers change on each step of the quiz are examples of good uses for dynamic entities.

The depth in which we examine the nested `slots` objects and subobjects represents the new complexity brought by entity resolution. The benefit of this complexity is abstract on first usage. You will be tempted to ignore it and go straight for the entity ID, but you will find problems. The most immediate is the explosion when a user doesn't provide a sleep quality and the nested objects are no longer present to provide the final ID. This is why we check at each nested level. Because the sleep quality isn't always expected, we want a way to signify when it isn't present without a runtime error. Ultimately, if the user has provided a sleep quality, `resolutionValues` receives an array of objects, each with the canonical value and entity ID that the slot value maps to. For example, the value "wonderfully" in our skill will return an object that has both a canonical value and ID of "good."

There is something we're ignoring in our latest code. We went straight for the first item inside the `values` array (set to the variable `resolutionValues`). This isn't because there will only ever be a single item inside that array. If you place the same synonym in multiple groupings, you will get multiple values back. In this case, though, how could someone have both "good" and "bad" sleep? They can't, so we don't have any crossover across groupings, and we don't need to worry about multiple values.

You can have situations where you do have the same values across multiple groupings. In a skill for baseball scores, some teams will be referenced in the same manner. A user could ask for the White Sox by asking for the "White Sox," "Chicago White Sox," or "Chicago." The crosstown Cubs map to the "Cubs," "Chicago Cubs," or, again, "Chicago." When a user asks for "Chicago," Alexa will send two separate resolution values, and you might then ask the user for clarification—"Did you want the Cubs or the White Sox?"—or perhaps provide the scores for both teams.

> **NOTE** Entity resolution only works for slots with custom values. This includes custom slots and built-in slots that you have extended with custom values. Our skill can't use entity resolution for the number of hours. Our reliance on the `AMAZON.NUMBER` built-in slot precludes that, and so we go straight for the slot value.

Now that you have the interaction model and the fulfillment, you can deploy it. This time, we'll avoid the browser—the ASK CLI will handle the process. Run the following `deploy` command with no options from inside the root of the skill directory.

**Listing 4.6 Deploying the skill configuration and fulfillment**

```
$ ask deploy
-------------------- Create Skill Project --------------------
Profile for the deployment: [default]
Skill Id: amzn1.ask.skill.fcaf69830-3cf2-4980-b1a2-3b9999e8a34c    ◄────┐
Skill deployment finished.                          Your skill ID will be different.
Model deployment finished.
Lambda deployment finished.
Lambda function(s) updated:
  [URI] arn:aws:lambda:us-east-1:87698204184078:function:ask-custom-super-
    sleeper-default
```

```
No in-skill product to be deployed.
Your skill is now deployed and enabled in the development stage.
Try invoking the skill by saying "Alexa, open {your_skill_invocation_name}"
     or simulate an invocation via the `ask simulate` command.
```

> **NOTE**  If you have difficulties with the `deploy` command, you may need to first run this command: `touch ~/.aws/config`.

When you run the deployment, the CLI will perform a few actions. First, it will take the skill.json file and the interaction model file (or files, if you're targeting multiple locales), and use them to assemble the skill metadata and train the NLU. This is the same as what was previously done in the Amazon Developer Console. Next, it takes the code inside lambda/custom and sends it to AWS Lambda, creating a function with a name of `ask-custom` plus the skill name and profile name. Then it stores the new Alexa skill ID and Lambda ARN (Amazon Resource Name, which is how AWS services can identify specific AWS resources) inside .ask/config. You can see where each directory or file heads in figure 4.4. Each time you run the `deploy` command from now on, the CLI will update the configuration and the Lambda function, but it won't create a new skill or function.

After it is deployed, the Super Sleeper skill can handle `WellRestedIntent`, but that makes for just the beginning of a skill. A couple of common interactions are when a user wants to cancel the current flow and start over, or instead stop entirely. These are common interactions, and ones that the Alexa team foresaw. They created built-in intents for this purpose.

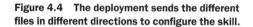

Figure 4.4   **The deployment sends the different files in different directions to configure the skill.**

### 4.2.2   *Built-in intents*

Each time intents appear in the interaction model, they feed the NLU and are available to be invoked by the user. In `WellRestedIntent`, we specified the intent name, the sample utterances, and the slots a user could fill. `WellRestedIntent` is very specialized, and few other skills will have the same utterances and slots mapping to an intent. Stopping and cancelling, however, are intents that any skill will likely have. Indeed, to appear in the Alexa skill store, Amazon *expects* developers to add these intents, and the Alexa platform benefits when users know there will be consistency between different skills in the vocabulary for cancelling, stopping, and other common behaviors.

Amazon has made it as easy as possible to integrate the built-in intents with the interaction model.

**Listing 4.7   Adding intents to the interaction model (./models/en-US.json)**

```
{
  "interactionModel": {
    "languageModel": {
      "invocationName": "super sleeper",
      "intents": [
        {
          "name": "AMAZON.CancelIntent",
          "samples": []           ◄──────────┐  Developers can extend what a user can
        },                                    │  say to trigger built-in intents.
        {
          "name": "AMAZON.StopIntent",
          "samples": []
        },
        ...
      ],
      ...
    }
  }
}
```

Even though the stop and cancel intents are prebuilt and expected by Amazon in any public skill, developers must still add them to the intent model. Alexa natively creates a mapping between phrases like "stop" and "cancel" and their related intents, but developers can also add their own phrases. Maybe "It's time for bedtime" maps to the stop intent? Hey, it's your skill. Add a little bit of flavor to it.

There always needs to be a handler in the fulfillment for any new intent, though as you'll soon see, there need not be one handler per intent. Determining which handler is responsible for a given intent is not the role of Alexa but of the fulfillment. Alexa merely provides information about the request, such as the desired intent, the slot values, and attributes about the user. The SDK takes this information and feeds it into each handler's `canHandle` method, in the order the developer listed them in the `addRequestHandlers` arguments, until it hits `true`, and it passes control to that handler's `handle` method.

The flow of information starts with the user saying something, and with that being passed through device and platform to the fulfillment, but it doesn't stop there. The information continues to flow within the fulfillment, as in figure 4.5, until it finds a handler and reverses with the response. One opportunity that arises from this continued flow is that there needn't be a direct link between intent and handler. The fulfillment can have different handlers for different intents, for different intent and slot combinations, for different times of day, or even for different results of a request to an outside source. Conversely, because each `canHandle` method is invoked until one returns `true`, processing time becomes a consideration. The order in which you register handlers should take into consideration how often they are invoked (the more common go first), how expensive they are (the more expensive go last), and whether they are more or less specific (the least-specific go last).

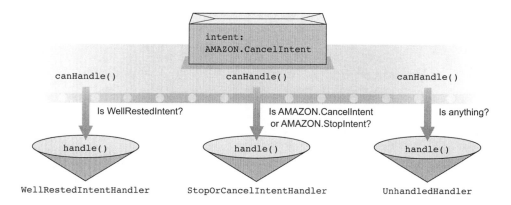

**Figure 4.5**   **The flow for determining which handler will respond to a request is like a conveyor belt, with the request coming off the belt once a condition is met.**

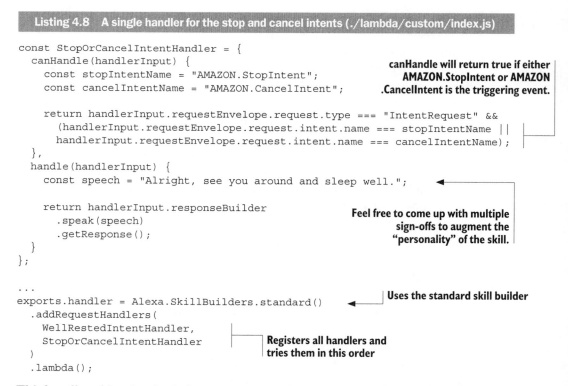

Listing 4.8   A single handler for the stop and cancel intents (./lambda/custom/index.js)

```
const StopOrCancelIntentHandler = {
  canHandle(handlerInput) {
    const stopIntentName = "AMAZON.StopIntent";
    const cancelIntentName = "AMAZON.CancelIntent";

    return handlerInput.requestEnvelope.request.type === "IntentRequest" &&
      (handlerInput.requestEnvelope.request.intent.name === stopIntentName ||
      handlerInput.requestEnvelope.request.intent.name === cancelIntentName);
  },
  handle(handlerInput) {
    const speech = "Alright, see you around and sleep well.";

    return handlerInput.responseBuilder
      .speak(speech)
      .getResponse();
  }
};

...
exports.handler = Alexa.SkillBuilders.standard()
  .addRequestHandlers(
    WellRestedIntentHandler,
    StopOrCancelIntentHandler
  )
  .lambda();
```

canHandle will return true if either AMAZON.StopIntent or AMAZON .CancelIntent is the triggering event.

Feel free to come up with multiple sign-offs to augment the "personality" of the skill.

Uses the standard skill builder

Registers all handlers and tries them in this order

This handler object has both the canHandle and handle methods. The handle method says goodbye to the user, but the canHandle method is more interesting—it checks to see if the inbound request is either to stop or to cancel. In many skills, these two requests will be different from each other. In a banking skill, a user canceling a transaction doesn't mean the interaction is over; it just means that Alexa should follow up and ask what they want to do instead. In skills where a user isn't trying to change data or progress along a flow, like the Super Sleeper skill, stopping and canceling can be treated as equivalent. This equivalence inside the `canHandle` method demonstrates that a handler object need not be constrained to a single handler. The beauty of this intra-fulfillment flow is that you can create handler objects for situations as narrow or as broad as you want, using any condition you desire.

> **TIP** I recommend that you test your skills each time you change the fulfillment by redeploying and testing with your device. I won't explicitly point that out except when we're discussing *how* to test the new code, so remember that as you progress through the book. If you only want to update the fulfillment code, use the command `ask deploy --target lambda`. This command won't update the interaction model, which is generally the slowest part of the deployment process.

Alright, a built-in intent will handle common requests. What happens if the user launches the skill without saying anything else?

### 4.2.3 *LaunchRequest*

"Alexa, open Super Sleeper."

We can reason about what will happen next. The skill *launches* in this scenario; that much we know. We also know that every request must be handled. Will the built-in cancel and stop intents handle this kind of bare request? That wouldn't make sense. How about our custom-built intents? That makes even less sense.

For this situation, we need not an intent request but instead the `LaunchRequest`.

**Listing 4.9 Handling the `LaunchRequest` (`./lambda/custom/index.js`)**

```
const LaunchRequestHandler = {
  canHandle(handlerInput) {
    return handlerInput.requestEnvelope.request.type === "LaunchRequest";
  },
  handle(handlerInput) {
    const speech = "Welcome to the Super Sleeper skill. You can ask for " +
                   "how well rested you'll be or tell me how you slept.";
    const reprompt = "Try saying 'I slept well last night.'";

    return handlerInput.responseBuilder
      .speak(speech)
      .reprompt(reprompt)
      .getResponse();
  }
};

...

exports.handler = Alexa.SkillBuilders.)
  .addRequestHandlers(
    ...
    LaunchRequestHandler
  )
  .lambda();
```

*The `LaunchRequest` is a request type, not an intent.*

The launch request responds to a different type of request. There's no intent name and only the request type of LaunchRequest. The launch request only comes around at the very beginning of an interaction, when the user doesn't ask for anything beyond launching a skill. As a result, the handler welcomes the user and provides some guidance on what the user can do.

> **Little VUI touches that make a difference**
>
> Notice the use of the first-person singular in listing 4.9. The skill is using the Alexa voice, so it piggybacks on the Alexa personality. For many users, this feels like speaking to a real person, whereas using the first-person plural ("tell us") or third-person ("tell Alexa") would seem out of place.
>
> I think, though, that the response could be improved. Can you catch the unnatural phrasing? "Welcome to" isn't a phrase people use to start a conversation, yet voice applications do it all the time. Try to devise a better way to greet users when they launch your skills.

If you deploy this again and test it by saying "Alexa, launch Super Sleeper," you will hear Alexa guiding you in how to use the skill. You don't need to use voice, though. You can also invoke the skill from the terminal.

## 4.3   *Invoking the skill locally*

So far we have been testing our skills with a device or inside the Developer Console, and each of those has its uses. A skill is not fully tested until it's tested with voice on a device, because the interaction of speech between the human and device is otherwise lost. The Developer Console, on the other hand, can show the response and a history of interactions.

The ASK CLI has its own tooling for testing in the simulate command. This command takes a written utterance and sends it to the Alexa platform, and back, ultimately, to the terminal. In doing so it offers up the request, response, and execution metrics. This won't replace testing through directly invoking the fulfillment or testing on a device, but it adds another tool for ad hoc or automated testing.

> **Listing 4.10   Using the ASK CLI** simulate **command to test the** LaunchRequest

```
$ ask simulate \
--locale en-US \
--skill-id amzn1.ask.skill.fcaf69830-3cf2-4980-b1a2-3b9999e8a34c \
--text "launch super sleeper"     ◄─────┐
                                  │ The utterance a user would say to Alexa
```

> **TIP**   There is also a validate command that checks the skill configuration in skill.json for readiness to submit to the skill store.

This command snakes its way through the entire skill flow, as you can see in figure 4.6, and returns JSON containing both the request sent to the fulfillment and the response the fulfillment created. You already know that a voice application is simply data flowing

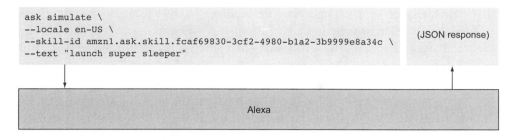

```
ask simulate \
--locale en-US \
--skill-id amzn1.ask.skill.fcaf69830-3cf2-4980-b1a2-3b9999e8a34c \
--text "launch super sleeper"
```

(JSON response)

Alexa

**Figure 4. 6   The simulate command communicates with Alexa and returns the request and response.**

through services. With that in mind, and considering that the simulate command pro-vides the data coming and going, plus the fact that an AWS Lambda function is really just a function that we can call with arguments, we can use the returned JSON for test-ing the fulfillment locally.

Because the simulate command outputs a JSON response, we can send that directly to a file.

**Listing 4.11   Storing the simulation response in a JSON file**

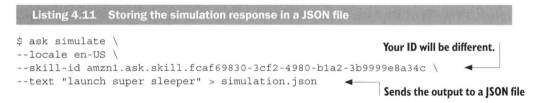

```
$ ask simulate \
--locale en-US \
--skill-id amzn1.ask.skill.fcaf69830-3cf2-4980-b1a2-3b9999e8a34c \
--text "launch super sleeper" > simulation.json
```

**Your ID will be different.**

**Sends the output to a JSON file**

The newly created JSON file contains the round-trip data, including details on the request itself, such as the ID, whether it was successful, which fulfillment endpoint it hit, and the body of the request. It also contains the response and records how many milliseconds the entire execution took. Because a Lambda function takes in that request body, writing code to run the fulfillment requires only a few lines.

**Listing 4.12   Using the stored response to invoke the fulfillment directly (./test.js)**

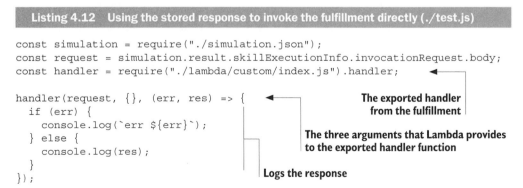

```
const simulation = require("./simulation.json");
const request = simulation.result.skillExecutionInfo.invocationRequest.body;
const handler = require("./lambda/custom/index.js").handler;

handler(request, {}, (err, res) => {
  if (err) {
    console.log(`err ${err}`);
  } else {
    console.log(res);
  }
});
```

**The exported handler from the fulfillment**

**The three arguments that Lambda provides to the exported handler function**

**Logs the response**

AWS Lambda invokes the skill fulfillment by calling the exported handler function and providing it with three arguments: the inbound request, a context object with informa-tion about the Lambda invocation, and a callback that receives an error or response object to send back to the caller. The exported handler function, you'll recall, is created by the ASK SDK, which ultimately calls the callback and sends it the assembled response.

This code mimics the data's first entry into the fulfillment as well as its final point before the response returns to Alexa. By calling the function, you can test changes in the fulfillment and confirm that you get back the expected response. This code will not test the Alexa service—that must be done through the simulator, the Developer Console, or a device—but you can edit the simulation file to change any of the incoming details, like session attributes or slot values, to provide a quick check without a redeployment of the fulfillment.

We now have a fuller-featured skill than before. By using the built-in intents, we can take advantage of Amazon's wealth of training data to better understand when someone asks our skill for help, aid, or information on what it can do. LaunchRequest allows users to invoke the skill directly, without an intent. Plus, we've unshackled our development process from the browser, using the ASK CLI to speed up our work and give us new ways to manage skills. We'll continue with this skill in the next chapter, making it conversational.

## Summary

- Using the ASK CLI creates a central, local place for skill creation and configuration, and it demonstrates the relation between the fulfillment and interaction configuration.
- People will use different words and phrases for the same thing, and entity resolution provides a tidy way to organize these synonyms with a canonical value and an ID.
- Some intents are common enough for Alexa to provide established interaction models. Developers can add these built-in intents to any skill.
- The flow of information that starts with the user's utterance doesn't stop at the fulfillment, but instead shuffles through each handler object's canHandle method until one returns true.
- LaunchRequest is triggered when a user asks for a skill without an explicit intent. A handler must be created by the developer to catch and respond to this request.
- The ASK CLI's simulate command will simulate an Alexa invocation without using a device or the Developer Console.
- Capturing the request created by the Alexa service and sending it to the fulfillment handler directly allows for quick, local invocation of the skill fulfillment without deploying.

# Making a conversational Alexa skill 5

**This chapter covers**

- Sketching out a skill's conversational flow
- Keeping track of skill flow by using state
- Connecting to a database for cross-session storage

So far the Sleep Tracker and Super Sleeper skills have been of the call-and-response variety: when I say X, you say Y. Adding a number of different responses gives the skill more of a personality: when I say X, you randomly say U, V, W, Y, or Z. That's where the skill ends, though. That's not how real conversations work.

In human conversation, even the most perfunctory requests for information have the opportunity for back-and-forth. For example, you need to know the next arrival for an uptown train, so you look at someone standing on the platform and ask, "When's the next uptown train?" Your fellow commuter could say, "In about five minutes," and that would be the end of it. But it's also possible that there are several uptown trains, so the question comes up, "Do you need the express or the local?" Now you're having a conversation.

This back-and-forth is possible with voice-first skills, too. There wouldn't be much value in voice first otherwise. That we can create conversations is good news. Even better is that the code to do this is not very difficult to write. The bad news is that keeping the flow in your head while you code can be difficult. This is one situation where sketching out a flow with pen and paper is a good idea.

## 5.1    *Creating a conversation*

In this chapter we'll start with the Super Sleeper skill from chapter 4 and tackle the next iteration. The new version will be similar to the old, but it will introduce some conversational aspects. We'll change the behavior of `WellRestedIntent` to handle back and forth between the user and Alexa.

> **NOTE**   You can find the code for the Super Sleeper skill as it was at the end of chapter 4 on the book's website at www.manning.com/books/voice-applications -for-alexa-and-google-assistant and also on GitHub, at https://github.com/ dustincoates/voice-applications/tree/master/chapter-4/super-sleeper.

In this version of Super Sleeper, users will still be able to get an estimate of the level of drowsiness they will feel after a number of hours of sleep. But let's be honest—how often do people sleep for more than 12 hours? If a user says a number greater than 12, Alexa will ask, "Are you sure?" and allow them to confirm the number. This will probably lead to a "yes" or "no" response, which the fulfillment needs to handle differently than the same answer in a different context.

There are a few ways to handle this. One is to keep track of how many hours the user said, store it, and then have a condition that checks to see if that value is more than 12. This will work for a smaller skill, but it will become overly brittle and difficult to reason about when the skill becomes more complex. The developer will need to keep in mind all the different attributes and which values lead to which handlers. Furthermore, the code must make sure that the values that lead to different handlers don't conflict in unexpected ways, and that the attributes are cleared out when they're no longer needed.

Another approach is to use state management. If you come from a computer background, "state" is familiar to you. If you're a self-trained developer, you may not know what a "state machine" refers to specifically, but you've likely worked with one in the past.

### 5.1.1    *State management*

A *state machine* is a concept that allows code to route events based on a current context. The simplest possible state machine might determine whether an array is in state A or state B based on whether `true` or `false` was the last item popped.

Suppose we have a state machine with the following rules: if it is in the A state, it will change to the B state if the next input is `false`; if it is in the B state, it will change to the A state when the next input is `true`; if the input is `true` in the A state or `false` in the B state, it stays put. Figure 5.1 illustrates these rules.

This might sound theoretical, but it has practical implications you've likely worked with before. If you're creating a music player, what happens when the listener presses Play when music is already playing? Probably nothing. What about the Pause button? Playing music stops, and paused music does nothing.

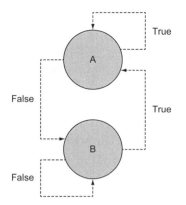

**Figure 5.1  The state machine moves between states A and B depending on the previous state and the current input.**

A state machine can be more complex and can represent an entire flow in an application. There aren't always just two possibilities (move or stay)—there can be many different transitions between states. You can see this in a banking skill, where a user can go from a start state to the checking, savings, or mortgage states, each with their own branches, and these all can lead back to the base state, as in figure 5.2.

Truthfully, this complex state machine is quite simplistic. There are several states, but there are at most only two possible moves from each state, and one of those is always heading back.

You might think that a voice application state machine would be much more complex because users can jump from intent to intent at any time. But we won't use state machines to select intents—users do that by what they say. Instead we'll use state to route the intents to specific handlers.

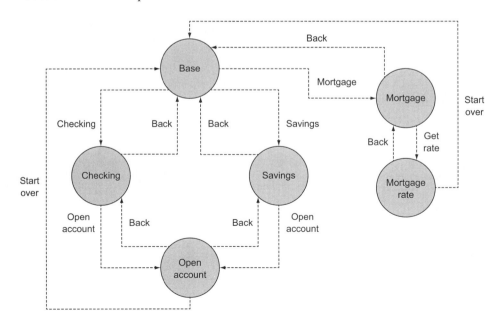

**Figure 5.2  This complex machine moves between many states.**

#### USING STATE TO ROUTE TO DIFFERENT HANDLERS

We discussed earlier that the Super Sleeper skill will ask users for confirmation if they say they will sleep for a long time. We'll start off by thinking about how a user might respond, before thinking about how we might route that response in the skill.

The skill will ask the user for confirmation if the skill has heard the user ask for more than 12 hours of sleep. Then, if the skill has asked the user for confirmation, the user will likely respond with a "yes" or "no." This plain English description of the behavior is useful. When you describe an intent with "if something has happened, then a user will respond with something," you have identified a probable use of state for intent routing. In this scenario, we'll set a state called TOO_MUCH_CONFIRMATION to signal that the user is in the confirmation state for too much sleep, and we'll use two built-in handlers to handle the possible responses.

Conceptually, the simplest way to think about handling states is to think of "intent-first" wherein you first sketch out the intents, then think of different conditions that would lead to different handlers for the intent. This is more natural for most skills because it mimics the interaction model, which defines intents, but not state or other conditions. Because an intent defined in the model is available no matter what a user has been doing, thinking first about intents is useful because it emphasizes that every intent has a handler, and that intents can be further served by multiple handlers if different conditions call for different actions.

Because the request handlers are registered in order, figure 5.3 illustrates the flow the request will take as the SDK looks for the right handler. If the request type is IntentRequest and the intent name is WellRestedIntent, the request goes to the WellRestedIntentHandler.

To implement state handling in the skill, we need to first have the states in the code. A best practice is to define a top-level object that contains all of the states. This allows you to see and understand clearly all the states that are available and that might guide the user flow and the intent handling. State management in skills can be confusing with all the back and forth between states, so it's best to do what you can to keep it simpler.

We'll start with a single state that we'll define as TOO_MUCH_CONFIRMATION. Think of this as if the user has had "too much sleep" and we're now asking for confirmation. CONFIRMATION_AFTER_TOO_MUCH_SLEEP is just excessive, after all.

> **Listing 5.1   An object that contains all possible user states (./lambda/custom/index.js)**

```
const states = {
  TOO_MUCH_CONFIRMATION: "TOO_MUCH_CONFIRMATION"
};
```

The user will enter the "too much sleep" state after telling Alexa that the amount of expected sleep is greater than 12 hours. Alexa will follow up like a worried parent, asking, "Are you sure?" By bouncing information between participants, with each remembering where the conversation stands at a given moment, we form a conversation.

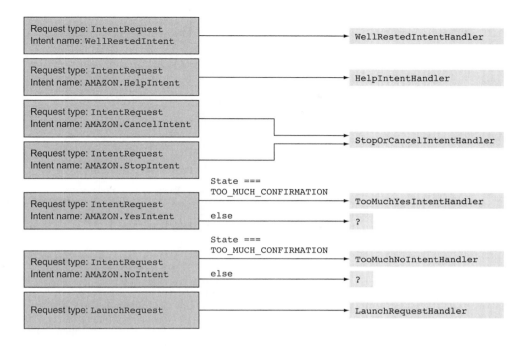

**Figure 5.3   Handlers are mapped to request types, intents, and state.**

The state will be identified inside *session attributes.* There are three types of attributes inside a skill: request, persistent, and session.

- *Request attributes* live only as long as a request. The user asks for something, the fulfillment responds, and the attribute goes away.
- *Persistent attributes* live in a data store and are generally tied to either a user or device ID.
- *Session attributes* live for a session. They aren't stored but are passed back and forth between Alexa and the fulfillment for as long as the session continues. There can be a lot of reasons for a session to cease. Perhaps the user's kids come into the room to ask their parent a question, or the user needs to look up some information that Alexa requested. Or perhaps the Alexa device could not hear the user and assumes that the conversation is over.

Information about the user that needs to be kept for a long time shouldn't be stored in the session. A flag to denote whether the user is new or existing doesn't go in the session, nor does the furthest step the user has reached in a multi-step interactive story. Rather, use session attributes for any information that you could lose without adversely affecting the user's enjoyment of the skill. For everything else, persist skill attributes in a database. We'll look at this later in the chapter.

Session attributes are ideal for storing the current state, such as whether the user is planning to sleep for a long time.

Listing 5.2   The current state lives in the session attributes (./lambda/custom/index.js)

```javascript
const WellRestedIntentHandler = {
  ...
  handle(handlerInput) {
    ...

    if (Number.isInteger(adjustedHours)) {
      let speech = "";
      const attributes = handlerInput.attributesManager.
    getSessionAttributes();                    ◀──────┐ Grabs the session attributes

      ...                                     The user's session now has a state attribute
                                                set to TOO_MUCH_CONFIRMATION.
      if (adjustedHours > 12) {
        attributes.state = states.TOO_MUCH_CONFIRMATION;
        handlerInput.attributesManager.setSessionAttributes(attributes);

        const speech = "I want to make sure I got that. " +
                       "Do you really plan to sleep " +
                       numOfHours + " hours?";
        const reprompt = numOfHours + " hours? Did I hear right?";

        return handlerInput.responseBuilder              numOfHours refers to
               .speak(speech)                             what the user said.
               .reprompt(reprompt)
               .getResponse();
      }                                        Returns early because this is the
      ...                                      only response with a prompt

      return handlerInput.responseBuilder.speak(speech).getResponse();
    }
    ...
  }
};
```

The code first grabs the session attributes, which are passed back and forth between the fulfillment and Alexa. At this point in the code, `getSessionAttributes` is functionally the same as retrieving `session.attributes` directly from the request object (request-Envelope). Later, the `state` attribute is set and passed to `setSessionAttributes`, which stores the session attributes in the response object that will be sent to Alexa.

The skill then has Alexa voice her concern. More than 12 hours in one go is a long time. When Alexa replies to the user, the response includes the slot value—this is a subtle, but important, addition. Speech-to-text mistakes are unavoidable but can be made worse if the voice application doesn't give the user the opportunity to understand what happened. In this case, the user may have said "four" and Alexa heard "fourteen." Being transparent helps the user correct the error.

**NOTE** Falling into wooden dialog is easy. My first draft of the preceding code had the prompt, "I heard you say 14 hours. Did I get that right?" No one speaks like this! After speaking it out loud, I changed it to what's in the code: "I want to make sure I got that. Do you really plan to sleep 14 hours?"

Now that the user has been flagged as being in the "too much sleep" state, and the skill has asked for confirmation, the code needs to handle the response that comes back.

### 5.1.2 Per-state handlers

The skill will now handle the user's request on two axes: what the user said, which maps to the intent, and the state the user is in when responding, as defined by the session attributes. This combination calls for a separate handler that uses the `canHandle` method to check both of those conditions.

Think about how you might respond to the question, "Do you really plan to sleep 14 hours?" The two answers that come immediately to mind are the most simple: "yes" or "no." To capture those responses, we can create handlers for the built-in intents that map to yes and no responses. These are pretrained by Amazon, so they can handle the base answers, but they can also map "sure," "nope," "yeah," and others to the correct intent.

> **Listing 5.3   Handling an affirmative user response (./lambda/custom/index.js)**

```
const TooMuchYesIntentHandler = {
  canHandle(handlerInput) {                           Checks that all conditions are fulfilled
    const intentName = "AMAZON.YesIntent";
    const attributes = handlerInput.attributesManager.getSessionAttributes();

    return handlerInput.requestEnvelope.request.type === "IntentRequest" &&
      handlerInput.requestEnvelope.request.intent.name === intentName &&
      attributes.state === states.TOO_MUCH_CONFIRMATION;
  },
  handle(handlerInput) {
    const speech = "Okay, " + pluck(WellRestedPhrases.tooMuch);

    const attributes = handlerInput.attributesManager.getSessionAttributes();
    delete attributes.state;                          Resets the attributes to remove the state
    handlerInput.attributesManager.setSessionAttributes(attributes);

    return handlerInput.responseBuilder
      .speak(speech)
      .getResponse();
  }
};

exports.handler = Alexa.SkillBuilders.standard()
  .addRequestHandlers(
    TooMuchYesIntentHandler,          ◄──── Registers the new handlers
    WellRestedIntentHandler,
    StopOrCancelIntentHandler,
    LaunchRequestHandler
  )
  .lambda();
```

The first handler is for when users respond in the affirmative. Its `canHandle` method requires that the intent is `AMAZON.YesIntent` and that the user is in the "too much sleep" state. Because the handler has this extra level of specificity arising from the state, we register the handler at the very beginning. In the fulfillment of the intent, we'll create the response as normal and remove the state from the session attributes, because the user has now closed the conversation by saying that Alexa heard correctly.

If the user says Alexa made a mistake, the code needs to rectify it.

**Listing 5.4    Handling a negative user response (./lambda/custom/index.js)**

```
const TooMuchNoIntentHandler = {
  canHandle(handlerInput) {                        Checks for the state and the "no" intent
    const intentName = "AMAZON.NoIntent";
    const attributes = handlerInput.attributesManager.getSessionAttributes();

    return handlerInput.requestEnvelope.request.type === "IntentRequest" &&
      handlerInput.requestEnvelope.request.intent.name === intentName &&
      attributes.state === states.TOO_MUCH_CONFIRMATION;
  },
  handle(handlerInput) {
    const speech = "Oh, sorry. How many hours of sleep did you want?";
    const reprompt = "Once more, how many hours?";

    const attributes = handlerInput.attributesManager.getSessionAttributes();
    delete attributes.state;
    handlerInput.attributesManager.setSessionAttributes(attributes);

    return handlerInput.responseBuilder
      .speak(speech)
      .reprompt(reprompt)
      .getResponse();
  }
};

...
exports.handler = Alexa.SkillBuilders.standard()
  .addRequestHandlers(
    TooMuchYesIntentHandler,
    TooMuchNoIntentHandler,
    WellRestedIntentHandler,          Registers the new handler
    StopOrCancelIntentHandler,
    LaunchRequestHandler
  )
  .lambda();
```

In this handler, we need to make it clear that something happened. We have Alexa apologize. No one trusts an apology from a robot, but this isn't about making amends. "Sorry" is instead an indication that the conversation is turning, confirming that the user is exiting this particular state. The user isn't aware that we are deleting the state from the session attributes, but instead gets an indication of where the conversation stands and what the current expectations are, as we do in every working conversation.

**NOTE**  Notice how the responses start with "oh" and "okay." These are discourse markers, and we'll discuss them in chapter 7.

If you stopped here, you would make a common and difficult-to-debug error. Alexa would ask "Did I hear right?" and you might say "yes," expecting the AMAZON.YesIntent to kick in. The problem is, every intent must be specified in the interaction model. AMAZON.YesIntent and AMAZON.NoIntent aren't there yet, and Alexa won't map "yeah," "nope," and other utterances without this update.

**Listing 5.5  Including yes/no intents in the interaction model (./models/en-US.json)**

```
{
  "interactionModel": {
    ...
    "intents": [
      ...
      {
        "name": "AMAZON.YesIntent",
        "samples": []
      },
      {
        "name": "AMAZON.NoIntent",
        "samples": []
      }
    ]
  }
}
```

**NOTE**  You can deploy the entire skill with the ask deploy command on its own or ask deploy --target model to only update the interaction model if you've already updated the fulfillment code.

Alexa is now set up to listen for yes and no responses, but there's another way you might respond, at least if Alexa didn't hear you correctly or if you wanted to correct yourself. You'll say, "How rested will I be if I sleep for 4 hours?" instead of the 14 that Alexa heard. This phrase lines up well with the WellRestedIntent.

There's no need for a new handler because the behavior will be the same as if there hadn't been a call for confirmation and if the user had said 4 hours from the beginning. But we do need to clear the state in the WellRestedIntent— it's not necessary for those not sleeping for over 12 hours.

**Listing 5.6  Clearing the user's state (./lambda/custom/index.js)**

```
const WellRestedIntentHandler = {
  ...
  handle(handlerInput) {                          Deletes the state attribute
    ...

    delete attributes.state;
    handlerInput.attributesManager.setSessionAttributes(attributes);

    ...
  }
};
```

Here we clear the user's state because either it will not be necessary (the user clarifies with a lower number), or it will be added back on (the user specifies higher than 12 again).

> **TIP** The user might also get more to the point and simply say "four" or "four hours." This isn't in the interaction model, but Alexa will handle the intent and slot correctly anyway. For a more complex skill, particularly one in which multiple intents have numeric slots, that wouldn't necessarily be the case and {NumberOf-Hours} hours and {NumberOfHours} would need to be added to the model.

Just as in the bare state, the user in the "too much sleep" state can reasonably ask to cancel or stop the skill, or ask for help. The first question to always ask when we encounter a new combination of state and utterance is: "Will this intent be sufficiently different from what exists to create a new intent?"

For the stop intent, probably not. If the user wants to stop, it doesn't matter what state or step of the flow is active. For other skills, it might matter. In the middle of a role-playing game, Alexa might remind the user that the game has been saved at that point.

The cancel intent could be unique, but in this skill you can assume that canceling is the same as quitting.

### 5.1.3 *Handling the unhandled*

What if the user requests an intent that isn't handled in the code? Some intents, like the yes and no intents, don't fit within the "too much sleep" state. We *could* add handlers for any missing intents, no matter the state, whether they're appropriate or not. Or we could use the cascading nature of request handlers and canHandle to create a handler that takes in any request that doesn't otherwise have a home. Remember, the first handler object whose canHandle method returns true handles the request.

> **Listing 5.7 Handling all unhandled requests (./lambda/custom/index.js)**

```
const Unhandled = {
  canHandle(handlerInput) {
    return true;                          The handler will take care of anything
  },                                      that reaches this point.
  handle(handlerInput) {
    const speech = "Hey, sorry, I'm not sure how to take care of that. " +
                   "Try once more?";
    const reprompt = "How about this. Tell me instead how many hours " +
                     "you want to sleep.";

    return handlerInput.responseBuilder
      .speak(speech)
      .reprompt(reprompt)
      .getResponse();
  },
};

...
exports.handler = Alexa.SkillBuilders.standard()
  .addRequestHandlers(
```

```
    TooMuchYesIntentHandler,
    TooMuchNoIntentHandler,
    WellRestedIntentHandler,
    StopOrCancelIntentHandler,
    LaunchRequestHandler,
    Unhandled
)
.lambda();
```

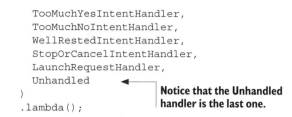 **Notice that the Unhandled handler is the last one.**

The `Unhandled` handler is the orphanage that takes in all of the intents that don't otherwise have homes. Including such a handler is a good practice to get into, but think about how you want Alexa to respond. Because you never know precisely what utterance will trigger this handler, your best approach is to be noncommittal. Tell the user that Alexa didn't understand, and give them a way forward.

> **TIP** Amazon has also added an intent for situations where it can't match what the user is saying. It is called `AMAZON.FallbackIntent`, and you would need to add it, like any other built-in intent. First add the intent to the interaction model, and then add an intent handler to handle it when it arrives in the fulfillment. This intent is useful for tracking what users expect your skill to do but that you haven't yet implemented.

## 5.2 *Maintaining long-term information*

Session attributes are great for directing the flow of the conversation, but you already saw that the data is temporary. Cross-session information must be recorded somewhere. On a website, developers have access to cookies, or, for truly long-term storage, databases. There are no cookies for skills, but databases are available. This extends the voice application's flow of data, offering a new place for the data to go.

Previously, data flowed between the user and the fulfillment via Alexa. Now look at figure 5.4, and see that data can also flow between the user and the database, with the fulfillment and Alexa in between.

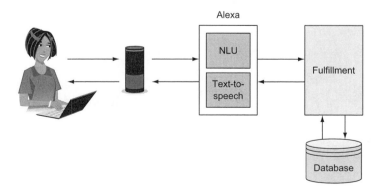

**Figure 5.4   Introducing a database adds another branch where data can flow.**

Alexa doesn't require a specific database, but you can expect that Amazon wants you to use one on AWS. To encourage your skill to stay within the Amazon ecosystem, Amazon has made the SDK integrate easily with DynamoDB.

To set up DynamoDB with a skill, you have to do three things:

1  Set the correct permissions on the Lambda function.
2  Set the name of the DynamoDB table inside the Lambda code.
3  Set an attribute.

There truly are no other steps.

> **NOTE**  DynamoDB is a NoSQL database hosted on AWS. Schema-less and designed for performance, it's one of several data-store options on AWS and the only one directly integrated with the ASK SDK. Using the custom skill builder (`Alexa.SkillBuilders.custom`), you can also add your own data store through a persistence adapter if you'd prefer not to use DynamoDB. Although this chapter focuses on using DynamoDB, storing data through the attributes manager is much the same, irrespective of where the data lives.

The hardest step is adding permissions to the skill so it can interact with the DynamoDB service, and that's not difficult. It just involves a large series of tiny steps to add permissions so you can create a table and work with items in the database. Appendix B outlines how to do this inside AWS with IAM.

> **WARNING**  To continue testing the skill by invoking the fulfillment locally, you must also add the DynamoDB permissions to your local profile—the one created when you set up the ASK CLI. Do this the same way you added it to the Lambda function, with the directions in appendix B.

Once you have the permissions set up, you're ready to communicate with DynamoDB from your skill and save information for the long haul. The skill needs to know *which* DynamoDB table to add to and retrieve from.

**Listing 5.8  Connecting DynamoDB to the skill (./lambda/custom/index.js)**

```
const AWS = require("aws-sdk");

...

exports.handler = Alexa.SkillBuilders.standard()
  .addRequestHandlers(
    ...
  )
  .withSkillId(skillId)
  .withTableName("super_sleeper")
  .withAutoCreateTable(true)
  .withDynamoDbClient(
    new AWS.DynamoDB({ apiVersion: "latest", region: "us-east-1" })
  )
  .lambda();
```

This is only necessary for testing locally.

The table does not need to be created beforehand.

You're probably thinking, "I didn't create a table." That's true, and it's not. By specifying the name of the table and setting `withAutoCreateTable` to `true`, the SDK will create a table if one with that name doesn't exist. The implication, of course, is that on the very first run of the Lambda function, the skill will run more slowly. Every subsequent connection, however, will start up with the same speed.

> **NOTE** In the preceding code, the `withDynamoDbClient` method does not need to be there for deploying to Lambda. We add it instead so we can do local testing. When adding it, you also must pull in the AWS SDK (already a dependency through the ASK SDK). Set the region the same as the skill's Lambda function for the minimum latency.

Storing data about the user empowers the skill to do much more. Immersive voice games and applications aren't possible without users being able to return to a skill that remembers them. Especially when considering the narrowness of the voice interface, skills need to present users with information precisely tailored to them, removing all impediments to completing actions. One shape this can take is using user behavior to illuminate actions that perhaps the user doesn't know are possible.

Right now, Super Sleeper's primary focus is telling users how well rested they'll be, depending on how many hours of sleep they'll get. It also has the ability to factor in how the previous night's sleep was. The previous night's quality isn't required, unlike the upcoming amount of sleep, and it isn't called out significantly when the user asks for help. As a result, users might forget or not be aware that it's there for them.

To rectify this, the skill could tell users about this option any time they launched the skill or asked for help, but this probably is not the best approach. The skill should focus on the most important actions the user can take, and specifying the previous night's sleep quality isn't one of them. But just because the user doesn't need to hear about the secondary capability every time doesn't mean that the user *never* needs to hear about it. Instead, the skill could educate the user after a number of interactions that use only the primary functionality.

**Listing 5.9  Tracking use of the skill and functionality (./lambda/custom/index.js)**

```
const WellRestedIntentHandler = {
  canHandle(handlerInput) {
    ...
  },
  async handle(handlerInput) {
    const slots = handlerInput.requestEnvelope.request.intent.slots;
    const data = await handlerInput
                        .attributesManager
                        .getPersistentAttributes();

    if (data.wellRested) {
      data.wellRested.invocations = data.wellRested.invocations + 1;
    } else {
      data.wellRested = {
        invocations: 1,
        sleepQuality: false,
```

The attributes manager reaches out to DynamoDB asynchronously; thus the use of the await keyword.

Stores user-level information about skill interaction

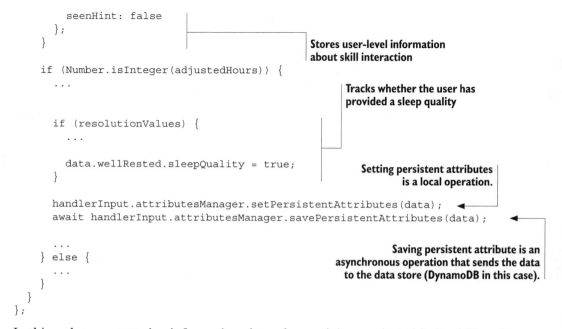

```
          seenHint: false
      };
   }
   if (Number.isInteger(adjustedHours)) {
      ...

      if (resolutionValues) {
         ...

         data.wellRested.sleepQuality = true;
      }

   handlerInput.attributesManager.setPersistentAttributes(data);
   await handlerInput.attributesManager.savePersistentAttributes(data);

      ...
   } else {
      ...
   }
  }
};
```

Stores user-level information about skill interaction

Tracks whether the user has provided a sleep quality

Setting persistent attributes is a local operation.

Saving persistent attribute is an asynchronous operation that sends the data to the data store (DynamoDB in this case).

In this code, we are storing information about the user's interaction with the skill, such as the number of invocations and whether the user has provided a sleep quality or seen a hint about the skill's functionality. This data flow begins by asynchronously retrieving information about the user from DynamoDB, holding on to it locally, and then asynchronously storing it again on DynamoDB.

> **NOTE** There are now asynchronous calls to the database inside the function, and the `async` keyword tidies up the code. This is not necessary, but `async` and `await` are used here to cut down on the number of changes in this chunk. Use whichever style you prefer.

Next, we'll use this information to give users relevant guidance about the skill's functionality.

**Listing 5.10    Providing guidance on an unused feature (./lambda/custom/index.js)**

```
const WellRestedIntentHandler = {
  ...
  async handle(handlerInput) {
    ...
    if (Number.isInteger(adjustedHours)) {
      ...
      let endSpeech = "";
      const regularUserCount = 1;
      if (
        data.wellRested.invocations > regularUserCount &&
        !data.wellRested.sleepQuality &&
        !data.wellRested.seenHint
      ) {
        endSpeech = " By the way, you can also tell me how " +
                    "you slept last night. I'll take it into account " +
```

Provides a friendly tip if the user has invoked the skill enough to become a "regular" but hasn't provided a sleep quality

```
                          "with your upcoming sleep.";
        data.wellRested.seenHint = true;
      }


      handlerInput.attributesManager.setPersistentAttributes(data);
      await handlerInput.attributesManager.savePersistentAttributes(data);

      if (adjustedHours > 12) {
        ...
      } else if (adjustedHours > 8) {
        speech += pluck(WellRestedPhrases.justRight) + endSpeech;
      } else if (adjustedHours > 6) {
        speech += pluck(WellRestedPhrases.justUnder) + endSpeech;
      } else {
        speech += pluck(WellRestedPhrases.tooLittle) + endSpeech;
      }
      ...
    } else {
      ...
    }
  }
}
```

**Appends the tip to the response, but only if the user has given a time of 12 hours or less**

**Provides a friendly tip if the user has invoked the skill enough to become a "regular" but hasn't provided a sleep quality**

Let's examine what's going on. From the VUI side, if the user has invoked the intent more than once and hasn't provided a sleep quality, we assume that it's because that part of the intent is hidden. We provide the information the handler is meant to provide, but we also provide a bit of guidance at the end. (To keep things simple, a "regular" here is someone who is a returning user, but you might want to increase this threshold in your own skill.)

There are a couple of small, but important things to note. First, we only provide the tip once. We could change it so that we provide the tip every five times or so, but what we are ultimately avoiding is sharing it every time. That's too much. Second, the tip only shows up if the user has mentioned an expected slumber of 12 hours or less. That's because anything more than 12 hours leads Alexa to ask the user for confirmation, and we don't want a confirmation followed by "By the way, did you know…?"

> **TIP** This same flow could easily be configured to ask a user to rate or share the skill. You could also bump up the number of times users need to interact with the intent before they hear the message, depending on how important it is to get the information to them.

## How attributes are saved

In the SDK, saving to DynamoDB works through three pieces of information: the table name, the attributes to save, and the user ID. The user ID is not a true identifier of a user but is more precisely a user-installation mapping. When users disable and re-enable a skill, their user IDs change, and they are no longer tied to their data.

If you want to confirm that your attributes now exist in DynamoDB, you can go to DynamoDB in the AWS console, find your table name, and click on the Items tab. There you'll see all of the saved attributes by user ID.

## 5.3    *Putting it all together*

The Super Sleeper skill isn't fulfilling its promise of tracking sleep just yet. Thankfully, with state management and user attributes, we have a base to build that functionality. To complete it, we'll need new intents, new sample utterances, and new fulfillment code (namely, intent handlers).

### 5.3.1    *New intents*

For tracking sleep, we'll build something similar to a stopwatch, and we will need two new intents: one to start sleep and one to wake up. The time elapsed between the two will be the length of the sleep. The user shouldn't need to provide any extra information, which means there will be no slots for the intents.

You might be thinking that "going to sleep" and "waking up" could be different slots, and you could use the same utterances. There may be some overlap in the utterances, but the behaviors for those two actions are sufficiently different that separating them is better.

### 5.3.2    *New utterances*

Take some time and think about each intent separately. How might a tired person tell the Super Sleeper skill that it's time for bed? What are the different ways an early riser could tell Super Sleeper that the time for sleep is through? Say them out loud and then write them down.

Listing 5.11    Adding new intents to track sleep (./models/en-US.json)

```
...
{
  "name": "GoingToBedIntent",
  "slots": [],
  "samples": [
    "I'm going to bed",
    "I'm headed to bed",
    "I'm off to bed",
    "Time for bed",
    "I'm going to sleep",
    "I'm headed to sleep",
    "I'm off to sleep",
    "Time for sleep",
    "Time to sleep",
    "Goodnight",
    "Taking a nap",
    "Laying down to sleep"
  ]
},
{
  "name": "WakingUpIntent",
  "slots": [],
  "samples": [
    "I'm up",
```

```
      "I'm awake",
      "I'm done sleeping",
      "I've gotten up",
      "I got up",
      "I'm out of bed",
      "How much I slept",
      "How long I slept",
      "How long I was sleeping",
      "How long I was out for last night",
      "How long my nap was",
      "How long my sleep was",
      "For the mount of sleep",
      "I've woken up"
    ]
  }
...
```

Add the new intents and sample utterances to the interaction model. I came up with a few examples, but I'm sure you thought of some that I didn't. Again, the more you can add, the better Alexa's understanding will be. The incremental increases become less powerful as you add more and more utterances, so focus on crafting a good VUI if you already have a good start on the utterances.

The slot arrays for each intent are empty here, because none of the samples have spaces for slots—there won't be any variable information. And note that there's no state information. State only lives in the fulfillment, not in the interaction model.

### 5.3.3 *New fulfillment*

Often, a night's sleep isn't a straight line but a repeating cycle of sleeping and waking. Super Sleeper should account for this. Alexa can respond to "I've woken up" with a confirmation: "Are you up for good?" There's not much sense in saying how long has passed each time the user gets up to use the bathroom. If anything, this could become quickly irksome. "I know it's only been an hour since I last got up!"

This flow raises a question for the design of the VUI. Do we assume that people generally wake up multiple times throughout the night? If so, we shouldn't ask for confirmation each time and instead assume that unless they tell us otherwise, they'll be back to sleep soon. The alternative is to adopt the opposite approach and ask on every awakening whether it's temporary.

Ultimately, I think the latter approach is better. I'd wager that most people don't get up several times a night. Those who do are likely in a half-asleep, half-awake daze that would preclude speaking to a voice assistant. Even more, what are the drawbacks of not confirming? The user might go to the bathroom at 2 A.M. and forget to re-engage on the way back, throwing the tracking off. With this considered, let's prompt on each announced wake-up.

You may already be pattern matching and seeing that this is similar to the earlier confirmation when Alexa thought the user was going to sleep too much. Taking the same state-based approach, we'll set a state (let's call it WAKING) when the user invokes the WakingUpIntent. Add it to the states object at the top of your index.js file.

**Listing 5.12    Adding the waking state string (./custom/lambda/index.js)**

```
const states = {
  TOO_MUCH_CONFIRMATION: "TOO_MUCH_CONFIRMATION",
  WAKING: "WAKING"
};
```

To calculate how long the user has slept, we need to track when the user went to sleep. That means we need to store information on a per-user basis. We need, in short, a persistent attribute.

The value will be set inside the `GoingToBedIntent` and will be cleared out each morning (or after a nap for midday sleepers) after Alexa confirms that the user's up for good. And let's also track how many times the user woke up since going to bed.

Keeping track of the state, the user attributes, and the different handlers gets confusing very quickly. A figure might help. Take some time to sketch it out before getting into the code. There's the `WAKING` state, an intent (`GoingToBedIntent`) that handles the beginning of the sleep, and an intent that stops the sleep. What does that look like, and which intents might be missing?

The first new handler is responsible for the intent the user triggers on going to bed. It needs to be the equivalent of setting a stopwatch.

**Listing 5.13    Starting the sleep tracking (./custom/lambda/index.js)**

```
const GoingToBedIntentHandler = {
  canHandle(handlerInput) {
    const intentName = "GoingToBedIntent";

    return handlerInput.requestEnvelope.request.type === "IntentRequest"
    && handlerInput.requestEnvelope.request.intent.name === intentName;
  },
  async handle(handlerInput) {
    const data = await handlerInput
                       .attributesManager
                       .getPersistentAttributes();

    data.sleepStart = (new Date()).toString();        Resets the tracking data
    data.timesRisen = 0;
                                                       Saves the data to the data store
    handlerInput.attributesManager.setPersistentAttributes(data);
    await handlerInput.attributesManager.savePersistentAttributes(data);

    const speech = "Sleep well and let me know when you're awake.";

    return handlerInput.responseBuilder
      .speak(speech)
      .getResponse();
  }
};

exports.handler = Alexa.SkillBuilders.standard()
  .addRequestHandlers(
```

```
    TooMuchYesIntentHandler,
    TooMuchNoIntentHandler,
    WellRestedIntentHandler,
    GoingToBedIntentHandler,
    ...
  )
  ...
```

This handler's most important job is to initiate the tracking. It sets the time at which tracking started, and it sets the number of times the user rose to 0. The handler also responds with a message that serves two purposes. First, it indicates that tracking has started, and it guides the user on how to end the tracking.

The handler for waking up is where the response guides the user.

**Listing 5.14  The intent for when a user wakes up (./custom/lambda/index.js)**

```
const WakingUpIntentHandler = {
  canHandle(handlerInput) {
    const intentName = "WakingUpIntent";

    return handlerInput.requestEnvelope.request.type === "IntentRequest"
    && handlerInput.requestEnvelope.request.intent.name === intentName;
  },
  async handle(handlerInput) {
    const data = await handlerInput
                       .attributesManager
                       .getPersistentAttributes();
    const attributes = handlerInput.attributesManager.getSessionAttributes();

    if (data.sleepStart) {
      attributes.state = states.WAKING;            ◄——— Tracks the number of
      data.timesRisen = data.timesRisen + 1;             times the user wakes up

      const speech = "Are you up for good?";
      const reprompt = "Should I stop the sleep timer?";

      handlerInput.attributesManager.setSessionAttributes(attributes);

      handlerInput.attributesManager.setPersistentAttributes(data);
      await handlerInput.attributesManager.savePersistentAttributes(data);

      return handlerInput.responseBuilder
        .speak(speech)
        .reprompt(reprompt)
        .getResponse();
    } else {
      const speech = "Oops, by my measure you were already awake.";

      return handlerInput.responseBuilder.speak(speech).getResponse();
    }
  }
};

exports.handler = Alexa.SkillBuilders.standard()
```

```
.addRequestHandlers(
  ...
  GoingToBedIntentHandler,          ◄─────┤  Registers the new handler
  WakingUpIntentHandler,
  ...
)
...
```

Waking up isn't the end of the cycle; it's just a waypoint due to our assumption that people could wake up several times a night. The handler increments `timesRisen` by 1, while placing the user in the `WAKING` state and asking if this is indeed the end of the slumber. This is only if the user had started sleeping in the first place.

This branching of responses (whether the user had started sleeping or not) could occur in the `canHandle` method instead, with two handler objects. That's a completely valid approach to organizing handler flow. Instead, I put this within a single handler object because the code to handle non-sleepers was minimal. Also I try to avoid going to the data store inside the `canHandle` methods. Remember that each `canHandle` method is invoked in order until one returns `true`. A trip to a data store before it's necessary can slow down finding the right handler.

The `WakingUpIntentHandler` asks the user if they're up for good or just temporarily, and it places the user in a new state in order to handle any responses in a way that's specific to where the user is in the flow. Thinking about how a user might respond, the most obvious responses are "yes" and "no." Users might also respond, though, with "stop" or "cancel," and these require some assumptions on our part. User testing is the best way to understand what these two utterances mean to people in this context. We will assume that "stop" means that the user wants to stop sleeping for the night, and "cancel" means that the user instead wants to cancel waking up.

With those considerations, we start handling the requests with the handler for users who are waking up for good.

> **Listing 5.15   Checking if a user replies (./custom/lambda/index.js)**

```
const WakingForGoodHandler = {
  canHandle (handlerInput) {
    const yesIntentName = "AMAZON.YesIntent";
    const stopIntentName = "AMAZON.StopIntent";
    const attributes = handlerInput.attributesManager.getSessionAttributes();

    return handlerInput.requestEnvelope.request.type === "IntentRequest" &&
      (handlerInput.requestEnvelope.request.intent.name === yesIntentName ||
      handlerInput.requestEnvelope.request.intent.name === stopIntentName) &&
      attributes.state === states.WAKING;
  },
  ...
};
```
The user must invoke the yes intent or the
stop intent, and be in the WAKING state.

The `canHandle` method combines both the invoked intents and the state. The user must invoke either the yes or stop intent, plus be in the `WAKING` state. This dual condition, if we register the handler correctly, ensures that users don't accidentally enter this handler if they aren't in the right state to do so. This handler's `handle` method is there to provide rousing users with their sleep statistics.

**Listing 5.16 Reporting on the slumber (./custom/lambda/index.js)**

```
const WakingForGoodHandler = {
  canHandle (handlerInput) {
    ...
  },
  async handle (handlerInput) {
    const data = await handlerInput
                    .attributesManager
                    .getPersistentAttributes();
    const attributes = handlerInput.attributesManager.getSessionAttributes();

    const current = new Date();
    const past = new Date(data.sleepStart);
    const diff = Math.abs(current.getTime() - past.getTime()) / (1000 * 60 *
      60);
    const hours = Math.floor(diff);
    const minutes = Math.round(60 * (diff - hours));
    const timesRisen = data.timesRisen;

    let speech = `You slept ${hours} hours and ${minutes} minutes.`;

    if(timesRisen > 1) {
      speech += ` You woke up ${timesRisen} times.`;
    }

    delete attributes.state;
    handlerInput.attributesManager.setSessionAttributes(attributes);

    return handlerInput.responseBuilder
      .speak(speech)
      .getResponse();
  }
};

exports.handler = Alexa.SkillBuilders.standard()
  .addRequestHandlers(
    TooMuchYesIntentHandler,
    TooMuchNoIntentHandler,
    WakingForGoodHandler,
    ...
  )
  ...
```

> **Extrapolates the hours and minutes slept from the time elapsed**

> **Retrieves the number of times the user reported waking up**

> **Places this handler early among the request handlers**

The `handle` method for when the user is waking up for good is complex only in its calculation of the elapsed time. The meaty voice-interaction part of the response involves reporting on the user's request after grabbing the data from the data store, and then returning the user to the bare state. We again register the more specific handlers first, so that they will be invoked before those that share similar conditions but are less specific.

Of course, we also need to handle the case where the user is simply marking a temporary pause from sleep. I'll leave that for you to do on your own—visit the online code listings if you want to see how I did it, but ask yourself in which ways people might say they haven't woken up for good, and what people would want to hear when they're still half asleep.

When people are half asleep, they might also invoke intents that are unrelated to the question "Are you up for good?" We need a way to get them back on track.

> **Listing 5.17    Handling all other `WAKING` intents (./lambda/custom/index.js)**

```
const WakingUnhandled = {
  canHandle (handlerInput) {
    const attributes = handlerInput.attributesManager.getSessionAttributes();

    return attributes.state === states.WAKING;
  },
  handle (handlerInput) {
    const speech = "Would you like to wake up for good?";
    const reprompt = "Are you waking up for good?";

    return handlerInput.responseBuilder
      .speak(speech)
      .reprompt(reprompt)
      .getResponse();
  }
};

exports.handler = Alexa.SkillBuilders.standard()
  .addRequestHandlers(
    ...
    WakingForGoodHandler,
    NotWakingForGoodHandler,
    WakingUnhandled,
    ...
  )
  ...
```

Checks if the user is in the **WAKING** state

Try to create this one on your own, using the others as a guide.

Comes after all of the other waking intents, but before everything without a state

This `canHandle` method is very generic, requiring only that the user be in the `WAKING` state. It is more generic than any other handler object outside of the `Unhandled` handler that vacuumed up everything that came to it. We can think of it as an `Unhandled` handler for a specific state, because we don't want users going off on a wayward flow before we've closed this flow. Because the `canHandle` method is widely generic, we can place it right after the other objects pertaining to the same state, including `WakingUpIntentHandler`, but before any objects with no state, because those would handle these requests before reaching `WakingUnhandled`.

> **TIP**  In reality, you would probably also want to handle requests for help and maybe other intents while in the `WAKING` state, but having a handler for all intents otherwise handled is a useful practice.

### 5.3.4  *Correcting a mistake*

There's something about the skill that's bothering me. Something in the response that would make me cringe if I heard it in a deployed skill. Consider some of the responses:

> *ALEXA: Would you like to wake up for good?*

That sounds good.

> *ALEXA: You slept eight hours and forty-five minutes.*

This one checks out, too. Except…

> *ALEXA: You slept eight hours and one minutes.*

Ahh, yes, there it is. This is a common problem in conversation interactions, and one reason why I always include a simple pluralization function in every voice application I build.

---

**Listing 5.18  Pluralizing words (./lambda/custom/index.js)**

```
function pluralize(count, singular, plural) {
  if(count === 1) {
    return `${count} ${singular}`;
  } else {
    return `${count} ${plural}`;
  }
}
```

All this function does is return a string with the count and the word in either its singular (if the count is equal to 1) or plural (everything else) variant. It doesn't do much, but any voice application that has dynamic, countable data will need some instance of this, enough that packaging it up in its own function is useful. You can then use it inside the handler when reporting how much sleep had occurred.

---

**Listing 5.19  Pluralizing the response (./lambda/custom/index.js)**

```
let speech = `You slept ${pluralize(hours, "hour", "hours")} and ` +
             `${pluralize(minutes, "minute", "minutes")}.`;
```

Now, the response is much better. "You slept eight hours and one minute." This doesn't make the skill conversational, but it does make it better.

We needed a lot of code to make the Super Sleeper skill conversational, but all of it builds on what you saw earlier. State that lives in session attributes directs users through the skill flow. Persistent attributes keep information about users between uses of the skill. And combining the two with Alexa's text-to-speech turns it all into a conversation with the user. Deploy the skill again and test it out. You now have a fully featured skill.

There's still room for improvement, though, as you'll see in the next chapter.

## *Summary*

- Use the notion of state in session attributes to enter into a temporary branch of a conversation between computer and user.
- Track how a user interacts with the skill, and use that information to guide users who haven't discovered all of the skill's functionality.
- Sketching the user's possible flow between intents can uncover missing steps that the skill needs to handle.

# VUI and conversation best practices

You already saw in chapter 3 that people have certain expectations of a conversation and are surprised when those aren't upheld. Developers new to voice applications tend to create stiff conversations that ignore these user expectations. Newcomers, perhaps, are so deep in the terse, mechanical language of code that they temporarily forget what they've been doing since they were young. Thankfully, only a little bit of effort is needed to elevate the conversation, and only a little bit more to take it within sight of natural dialog.

## 6.1 Conversations and context

One of the conversations we built in chapter 5 was a back-and-forth between Alexa and the user, discussing whether the user was waking up for good, and how long had elapsed during their sleep. An example might go like so:

> USER: Alexa, tell Super Sleeper that I'm awake.
>
> ALEXA: Are you up for good?

91

> USER: *Yes.*
>
> ALEXA: *You slept six hours and ten minutes. You woke up five times.*

We can look at this conversation and examine it using Grice's maxims, introduced in chapter 3, which outline well-formed interactions. The maxims were quantity, quality, relation, and manner:

- *Quantity*—Say enough, but not too much.
- *Quality*—Say the truth.
- *Relation*—Say something relevant to the conversation.
- *Manner*—Say it clearly.

Alexa's response was surely true, of the right length, and related to the user's request. The manner could be more conversational, but that's on the margins.

The maxims, though, are not the only things underpinning a conversation. There is also the context behind the conversation. More is unsaid in a conversation than is spoken. Who are the participants, and what are their relationships to each other? What were they talking about before? Where are they? This is an area where computers and voice applications usually fall short. Keeping the context in mind is a challenge, and a host of talented engineers are working on improving "context detection." But even in the skills that we build without the benefit of AI and machine learning, we can use context to make a better experience for our users.

Context is lurking in the conversation between Alexa and the person waking up:

1  "Are you up for good?" The implicit context is that Alexa is referring to what the user just said, that the user is awake.

2  The user responds, "Yes."

3  Alexa responds with how much time that user slept. The context being used here is the knowledge of the user's bedtime and the fact that the conversation is about the user waking up.

As far as context goes, this is a good start. The user still has to respond directly to what Alexa said. In fact, the main unspoken subject ("Are you up for good?") is spoken by Alexa, not the user.

What if a skill could remember what the conversation was about and let the user respond in a more natural way? That might look something like this:

> USER: *Alexa, ask Name Info what the first letter of Sandy is.*
>
> ALEXA: *The first letter is "s."*
>
> USER: *And how many letters is it?*
>
> ALEXA: *Sandy is five letters long.*

This is closer to how humans speak. Humans don't always use a specific noun. Conversations are fluid enough that the noun can be replaced with a pronoun— such as "he," "she," or "it"—unless the context has become so muddled that one of the participants needs to disambiguate. The conversation here comes close to that goal. For humans, context clues work because we can make a best guess based on what the question is. If the question, "How many letters is it?" follows an answer about the meaning of a name, we can safely guess the question refers to the name and not the length of the meaning.

Understanding context can be a difficult job. In the late 80s and early 90s, DARPA, the organization behind an early internet precursor, initiated the ATIS project to build up voice-recognition and voice-understanding technology. The project had researchers from all around attempting to build a system that would understand air traffic information requests. One of their tasks was to define the assumptions, such as what does a "red-eye" flight mean, or even whether "between 7 and 8 in the morning" refers to 7 to 8 inclusive, or 7:01 to 7:59.

> *The researchers involved in the ATIS project soon realized that, to accurately evaluate and compare the understanding capability systems built by the various labs, they had to define the air travel domain with the utmost lawyerly precision. To that end, they put together an ad hoc committee to create, maintain, and update the Principles of Interpretation (PofI) document. It took the committee more than two years of weekly calls and more than eighty interpretation rules to bring the PofI document to a final acceptable form...*
>
> *Members of the ATIS community still remember defining the Principles of Interpretation as a nightmarish experience.*
>
> — *Roberto Pieraccini,* The Voice in the Machine: Building Computers that Understand Speech *(MIT Press, 2012)*

A skill with a narrower focus, not built by committee, won't need two years of weekly meetings. But assumptions will still be present, and they should not be surprising. The code can rely on different heuristics. Like the baseball rule that the "tie goes to the runner," any ambiguous pronoun is assumed to refer to the last subject of discussion.

Let's look at the code needed to build a skill with smart context usage.

## 6.2 *A skill with context*

We're going to build a very simple new skill that can provide information about a first name. We could build a lot more onto the skill, but we'll start simple and focus just on introducing context into voice applications. Our aim is to enable people to achieve their goal more efficiently, which in this case will be to get information about names. The context of the last name discussed will empower the asker to ask for new information without needing to restate the name.

Here are the skill's details:

- *Skill name*—Name Info
- *Invocation*—"name info"
- *Intents*—LaunchRequest, GetNameIntent, SpellingIntent
- *Slots*—name with a type of AMAZON.US_FIRST_NAME

**NOTE** We won't add the intents that Amazon and users would expect in a published skill, such as help, stop, or cancel intents. We're just going to focus on a single topic. But if you were to publish this skill, you'd want to make sure those other intents were added.

Rather than looking at the entire code, we'll look at three intents: `LaunchRequest`, `Get-NameIntent`, and `SpellingIntent`. `LaunchRequest` will ask for the name, `GetNameIntent` will get the name and ask the user to complete the next step, and `SpellingIntent` will return the name spelled out:

> USER: *Alexa, launch Name Info.*
>
> ALEXA: *The name info skill needs you to just ask for a first name.*
>
> USER: *Lilou.*
>
> ALEXA: *Lilou sure is a nice name. What do you want to know about it?*
>
> USER: *How to spell it.*
>
> ALEXA: *You spell Lilou, L-I-L-O-U.*

### 6.2.1   *Frame-based interactions*

First up is the interaction model. Both `GetNameIntent` and `SpellingIntent` have the `AMAZON.US_FIRST_NAME` slot type (you could also use the built-in first name slot for your locale if you wish). This may seem a little weird for `SpellingIntent`, because shouldn't the `GetNameIntent` have gotten the name already?

Well, we have the name if the user performs the default "launch, provide name, ask for information" flow. That kind of linear thinking makes sense on a website or in an app, such as the flow for a form—even if all of the questions are on a single page, users generally won't jump around. With voice applications, however, users don't need to follow a set of steps in a specific order. There are smaller flows that are independent of each other, and users can move between them without having to back up or follow a defined path.

Figure 6.1 illustrates this difference between *graph-based* and *frame-based* user flows.[1] In a graph-based flow, users move in a predetermined path. They may branch off, but it's easy to know where the user can go at each step. Frame-based flows, however, are composed of individual frames. The user has a predetermined path within each frame, but they can jump between individual frames at will. Voice-first applications are more frame-based than graph-based. This is easier for the user, because they can go where they want in the skill when they want. It's more difficult for voice-first developers, because they need to be vigilant about supporting the interaction no matter where it starts from.

In the Name Info skill, we might receive a name outside of `GetNameIntent` because a user can jump into the frame that asks for the spelling of a name without going through `GetNameIntent` first. We want to support the default flow, while also supporting the shortcuts.

The default flow is where we'll add the record of what the current conversation is about. But because frame jumping is possible, we will support the `name` slot in multiple intents.

---

[1]  Paul Cutsinger, who is on the Alexa team at Amazon, presented this idea at a talk at the 2017 AWS re:Invent, Amazon's annual developer conference.

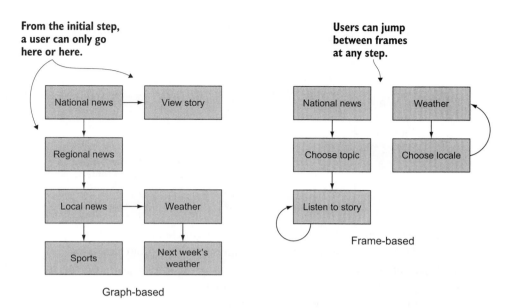

**Figure 6.1  Graph versus frame interactions**

Listing 6.1   Intents for getting the name and asking for spelling (./models/en-US.json)

```
...
"intents":[
    {
      "name":"GetNameIntent",
      "slots":[
        {
          "name":"name",
          "type":"AMAZON.US_FIRST_NAME"      ◁─── Biases toward US names
        }                                          and pronunciations
      ],
      "samples":[                            All the samples collect a name.
        "{name}",
        "the name is {name}",
        "{name} is the name",
        "facts about the name {name}",
        "facts about {name}"
      ]
    },
    {
      "name":"SpellingIntent",
      "slots":[
        {
          "name":"name",
          "type":"AMAZON.US_FIRST_NAME"
        }
      ],
      "samples":[
        "what is the spelling of {name}",
```

```
          "what the spelling of {name} is",
          "{name} spelling",
          "how to spell {name}",
          "what is the spelling of it",
          "what is the spelling",
          "what the spelling is",
          "how do you spell it",
          "how it is spelled",
          "spelled out",
          "spelling"
      ]
    },
    ...
  ]
  ...
```

**Some samples don't include a name and rely on context.**

In this interaction model, two things stand out. `GetNameIntent` has a sample utterance that is only the `name` slot. This can be dangerous. Remember that Alexa does best-effort matching for intents, and slots are not enums. If a user says nothing but "spelling," what do you expect to happen? If the interaction model contains a slot-only utterance (as is the case for `GetNameIntent`) but no utterance that contains "spelling" exactly, Alexa will match on the slot-only utterance. Alexa will consider "spelling" to be a slot value, even though we know that's—at best—a very rare first name. Adding an utterance for the single-word "spelling" solves this potential problem.

Perhaps it would be easier to force users to say "The name is…" Easier for the developer, sure, but more difficult for the user, and you should always optimize for the user's ease of use. There will be more of them than there are of you. If you ask for a name, allow the user to say just the name, and remember to include single-word sample utterances where they could be necessary. Coming up with these cases will be more work on your side, but worth it.

The other thing that stands out in listing 6.1 is that `SpellingIntent` has sample utterances with and without a slot. This is where we start to meet users who are using a conversational tone. Some users might ask, "How do you spell Sandy?" especially if they have been "trained" by other voice-first skills. Other users, though, will just ask, "What's the spelling?"

That's the interaction model. What does the intent fulfillment look like?

### 6.2.2   *The fulfillment*

For the sake of simplicity, we won't look at the `Unhandled` or other handlers, though these would be in a production-level skill. Instead, we'll focus first on the `LaunchRequestHandler`.

This will be the first time we'll see a handler serving two roles. `LaunchRequestHandler` will primarily build the response for the `LaunchRequest` and ask for a name from the user.

**Listing 6.2   Creates `LaunchRequestHandler` (./lambda/custom/index.js)**

```
const Alexa = require("ask-sdk");
const AWS = require("aws-sdk");

const LaunchRequestHandler = {
  canHandle(handlerInput) {                                    Matches the launch request type
    return handlerInput.requestEnvelope.request.type === "LaunchRequest";   ◄
  },
  handle(handlerInput) {                                       Provides guidance on skill abilities
    const speech =
      "The name info skill needs you to just ask for a first name.";
    const reprompt = "Try saying, 'give me facts about the name Dustin.'";

    return handlerInput.responseBuilder
      .speak(speech)
      .reprompt(reprompt)
      .getResponse();
  }
};

const skillId = "<YOUR SKILL ID>";
exports.handler = Alexa.SkillBuilders.standard()
  .addRequestHandlers(
    LaunchRequestHandler        ◄            Registers the handler
  )
  .withSkillId(skillId)         ◄            Verifies that the request matches the skill ID
  .withTableName("name_info")                you can get from the Developer Console
  .withAutoCreateTable(true)
  .withDynamoDbClient(
    new AWS.DynamoDB({ apiVersion: "latest", region: "us-east-1" })
  )
  .lambda();
```

**NOTE**   Notice that we also added ID verification in the preceding code. This prevents other people from hijacking your code, and it confirms that the request is coming from your skill, identified with a unique ID that the Alexa platform sends at each request.

In the `LaunchRequestHandler`, we're having Alexa instruct the user in the skill's capabilities and expectations. The primary expectation is that it needs a name, which it asks the user to provide. Because it is serving the name-collection purpose, we can reuse it in situations where we don't have a name.

**Listing 6.3   Passing control to `LaunchRequestHandler` (./lambda/custom/index.js)**

```
const GetNameIntentHandler = {
  canHandle(handlerInput) {
    const intentName = "GetNameIntent";
```

```
    return handlerInput.requestEnvelope.request.type === "IntentRequest" &&
      handlerInput.requestEnvelope.request.intent.name === intentName;
  },
  async handle(handlerInput) {
    const slots = handlerInput.requestEnvelope.request.intent.slots;
    const name = slots.name.value;

    if(name) {
      ...
    } else {
      return LaunchRequestHandler.handle(handlerInput);
    }
  },
};

...
```

**If the user hasn't specified a name, fall back to LaunchRequestHandler to provide direction.**

The `GetNameIntentHandler` is responsible for getting a name from the user, and we expect that a user will only trigger it when providing a name. However, we will be defensive here for the case where the user arrives and hasn't given a name. In that situation, there's nothing to do but ask for the information. This is exactly what the `LaunchRequest` handler does, so we'll reuse it.

The `canHandle` methods are there for routing, not for gatekeeping, and the `handle` method will accept any handler input, which is roughly the current event wrapped up with other event details. If the flow of data inside the fulfillment is normally checking a list of `canHandle` methods and then passing control to a `handle` method, our `GetName-IntentHandler` method adds another step when it forwards the request to yet another `handle` method.

Conversely, when the user provides a name to `GetNameIntent`, the event flow continues by sending a message back asking for the next step.

**Listing 6.4    Handling when the user provides a name (./lambda/custom/index.js)**

```
const GetNameIntentHandler = {
  ...
  async handle(handlerInput) {
    ...

    const data = await handlerInput
                    .attributesManager
                    .getPersistentAttributes();

    data.name = name;

    if (name) {
      handlerInput.attributesManager.setPersistentAttributes(data);
      await handlerInput.attributesManager.savePersistentAttributes(data);

      const speech = name + " sure is a nice name. " +
                "What do you want to know about it?";
      const reprompt = "I could spell it for you.";
```

**Takes the value of the name slot and saves it for later**

```
      return handlerInput.responseBuilder
        .speak(speech)
        .getResponse();
    } else {
      ...
    }
  },
};

...
exports.handler = Alexa.SkillBuilders.standard()
  .addRequestHandlers(
    LaunchRequestHandler,
    GetNameIntentHandler
  )
  ...
```

In the preceding listing, `GetNameIntentHandler` takes in a name via the slot and saves it for use later. This handler exists generally to create *context* for future interactions.

Context is the information that exists in a cloud around a conversation. Often unspoken, it is the common ground that conversational partners can use to reduce the quantity of responses, while still maintaining the quality of relation.

In practice, this handler wouldn't see much use, as users will be more likely to jump directly into the meat of the skill functionality. Still, this sets the context for other intents. For example, the spelling intent handler can spell out a previously given name without the need to ask for it again.

> **Listing 6.5 Spelling the user's name (./lambda/custom/index.js)**

```
const SpellingIntentHandler = {            Accepts the SpellingIntent request
  canHandle(handlerInput) {
    ...
  },                                       Retrieves the name slot and gets the
  async handle(handlerInput) {             persistent attributes
    ...  ◀                                 Stores the name on the persistent attributes

    if(name) {
      data.name = name;                    If there is a name from the slot or the
    }                                      data, respond; otherwise forward the
                                           request to LaunchRequestHandler.
    if(data.name) {  ◀
      handlerInput.attributesManager.setPersistentAttributes(data);
      await handlerInput.attributesManager.savePersistentAttributes(data);

      const speech = `You spell ${data.name}, ${data.name.split("").join("
      ➡")}.`;

      return handlerInput.responseBuilder
        .speak(speech)
        .getResponse();
    } else {
```

```
        return LaunchRequestHandler.handle(handlerInput);
    }
  },
};

...
exports.handler = Alexa.SkillBuilders.standard()
  .addRequestHandlers(
    ...
    SpellingIntentHandler
  )
  ...
```

> **NOTE**   To test the skill out once it's deployed, you'll again need to add the proper DynamoDB permissions, as outlined in appendix B.

`SpellingIntentHandler` uses the legwork that `GetNameIntentHandler` has already done, taking in the previously specified name and using that for the response. Passing data between services like this efficiently completes an action. The user passes the name to Alexa, the fulfillment and the database pass it back and forth, and the user can follow up, asking for information without having to be as explicit:

> *USER: Alexa, tell Super Sleeper the name is Carlos.*
>
> *ALEXA: Carlos sure is a nice name. What do you want to know about it?*
>
> *USER: What the spelling is.*
>
> *ALEXA: You spell Carlos, C-A-R-L-O-S.*

`SpellingIntentHandler` also stores the name for later use, because a user can come back directly to the spelling intent: "What is the spelling of Carlos?" This illustrates well the frame-based interaction model, where users jump in and out of different paths.

This interaction could be extended to add a length intent, popularity intent, Scrabble point intent, and more, all available one after another if the user wanted to keep going (and as a skill maker, you will probably want that kind of engagement). For sure, the user should never have to go "back" to `GetNameIntentHandler` to reset the context. Instead, as seen in the `SpellingIntentHandler`, all that's needed for a new name to become the center of attention is for the user to provide it.

### 6.2.3   *Decaying context*

We can extend context to skills that would benefit from having some knowledge of the user on a longer time frame. A skill for baseball scores highlights this well. An average interaction would involve the user asking for their favorite team's next game, and then for the last game. Then the user might ask for a different team altogether. Overall, there are many different stops the user could choose, and the most recent one is top of mind unless explicitly replaced.

"Most recent," though, is a time frame that can be scoped. When you're designing the interaction, the context could be intentionally forgotten after a set amount of time elapses. This is what happens in normal human interaction, usually with an intermediate step where the listener asks whether the context still holds true:

> USER: *When's the next game?*
>
> ALEXA: *Are you still asking for Houston?*

In the skill flow, the skill can remember two pieces of information: the most recently requested team and the time the user requested it. Then, each time the user speaks to the skill without explicitly specifying a team, the skill can check to see if enough time has passed that the context is effectively "cleared." By doing this, we avoid asking the user to do too much. Good VUI does the work for the user where possible, instead of requiring the user to do the work.

The following pseudocode illustrates how this potential "get team" intent handler could be implemented:

- Check to see if the user includes a team signifier, such as a name or city, in the request.
  - If so, save both the requested team and the time the user requested it.
- If the user didn't specify a team, see if the user specified one in the past:
  - If so, use that team.
  - Otherwise, ask for clarification.

The handler relies on either an explicit or implicit team value. The preference is for the explicit request. When the user directly asks for a team, that's the one the skill should use, no matter how recently the user asked for a different team. If there's no explicit request, the skill assumes that the most recent team is the one the user is still talking about. This is a reasonable assumption in most situations, and it creates the opportunity for follow-up requests:

> USER: *When does Houston play next?*
>
> ALEXA: *Houston's playing tomorrow at home.*
>
> USER: *And what is their record?*

The threshold that determines whether a request is recent *enough* will vary based on the skill. A gaming skill with quick rounds will have a lower threshold than a baseball-scores skill, where games last for hours.

**Listing 6.6   A function for determining value recency**

```
function recentlyRequested(data, recentKey) {
  const decay = 10;
  const decayedAgo = new Date(Date.now() - 1000 * 60 * decay);
  if (
    data[recentKey] &&
    data[recentKey].lastRequested &&
    decayedAgo < new Date(data[recentKey].lastRequested)     Checks to see if the user
  ) {                                                         last requested the
    return data[recentKey];                                  attribute before the
  }                                                          threshold for "forgetting"
};
```

The `recentlyRequested` function looks at the data we've stored about the user to see if the user requested the attribute, and, if so, whether that request hasn't yet gone stale. In this case, that time comes when 10 minutes have passed. This amount of time is a static limit, but you could have a dynamic threshold. If a user asks for a bus, you could set the request to go stale not long after the next bus arrives. As you've seen, the goal is consistency and intuitiveness. You can't rely on a countdown clock to show the user when the request is going stale, so choose a threshold that a user can understand without direction.

One thing about baseball teams (or bus stops or movie theaters) is that people tend to have their local or preferred teams and ask for them most of the time. A welcome VUI touch is to learn, over time, each user's preference and assume that "the usual" is what's needed when no value is explicitly stated. Pay attention to what your users are asking for, and once you have figured out that they keep going back to the same thing, tag it as their favorite and rely on it.

We can revise our earlier pseudocode so it now looks like this:

- Check to see if the user includes a team signifier, such as a name or city, in the request:
  - If so, save the requested team and when the user requested it, and increment the count of how often that team has been requested.
- If the user didn't specify a team, see if the user specified one in the past:
  - If so, use that team.
  - If not, see if the user has a favorite team, and use that one.
  - Otherwise, ask for clarification.

Instead of only relying on recent requests, the handler now relies on the explicitly requested, the recently requested, or the most requested values, in that order. This is, again, making an assumption about the user's behavior, but a reasonable assumption. If the user explicitly requests a value, certainly use that. If a user has requested a value recently, bias toward recency. But if there's nothing else to go on, rely on what the user has done most often in the past, if that's available.

> **TIP** If you want your users to know that they can ask for their usual without specifying it, you'll need to tell them. Consider letting them know once it takes effect: "By the way, it sounds like you ask for the Navy Yards stop a lot. Next time just say 'Next bus time,' and I'll assume you're talking about that one."

In all cases, the favorite should be the final option if you haven't gotten a value otherwise. Always prioritize the recent request.

One simple way of doing this is keeping count of which request has come in most often, as already mentioned. More complex but more like learning the user's favorite is to declare a favorite once it reaches a minimum threshold of requests and has accounted for a set percentage of all requests. For example, maybe the user needs to request a bus stop at least five times and that stop must account for at least 20% of all requests before you consider it the user's favorite.

Which approach you use will depend on the use case. A user will likely ask for the same baseball team nearly all the time, so checking only for the most popular is sufficient. But a user might go to three bus stops fairly evenly, and you won't want to assume a favorite that has only been asked for once more than the stop in second place.

> **NOTE** Any time you rely on implicit context, consider whether the user will know what the response is about. If the new request comes shortly after the previous one (within 15 seconds) or if the answer will otherwise make clear what the assumption was, you could probably be less clear and the user will understand. Otherwise, be explicit in your response and state the assumptions.

To determine what the user's favorite requests are, we'll need to keep track of what they're requesting. The following listing shows how we could do that.

**Listing 6.7   Storing the user's history**

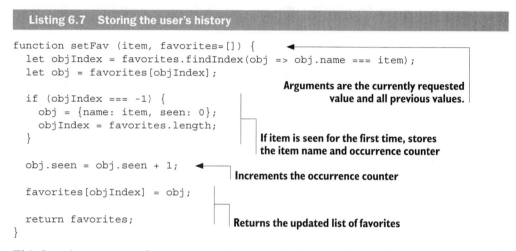

```
function setFav (item, favorites=[]) {
  let objIndex = favorites.findIndex(obj => obj.name === item);
  let obj = favorites[objIndex];

  if (objIndex === -1) {
    obj = {name: item, seen: 0};
    objIndex = favorites.length;
  }

  obj.seen = obj.seen + 1;

  favorites[objIndex] = obj;

  return favorites;
}
```

Arguments are the currently requested value and all previous values.

If item is seen for the first time, stores the item name and occurrence counter

Increments the occurrence counter

Returns the updated list of favorites

This function puts together an array of requested values and how often users request each value. The running total for every value is useful to know when a request was seen most often. Users might also change their favorite over time. A bandwagon fan might jump from Chicago to Houston, and the skill will need to account for the change in allegiance.

The previous function tracks the values. This function takes the tracked values and chooses the favorite.

**Listing 6.8   Selecting the overall favorite value**

```
function topFav (data, requestsKey) {
  const favorites = data[requestsKey];
  const minRequests = 3;

  if (favorites) {
    const favorite = favorites.sort((a, b) => b.seen - a.seen)[0];
    if (favorite.seen > minRequests) {
      return favorite;
    }
  }
}
```

Sorts favorites from most seen to least and selects the first

A threshold (here, three occurrences) is set to ensure that a user has asked for a value enough times that the skill can make assumptions that don't surprise the user. From there, the function simply returns the most requested value.

Depending on what the skill does, you might require the favorite to also make up an overwhelmingly large percentage of the overall request count. You might even decide to return a couple of favorites and have the user decide which they want. ("Which account? Your retirement account, savings, or another?") The overall goal is to take the user's preference and use it to make the action more efficient.

For some voice applications, consider allowing the user to explicitly set a favorite. In a cooking skill I built, the user could say, "I like cooking with garlic," or "My favorite type of food is Cajun." From that point on, the skill would bias its search to look for Cajun recipes or those with garlic.

Storing user favorites or conversation context is useful, but needing to save that data in each handler is annoying. Instead, we could use our knowledge of how data flows within a skill to save the data in a single place.

## 6.3    *Intercepting responses and requests*

All skills work by having a request come in from the Alexa service, the handler input ending up at the right handler, and a response heading back out to the Alexa service, such as in figure 6.2.

There is, of course, more to it than that. The SDK assembles the data into the handler input, or data heads off to the data store. This is still a good, if simplified, model of how the information flows within the skill.

Any actions that are shared among the handlers could be done in the parts of the flow that are common to all handlers. These commonalities are when the request comes in and when the response heads out.

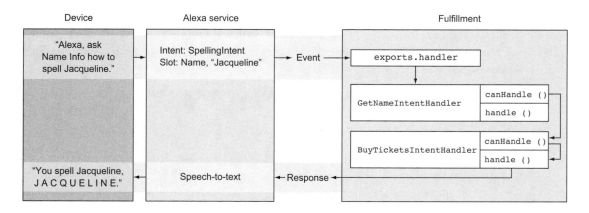

**Figure 6.2    Flow of data in the Name Info skill flow for** `SpellingIntent`

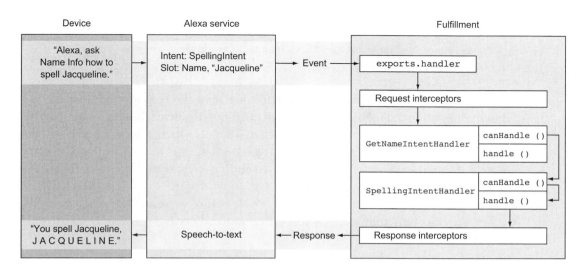

**Figure 6.3  Flow of data inside the Name Info skill flow for `SpellingIntent`, with request and response interceptors**

Interceptors, seen in figure 6.3, change the information flow to either take in the request before it hits the handler, or take in the response before it's sent back to Alexa. By introducing these extra steps, the skill can prepare data or call methods that need to be shared across handlers. On the back side, the skill can perform any closing tasks or clean up before the invocation ends. For example, the request interceptor could introduce logging or prepare localization. The response interceptor could be used to centralize the code to save persistent data.

**RESPONSE INTERCEPTORS**

The following interceptor runs right before the response is sent back to the Alexa platform.

**Listing 6.9  Saving before sending a response (./lambda/custom/index.json)**

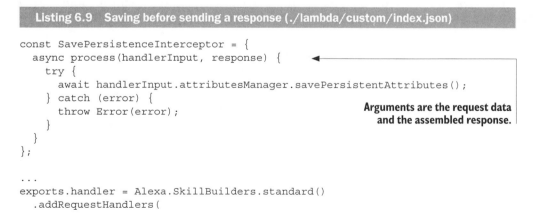

```
const SavePersistenceInterceptor = {
  async process(handlerInput, response) {
    try {
      await handlerInput.attributesManager.savePersistentAttributes();
    } catch (error) {
      throw Error(error);
    }
  }
};

...
exports.handler = Alexa.SkillBuilders.standard()
  .addRequestHandlers(
```

**Arguments are the request data and the assembled response.**

```
    ...
)
.addResponseInterceptors(SavePersistenceInterceptor)
...
.lambda();
```

The interceptor is registered on the skill builder.

We can save the attributes immediately before we send the response because the fulfillment does not need to save the persistent attributes inside each of the handlers. We can store the data in memory in an object first, which is what we do when setting attributes. The only requirement is that we must send that information to the data store before sending the response. That's because sending a response means the function's role in that step in the conversation is over.

As we are required to send the data away only before we send the response, we do not need to distribute that action across different handlers and can simply set the data without saving it.

> **Listing 6.10  Setting persistent attributes without saving (./lambda/custom/index.js)**

```
handlerInput.attributesManager.setPersistentAttributes(data);
// await handlerInput.attributesManager.savePersistentAttributes();
```

Doesn't save the persistent attributes in the handler

We need to continue setting the attributes throughout the fulfillment, but now we only save attributes to the data store in a central location.

The same reasoning applies to the other side of the fulfillment flow. Because we know that the conversation between user and device implies a complete circle of data, we can use the moment when the request enters the fulfillment to set up the skill or the necessary data.

#### REQUEST INTERCEPTORS

Saving the data in an interceptor was a good start. The next step is to consolidate *retrieving* data from the data store. The data needs to be available throughout the fulfillment, so the request interceptors are a good place to retrieve it.

But that brings up another question. How does the data get from the request interceptor to the handlers? We can't store it in a global variable, because Lambda will sometimes reuse a function execution. Global variables are a certain way for users to get information from other people. We could use session attributes, but those are overkill, as we don't need the data that's stored in a data store to be sent back to the Alexa service. Instead, we'll use *request attributes*, which are attributes that only live for the current request.

> **Listing 6.11  Retrieving persistent attributes (./lambda/custom/index.js)**

```
const GetPersistenceInterceptor = {
  async process(handlerInput) {
    try {
      const data = await handlerInput
                        .attributesManager
```

```
                            .getPersistentAttributes();
        const attributes = handlerInput
                            .attributesManager
                            .getRequestAttributes();

        attributes.data = data;          Gets the current request attributes

        handlerInput.attributesManager.setRequestAttributes(attributes);
    } catch (error) {                    Sets the persistent attributes
        throw Error(error);              on the request attributes
    }
  }
};

exports.handler = Alexa.SkillBuilders.standard()
  ...
  .addRequestInterceptors(GetPersistenceInterceptor)
  ...
```

The new `GetPersistenceInterceptor` centralizes the act of retrieving persistent attributes from the data store. You could do this in a function that you call in each handler, but the interceptor ensures that this occurs automatically on each request.

To share the persistent attributes with the rest of the fulfillment, we store them in the request attributes. These attributes only have the lifespan of a single request, and they're appropriate for data we want to share with other places in the fulfillment.

You should use request interceptors for actions that are generally common among requests. Don't perform expensive operations such as reaching out to the data store if those operations serve a minority of requests. You don't want to add latency to the person–computer conversation.

To close the loop, we need to get the request attributes inside the handlers rather than the persistent attributes.

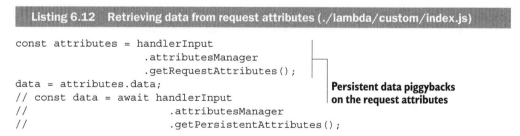

**Listing 6.12  Retrieving data from request attributes (./lambda/custom/index.js)**

```
const attributes = handlerInput
                    .attributesManager
                    .getRequestAttributes();
data = attributes.data;                  Persistent data piggybacks
// const data = await handlerInput        on the request attributes
//                    .attributesManager
//                    .getPersistentAttributes();
```

Everywhere that we previously reached out to the data store to retrieve attributes, we can now retrieve them from memory.

We've written a lot of code, and we've tested it when we interacted with it through a device, or when we sent a request to it locally. But we can go further and give ourselves more confidence that the skill will work when users interact with it. We can add unit testing.

## 6.4    *Unit testing*

We could implement unit tests by following the same approach we saw before of sending a local request object to the fulfillment, and then looking at the output. The downside of this approach is that it gets unwieldy, especially for interactions with multiple steps. A set of tools called *Bespoken* handles that much more easily and fluidly.

Bespoken is a suite created for voice developers, with tools to speed development. The proxy tool lets developers point to their local code during development while testing on an actual device. The speak tool takes text input from the command line and speaks it to the Alexa Voice Service (AVS) as if a real person were speaking to a real device before it returns the result to the command line. The utterance tool takes an utterance and feeds back a result. These interactions roll up to larger tools that provide end-to-end and unit testing. The unit testing tooling is built atop of Jest and uses a "virtual Alexa" that closely tracks the real Alexa platform, but is ultimately an emulator.

The Bespoken tools arrive like many testing tools, as an NPM package:

```
$ npm install -g bespoken-tools
```

With the Bespoken tools installed, you can start building your tests.

Bespoken uses YAML to write tests. The syntax mimics the conversation a user would have with the skill, and Bespoken uses it to test that the output is what the developer intended. The Bespoken tools work largely by convention, but they also leave room for configuration.

> **Listing 6.13   Configuring the test suite (./test/unit/testing.json)**

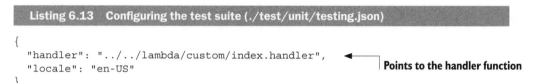

```
{
  "handler": "../../lambda/custom/index.handler",     ◄─────┐ Points to the handler function
  "locale": "en-US"
}
```

The configuration file (testing.json) houses options that set up Bespoken, such as which locales are to undergo testing or where the fulfillment handler lives. It can also include mocks, such as a user ID or a user address. The configuration should live inside the skill files and in the same test/unit/ directory as the tests themselves, which come in one or many YAML files.

> **Listing 6.14    Testing the launch request (./test/unit/index.test.yml)**

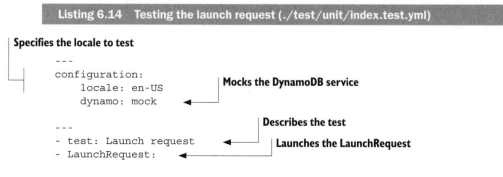

**Specifies the locale to test**

```
---
configuration:
    locale: en-US
    dynamo: mock        ◄───── Mocks the DynamoDB service

---
- test: Launch request    ◄───── Describes the test
- LaunchRequest:          ◄───── Launches the LaunchRequest
```

```
  - prompt: The name info skill needs you to just ask for a first name.
  - reprompt: Try saying, 'give me facts about the name Dustin.'
```

**Specifies the expected reprompt without user input**

**Specifies the expected response**

The preceding launch request test requests a specific action—remember that the launch request maps to when a user opens the skill without a follow-on utterance.

Once you've got a test, you can run it with the `bst-test` command in the terminal. You can specify specific files or even specific intents (for example, `bst-test GetName-Intent`), or run them all at once.

The `LaunchRequest` test checks to see if what's coming back from the fulfillment matches what you expect. The Name Info skill's `LaunchRequest` is static, but the testing also works with user utterances and dynamic responses.

**Listing 6.15  Testing a user utterance and response (./test/unit/index.test.yml)**

```
---
- test: Provide a name
- "the name is Roan":
    - prompt: Roan sure is a nice name. What do you want to know about it?
    - reprompt: I could spell it for you.
```

**What the user would say**

**Includes the variable information (the name)**

We could now run this test with the `bst-test` command, and it would run the request based on what the user would have said. Bespoken uses the virtual Alexa here to map the utterance to an intent. In the prompt, we're testing a response that has variable information. For this intent, the response takes the name the user said and returns it as part of the response, and that lines up here. We also notice—oh no!—that the test fails. We've got a reprompt string in the code, but we never use it. How to fix that?

Putting users at ease when speaking with computers is one of our most important jobs as voice applications developers. We can go a long way toward this goal by using context and user affinities, or favorites, to reduce the strain on the user's requests. We can also reduce the strain on us as developers by using interceptors to handle any necessary set-up and clean-up operations. We can put ourselves at ease through extensive testing, including unit testing with tools such as Bespoken.

In the next chapter, we'll dig back into the code and take these VUI best practices with us as we further enhance our skill functionality.

## Summary

- Remembering the context makes users comfortable by coming to them and not forcing them to be explicit with every reply.
- Context can be enhanced by decaying it over time so that the recent subject is only assumed to be the subject of conversation for a limited amount of time.

- Some skills benefit from using favorites, either explicitly provided by the user or assumed over time, to allow the user to invoke intents more implicitly.
- Data must enter and exit the fulfillment, and interceptors can capture it at both points to centralize common actions.
- Unit tests, using tools such as Bespoken, mimic conversations and ensure the conversation goes as you expect.

# 7

# *Using conversation tools to add meaning and usability*

---

**This chapter covers**

- Making skills users can connect with in their own way of speaking

- Adding Speech Synthesis Markup Language (SSML) and speechcons

- Using rate, pitch, and volume, and specifying pronunciation

- Making responses more natural with discourse markers

---

The first six chapters of this book provided you with the knowledge you need to build a skill that is more feature-rich and more polished than 90% of the skills available to users. This chapter helps you go further, such as using SSML to aid in understanding and usability, or using discourse markers to imbue meaning and make more natural responses.

## 7.1 Discourse markers

> *"Okay, what do we do now?"*
>
> *"Well, we can go back to the car and wait there."*
>
> *"Got it. Sounds like a plan. Let's go."*

Discourse markers are little parts of speech that have a huge impact, but that don't get much attention. They're probably not something you learned about when studying grammar, and yet they add to the meaning of conversations. These are words and phrases such as "okay," "well," or "got it," that link thoughts together and manage the flow of communication. They are used in written and verbal communication, but certain markers are more conversational and others are more geared toward writing.

Some examples of discourse markers common in written communication are "further," "therefore," and "in conclusion." There are people who use these in spoken communication, but their speech sounds stilted, patrician, or affected—or all three. Verbal discourse markers include "okay," "got it," and "so." When you're writing what the user will hear, avoid the written discourse markers and use the verbal ones. Speaking the response "script" out loud is important for this reason. You will hear the woodenness more easily when it's spoken rather than on a silent read-through.

Discourse markers make for more melodic speech, connecting phrases and sentences together. This is taken to an extreme by auctioneers, speaking rapidly as bids come in, sharing information about what's up for sale, and controlling the flow of the bids. Listen very closely (or perhaps slow down a video) and you'll hear discourse markers in abundance. Here's one from Barry Baker of Ohio Real Estate Auctions: "The auction's on, what are you going to give for it? Would you give $200? *Well then*, give a hundred. I've got a hundred. *Now* with a hundred and a quarter. Would you give a hundred and a quarter? *Now* a hundred and a half."[1] Those discourse markers of "well then" and "now" connect the phrases together.

Consider the following dialog, first without discourse markers:

> *MOVIEGOER: I want to see a movie.*
>
> *TICKET SELLER: Which movie? What time? How many tickets?*
>
> *MOVIEGOER: "Boyhood." 9:15. Two tickets.*
>
> *TICKET SELLER: Here are your tickets. Theater's on your left.*

This is stilted and truly robotic. Other than the subject matter, there's no connection between one phrase and another. In fact, it sounds brusque and rude.

Just a handful of additions opens it up:

> *MOVIEGOER: I want to see a movie.*
>
> *TICKET SELLER: Okay, which movie? Also, what time and how many tickets?*
>
> *MOVIEGOER: "Boyhood," 9:15, and finally, two tickets.*
>
> *TICKET SELLER: Alright, here are your tickets. By the way, theater's on your left.*

These little discourse markers aren't just the cotton candy of speech, providing fluff and color and little else, but you wouldn't be on your own if you thought so. Linguists

---

[1]   Barry Baker of Ohio Real Estate Auctions describes what the auctioneer is saying during the chant or bid calling during the auction, http://mng.bz/Wa8d.

didn't start studying them seriously until the 1980s.[2] They are very important for understanding, however, and they're full of meaning on their own.

A marker like "well then" can mean a number of things depending on the context. It could imply passive aggression, especially with a lengthy pause afterward. Conversely, it could mean "Here's another option instead." According to linguist Deborah Schiffrin, "well" itself indicates an attempt "to strike a balance" in both making the other party feel heard and providing unexpected or unwanted information.[3] That's quite a lot of meaning in just one four-letter word.

Discourse markers can communicate, "I'm still talking," "I've changed topics," "This is my last point," or myriad other messages. There is no definitive list of markers, but they do fall within certain categories. Linguist Bruce Fraser identified the groups listed in table 7.1, with examples of each, that can be added to a voice application.

---

[2]  Bruce Fraser, "Types of English Discourse Markers," *Acta Linguistica Hungarica* 38, no. 1/4 (1988): 19–33; http://www.jstor.org/stable/44362602.

[3]  Charles L. Briggs, "Review of 'Discourse Markers' by Deborah Schiffrin," *Language in Society* 21, no. 4 (1992): 683–87; http://www.jstor.org/stable/4168397.

**Table 7.1  Discourse markers**

| Purpose | Markers |
| --- | --- |
| Topic markers | back to my original point, before I forget, continuing, while I have you, incidentally, speaking of, on a different note, with regards to |
| Reinforcing | again, alright, indeed, in fact, listen, OK, see |
| **Activity** | |
| Clarifying | by the way, to clarify, to be clear |
| Conceding | admittedly, after all, anyhow, anyway, at any rate, of course |
| Explaining | to explain, if I may explain |
| Interrupting | if I may interrupt, to interrupt, just |
| Repeating | once again, repeating, to repeat |
| Sequencing | finally, first of all, on the other hand, third, to begin with, to finish |
| Summarizing | to sum up, in general, thus far, so far, overall, in conclusion |
| **Message relationship (connecting the current phrase to a previous topic)** | |
| Parallel (continuation) | also, and, otherwise, or, equally, likewise, similarly, too |
| Contrasting | all the same, but, despite, however, rather, regardless, still, that said |
| Elaborative | above all, also, besides, better, for example, for instance, further, in addition, indeed, more accurately, to cap it all off |
| Inferential (consequence) | accordingly, as a result, hence, of course, so, then, therefore, thus |

*Source:* Adapted from Fraser, "Types of English Discourse Markers."

Another common, and commonly maligned, discourse marker that appears in VUIs is "otherwise."[4] "Otherwise" deserves its scorn. No one except the most affected of speakers uses this in common speech, but it appears commonly in VUI and phone systems: "Press 1 for ticketing, press 2 for baggage, otherwise stay on the line and a customer service representative will be with you shortly." This is highly stilted and very common. This is much more natural: "If you need ticketing, press 1. Baggage, press 2. If you need something else, hold on for a moment and we'll get you to a representative." The extra change to put the numbers after the descriptions is also more friendly to callers—no longer do they need to hold the number in their mind while waiting to see if it connects with what they need. Now they hear what they need, and they hear the number immediately after.

Use discourse markers to enhance understanding, but not at the expense of unnatural speech:

- Show progression through a list with "first," "next," and "finally": "*First*, we've got Houston with 88 wins. *Next* there's Seattle with 82, and, *finally*, Oakland with 81."
- Demonstrate an outcome with "so": "Alright, *so* I'll close the account now."
- Clarify with "by the way": "*By the way*, you can also tell me how you slept last night."
- Avoid a professorial tone with "equally," "to sum up," or "indeed." Unless, of course, that's your application's persona. Even then, tread lightly: "*Equally*, you can *indeed* tell me how you slept last night."

Further, when providing help, Alexa could say, "*To start*, you can ask for the length or first letter of a name." This shows that Alexa is continuing the previous thought and not just saying things at random. When the user does provide a name, the response is, "*Alright*. You can ask me about the first letter or the length of (the name)." Here "alright" is a discourse marker that function as an acknowledgment that Alexa is truly listening. Even if users know they're speaking with a computer through code that's been programmed and then deployed, small touches like this can put them at ease.

Be mindful. Discourse markers, especially in situations where the responses are created ahead of time but read in an unplanned order, can sound right in one part of the conversation but wrong if the same sentence is placed elsewhere. Sequencing is, of course, an easy example. The marker "first" needs to come in a certain place, as do "third" and "finally."

Other examples are more subtle, but still important to note. For example, the marker "oh" can signify that what the speaker believes doesn't match with what the listener believes, and for that reason it isn't suited to all responses.[5] The response "I have just three left" could be said without a discourse marker to respond to a question like "How many tickets do you still have?" A single discourse marker like "oh" could change

---

[4]   Michael H. Cohen, James P. Giangola, and Jennifer Balogh, *Voice User Interface Design* (Addison-Wesley Professional, 2004), pp. 145–147.

[5]   Cohen, Giangola, and Balogh, *Voice User Interface Design*, p. 143.

the meaning subtly. "Oh, I have just three left," makes no sense when a customer asks specifically how many tickets remain, unless the speaker's goal is to project a Charlie Brown-style malaise. But it does sound natural when the customer has asked for five tickets: "Oh, I have just three left."

Your options, then, are to use discourse markers that always sound natural, no matter the order, or to craft different responses for each situation. The former is probably less work, but adding responses that are unique to each possibility will make for a richer overall application that communicates more fully.

Whereas discourse markers are words that we can use in a conversation, Speech Synthesis Markup Language (SSML) directs the platforms on *how* to say those and other words.

## 7.2 Controlling the application's speech with SSML

Old text-to-speech systems were famously bad. Forget sounding natural; those systems were nearly unintelligible. People take meaning from the pronunciation of words, of course, but the *way* we speak can also change the meaning. Find yourself a secluded space (or don't worry what people think of you) and speak the following sentence out loud.

> *"Today we're having hot dogs."*

Try it with no change of pitch, emphasis, or pause length between each word. Then take the same words and turn them into a question, a show of suspense, or a sarcastic rejoinder. Imply that your group is having hot dogs, but that someone else isn't. Indicate that while hot dogs are on the menu today, they aren't tomorrow. You'll notice that speaking in a way that's not like a robot adds just as much to the meaning as the words themselves.

Alexa, Google Assistant, and others do a much better job than older text-to-speech systems of speaking in a human-like manner, but they're not perfect and they could use your help. Providing the platforms with guidance on how to speak, particularly for responses that get said a lot, can make a skill feel polished. Developers can do this through the use of SSML.

> **NOTE** When determining which phrases to focus on polishing with SSML, use your analytics to determine which responses are being said most often. For brand-new or lightly trafficked skills, you can start off with anything that is said in `LaunchRequest` or the help intent.

SSML is not unique to these voice-first platforms. It comes from the World Wide Web Consortium (W3C) and it's nothing new: the W3C standardized version 1.0 of SSML in 2004 and it followed even earlier work, such as SABLE and Java Speech Markup Language. Speech properties have even been built into CSS, although SSML itself is XML-based.

The following listing shows the "Hello World" of SSML.

**Listing 7.1    SSML Hello World**

```
<?xml version="1.0"?>
<!DOCTYPE speak PUBLIC "-//W3C//DTD SYNTHESIS 1.0//EN"
                  "http://www.w3.org/TR/speech-synthesis/synthesis.dtd">
<speak version="1.0"
      xmlns="http://www.w3.org/2001/10/synthesis"
      xmlns:xsi="http://www.w3.org/2001/XMLSchema-instance"
      xsi:schemaLocation="http://www.w3.org/2001/10/synthesis
                  http://www.w3.org/TR/speech-synthesis/synthesis.xsd"
      xml:lang="en-US">
  <p>Hello, world.</p>                  The final, spoken output
</speak>
```
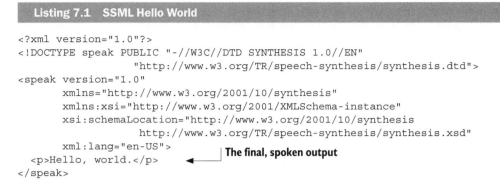

Thankfully, you don't have to provide all of this markup. All you need to provide in the response object for Alexa is the `<speak>` tag and any markup inside.

**Listing 7.2    Alexa SSML Hello World**

```
"outputSpeech": {
  "type": "SSML",
  "ssml": "<speak><p>Hello, world.</p></speak>"      The spoken output
}
```
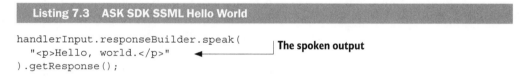

The ASK SDK in the following listing abstracts that away even further, leaving you to focus only on the markup.

**Listing 7.3    ASK SDK SSML Hello World**

```
handlerInput.responseBuilder.speak(      The spoken output
  "<p>Hello, world.</p>"
).getResponse();
```

> **NOTE**   To test your SSML, go to the Test tab of your skill configuration in the Amazon Developer Console. After enabling testing, look for the voice simulator. Add only the SSML—you can leave off the `<speak>` tag and the JavaScript.

### 7.2.1  *Breaks and pauses*

When you injected suspense into the hot dog sentence earlier, you probably did so with a pause, letting people wonder just what was for lunch: "Today we're having (pause) hot dogs."

Managing breaks and pauses is the simplest addition in SSML, and it's the one you'll probably use the most often, through sentences (`<s>`) or paragraphs (`<p>`). Or you can add more granular control with the `<break>` tag. Table 7.2 outlines these tags.

**Table 7.2  Tags to add pauses**

| Tag | Options | Details |
|---|---|---|
| `<break>` | `strength` or `time` | Can be used to change the amount of silence between words |
| `<p>` | | Specifies a paragraph; equivalent to `<break strength="x-strong">` |
| `<s>` | | Specifies a sentence; equivalent to `<break strength="strong">` or to adding a period at the end of a sentence |

The `<break>` tag is the base of all pauses in SSML. It gives you the flexibility to change the amount of silence between words. You can use it in conjunction with the `strength` or `time` attributes to add to or take away some silence. When used without any attributes, it represents a `medium` pause, which is the default amount of delay Alexa puts between any two words separated by a comma.

**Listing 7.4  Pauses using the `<break>` tag**

```
handlerInput.responseBuilder.speak(
  "Today, we're having hot dogs."
).getResponse();
handlerInput.responseBuilder.speak(
  "Today <break/> we're having hot dogs."
).getResponse();
handlerInput.responseBuilder.speak(
  "Today <break strength=\"medium\"/> we're having hot dogs."
).getResponse();
```

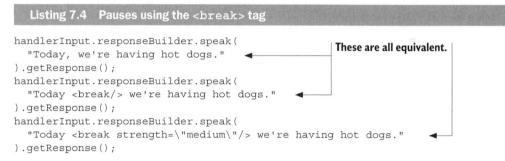

These are all equivalent.

The `strength` attribute can take six different values that correspond to four different lengths: `none` (or `x-weak`), `medium` (or `weak`), `strong`, and `x-strong`. In practice, you'll have difficulty hearing a significant difference between the strengths.

For more control, there's also the `time` attribute, where you can specify the number of milliseconds (`ms`) or seconds (`s`) of silence to add between words, up to 10 seconds.

**Listing 7.5  Specifying the amount of time in milliseconds**

```
handlerInput.responseBuilder.speak(
  'Wait <break time="300ms"/> hold up'
).getResponse();
```

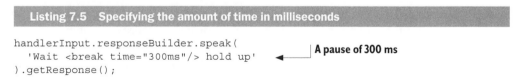

A pause of 300 ms

Adding suspense is perhaps the canonical use for pauses, but don't forget others. The popular audio story series *The Magic Door* uses pauses to allow listeners to catch up and digest what they're hearing. Andy Huntwork, the CEO of the company behind *The Magic Door*, says that adjusting the default pauses provided by the Alexa voice was so important to setting their skill apart from others that, after learning this lesson, he and his business partner (and wife) Laura went through and adjusted all of their existing content to provide a more natural pace. This is less applicable to brief responses, but adding some silence can give Alexa a little bit of time to breathe, add emphasis to information that a user especially needs to take in, or delineate between two independent thoughts.

**NOTE**   You can use breaks, paragraphs, and sentences in actions on Google, too.

Additional pauses can benefit cases where you want to teach the user how to interact with the skill, effectively creating "quotes" in sound through anticipatory pauses:[6] "You can (pause) 'get scores,' (pause) 'get stats,' or ask (pause) 'next game.'" Setting these phrases apart instructs the user that this phrasing is special and that the phrases are the keys for what they want to do. Saying this sentence without pauses doesn't indicate that there is anything special about the phrases, and indeed may simply describe the skill's functionality.

Another situation where you might add breaks is where you want to give the indication (real or imagined) that the skill is hard at work for the user. Alexa, for example, has "progressive response" functionality that does just this, providing longer pauses when real work is being done, such as going to an external API to look for data. But pauses for activities that take effectively no time can also provide value. This can suggest "that the system is taking the user's statement seriously"[7] or imply the arrival of new information that contradicts what the skill started to say, such as "I'm getting the weather for tomorrow. (pause) Hm, it looks like there's an issue with the weather service right now."[8]

Where breaks add meaning and understanding through silence, prosody does the same through sound.

### 7.2.2  *Prosody*

Robocalls are those annoying phone calls that come with a prerecorded message, often in the service of selling home or auto insurance. While writing this chapter, I received one that was so maddeningly clever I couldn't be too upset. It had prerecorded messages asking not only about whether I was a home owner, but also about the weather (replete with "ahhh, the weather's not so bad here in Florida") and what TV shows I was watching! About 30 seconds into the call, the prerecorded voice said, "I was hoping to talk to you about your home insurance andpressonetojointhedonotcalllist."

Sneakily, the part they didn't want me to hear, about the do-not-call list, was spoken twice as fast as everything else. They had used prosody, namely *rate*, to sneaky ends. You can use it for much more productive purposes, like increasing the perceived friendliness of your skill or adding emphasis.

*Prosody* describes the elements of speech that aren't *what* is said as much as *how* the speaker says it. Within the confines of SSML, when we discuss prosody, we're discussing three properties:

- *Rate*—The speed of the speech
- *Pitch*—The tone of the speech
- *Volume*—How loud (or quiet) the speech is

---

6   Clifford Nass and Scott Brave, *Wired for Speech: How Voice Activates and Advances the Human–Computer Relationship* (MIT Press, 2007).

7   From chapter 14 in Nass and Brave, *Wired for Speech.*

8   Cohen, Giangola, and Balogh, *Voice User Interface Design,* pp. 198–199.

Rate, pitch, and volume are all attributes of the <prosody> tag and can be combined in a single tag. All three can impact how a listener perceives what the speaker (or computer) is saying. Increase the rate and volume to express excitement. Decrease the rate and increase the volume, and you might have flashbacks to parental reprimands.

##### Listing 7.6 Speaking fast and with a high pitch

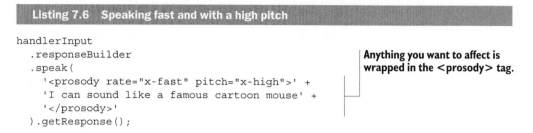

```
handlerInput
  .responseBuilder
  .speak(
    '<prosody rate="x-fast" pitch="x-high">' +
    'I can sound like a famous cartoon mouse' +
    '</prosody>'
  ).getResponse();
```

**Anything you want to affect is wrapped in the <prosody> tag.**

**NOTE** Actions on Google support rate, pitch, and volume as well.

#### RATE

Adjusting the speed at which words are spoken is done with the rate property. Again, *The Magic Door* uses this property to make their long-form audio more understandable—usually by slowing down the speech. But consider the effect you're going for. We already saw that people make assumptions about personality based on voice alone, and that you can't change perceptions on Alexa significantly—people spend more time with the Alexa voice outside of your skill than inside it—but you can influence how listeners react to what your skill is saying. For example, voices that are seen as more friendly are—among other traits—generally more rapid.[9] Rate can be used in your skills to show excitement through increased speed or to add emphasis with a slower response.

In SSML, you can adjust rate through keywords (x-slow, slow, medium, fast, or x-fast) or through percentages. For percentage-based adjustments, 100% is the default rate. Anything greater than 100% makes the speech faster, and anything less slows it down, with a floor of 20%.

##### Listing 7.7 Slowing down for understanding

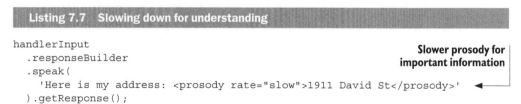

```
handlerInput
  .responseBuilder
  .speak(
    'Here is my address: <prosody rate="slow">1911 David St</prosody>'
  ).getResponse();
```

**Slower prosody for important information**

Unlike the robocallers, intent on selling home insurance, an address is something you want listeners to hear and understand. When you slow down the response, you give them the time to ingest the information.

---

[9] See "Personality of Voices: Similars Attract," in Nass and Brave, *Wired for Speech*.

**PITCH**

A change in pitch can take Alexa's voice from deep to chipmunk. Use pitch to make Alexa surprised, worried, concerned, happy, and so on. For example, a lower pitch combined with a slower rate can imply concern. A higher pitch can show excitement. If you're pulling in voices from other sources, such as AWS Polly, you can adjust the pitch to make a persona that is friendly (higher pitch with more pitch changes, plus a faster overall rate) or dour (deeper and slower with fewer overall changes in pitch).[10] The pitch can express a lot of emotion separate from the words themselves.

> **Listing 7.8    Showing excitement or disappointment through pitch**

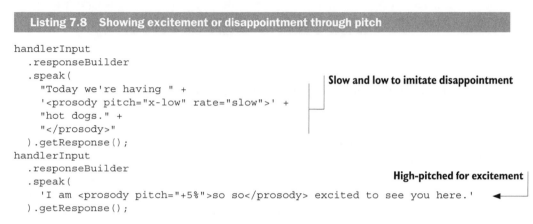

```
handlerInput
  .responseBuilder
  .speak(
    "Today we're having " +                      Slow and low to imitate disappointment
    '<prosody pitch="x-low" rate="slow">' +
    "hot dogs." +
    "</prosody>"
  ).getResponse();
handlerInput
  .responseBuilder
  .speak(                                          High-pitched for excitement
    'I am <prosody pitch="+5%">so so</prosody> excited to see you here.'
  ).getResponse();
```

The rate can range from x-low to low, medium, high, or x-high or it can use a positive or negative percentage. When providing a percentage, preface the value with a sign (+ or -) and note that the value must be between -33.3% and +50%. Lower the pitch to x-low, and you can hear the concern in Alexa's voice. Increase the pitch by 5%, and Alexa *is* excited that you were able to make it.

> **NOTE** Actions on Google also support adjusting pitch through adding or removing semitones. If you don't know semitones, imagine a piano. White keys that are next together without a black key between them are two notes separated by a semitone. The black keys themselves are a semitone away from their surrounding white keys. In more mathematical terms, a semitone is a measure of the separation between two tones where the frequency of the higher tone is 1.06 times the frequency of the lower tone. To adjust semitones, add + or - to a number followed by the st notation, such as +2st to increase by two semitones.

In conjunction with rate, you can use pitch to add emphasis. Current voice-first text-to-speech will vary the pitch for you—it's why these devices are more pleasant to use than older systems—but they can't predict everything. If you wanted to be clear that something is happening for the last time, bump up the pitch and slow the rate: "I would *never, ever* do that again."

> **TIP** Test your prosody changes on each platform. For Alexa, pitch would increase by 10% and the rate would slow by half for emphasis in "I would *never, ever* do that again." On Google Actions, those numbers are around 5% and 70%, respectively.

---

[10] "Personality of Voices: Similars Attract," in Nass and Brave, *Wired for Speech.*

### VOLUME

The last attribute for controlling prosody in SSML for Alexa is the volume. By using this, you can make Alexa shout or speak quietly relative to the volume setting of the device. You can't make Alexa wake up the neighbors if your listener has it set to be barely heard.

Values are set in keywords (silent, x-soft, soft, medium, loud, or x-loud) or in positive or negative decibels, with a maximum of just over 4 (about +4.08dB). Because decibels are measured on a logarithmic scale, +6dB doubles the volume, whereas -6dB halves it.

> **Listing 7.9   Reducing the volume**

```
handlerInput
  .responseBuilder
  .speak(                                            A reduced volume can imply distance.
    'Let me go to the other room... <break time="1000ms"/>.' +
    '<prosody volume="-32dB">Can you still hear me?</prosody>'
  ).getResponse();
```

Use volume to imitate physical changes (like Alexa "going into another room") or use it along with rate and pitch for emphasis. Overall, you'll notice more of an impact when lowering the volume than you will when raising it, which makes sense. The voice-first platforms don't want users to always wonder if a skill is going to shout at them.

### 7.2.3   amazon:effect

Lowering the volume seems like it should imitate whispering, but it's not perfect. Try this: say the word *whisper* at a normal volume with your hand on your throat. Say it more quietly now. Notice how each time your fingers feel a rumble. Now whisper it. You're no longer feeling the vibrations, and you may notice, too, that the sound is coming from further forward in your mouth. That's because whispering is not just a reflection of how loud the speech is, but where it's produced as well. The volume attribute affects one, but not the other, leaving out the breathy quality of a normal whisper.

For your whispering needs, Amazon added the amazon:effect tag to its SSML. The only effect is whispering, which you add through an attribute on the tag.

> **Listing 7.10   The whisper effect**

```
handlerInput
  .responseBuilder
  .speak(
    "Today, we're having " +                         Imitating a whisper
    '<amazon:effect name="whispered">hot dogs</amazon:effect>.'
  ).getResponse();
```

Give whispering a try, but in my opinion, you won't use this very often. The whispering seems off compared to the rest of the speech—there's almost a sense of distress in Alexa's voice. Maybe you'll need it, but if you're trying to decrease only the volume, use prosody instead.

### 7.2.4   *w, say-as*

Quick, how do you pronounce *wind?* It will depend on what the context is. If it's a verb, it's pronounced a different way than if it's a noun. Alexa is generally intelligent enough to tell the difference. Listen to Alexa's pronunciation of "Wind the watch and watch the wind." Other examples are more difficult. Even humans would have difficulty figuring out how to pronounce *read* in "I read the newspaper" with no further context.

With the w tag, you can specify the way the word should be pronounced. Use the role attribute and the values of amazon:VB for the present tense verb, amazon:VBD for the past tense, amazon:NN for the noun, and amazon:SENSE_1 for the less-common pronunciation. The secondary sense would be used in the case of *resign*, where the most common pronunciation refers to leaving a post and the secondary pronunciation means the opposite (effectively, signing again).

---

**Listing 7.11   Changing pronunciations with w**

```
handlerInput
  .responseBuilder
  .speak(
    'She refused to resign and wanted to ' +          Two different pronunciations
    '<w role="amazon:SENSE_1">resign</w> instead.'
  ).getResponse();
```

The pronunciation directions don't end there. The say-as tag offers control for different situations that people learn over time how to handle. Consider numbers, like 5125554912. Maybe that refers to 5,125,554,912 or the 5,125,554,912th. Or perhaps, it should be read as digits, 5-1-2-5-5-5-4-9-1-2. Maybe it's even an American phone number: 5-1-2 5-5-5 4-9-1-2. The say-as tag, coupled with the interpret-as attribute, provide the developer with control over how Alexa says this and many other potentially confusing parts of a response. There are many different values, shown in table 7.3.

---

### SSML implementation differences

There are some key differences between the w and say-as implementations in Actions on Google and Alexa:

- Google doesn't support the w tag.
- For dates, Google also supports the detail attribute. A detail value of 1 will have Google say "the third of January, 1997." A value of 2 will lead to "January 3rd, 1997."
- Times in Google SSML also accept a format attribute. Use it with a combination of h, m, s, Z, 12, and 24 to specify which parts of the text correspond to which parts of the time. The time can also be configured with a detail attribute, where the value 1 corresponds to 24-hour time and 2 is 12-hour time.
- Google will pluralize units in the spoken output, so that "10 foot" becomes "10 feet."
- Google doesn't add emphasis on interjection.

**Table 7.3** `interpret-as` **values**

| Use... | If you want Alexa to... |
| --- | --- |
| `characters` or `spell-out`, `digits` | Say each character separately |
| `cardinal` or `number`, `ordinal`, `telephone` | Specify how to interpret and say a string of digits |
| `fraction` | Pronounce a string like "1/2" as "one-half" |
| `unit` | Say "25s" as "twenty-five seconds" |
| `time` | Interpret 3'44" as "three minutes and forty-four seconds" |
| `address` | Say "245" as "two forty-five" rather than "two hundred forty-five"* |
| `date` | Say a string of digits as a human-friendly date |
| `expletive` | Bleep out words, adjusting the length for the amount of time it would normally take to say the words, and leaving a small bit of the beginning and end of the word or phrase.** |
| `interjection` | Speak with more *oomph* |

\* Alexa is smart enough to pronounce a number the more natural way if you provide a string like "245 Main St." without the `say-as` tag.

\*\* Alexa is generally demure even without `expletive`, so if you try to say a curse word, Alexa will clean it up.

There are a lot of different options here, reflecting the fact that there a lot of different ways for people to say what would otherwise be written in the same manner. Numbers, as you see, are the biggest category with the largest number of variations. The good news is that the text-to-speech on Alexa and Google can generally figure out what to say on their own. The better news is that you have the tools to step in when it doesn't work correctly, as shown in the following listing

**Listing 7.12   Adjusting number interpretation**

```
handlerInput
  .responseBuilder
  .speak(                                          Pronounced "one half"
    'Add <say-as interpret-as="fraction">1/2</say-as> a cup of sugar.'  ◄─┘
  ).getResponse();
handlerInput
  .responseBuilder
  .speak(                                          Pronounced "twenty sixteen"
    'The street number is <say-as interpret-as="address">2016</say-as>.'  ◄─┘
  ).getResponse();
```

An option of note is `characters`. In the Name Info skill, Alexa spelled out a name by first splitting the name into characters and then joining it back together with spaces. You can accomplish this, instead, with SSML.

**Listing 7.13    Spelling out a name without splitting letters (./lambda/custom/index.js)**

Pronounced "Kate"                                                                    Pronounced "K A T E"

```
const speech = `You spell ${data.name}, ` +
                    `<say-as interpret-as="characters">${data.name}</say-as>.`;
```

If SSML isn't enough, you should make an effort to tweak what Alexa or Google is saying by changing the text you're sending. Mistakes can be jarring to the user and can instantly remind them that they're talking to a computer that may not understand what they want. On a recent trip to Texas, my wife and I were driving around Houston when Google Maps told us to exit for "highway two-hundred eighty-eight." There's probably never been a native English speaker who has said the highway number like that. Instead, we speak highway numbers like "two eighty-eight" or "twenty-two twenty-two." If the platform you're working on doesn't do this automatically or have an SSML setting (Amazon does with `address`, Google does not), you may need to take your numbers and group them into smaller two-digit numbers before sending them along. It's a little extra work on your end, but a more natural response for your users.

The `interjection` value instructs Alexa to speak with more pep. This value should only be used with speechcons—words and phrases optimized for this purpose. These are region-specific, meaning you might use "oh brother" for US English and "oh my giddy aunt" in the UK. You'll find that speechcons humanize Alexa—and that's the problem with them. Your users will go from a good, but still robotic, voice to one that sounds a lot more human. It's jarring. If you are going to use speechcons, leave ample silence before and after, or use them on their own.[11]

### 7.2.5    *phoneme*

The `phoneme` tag is the most powerful of all. With it, you can specify exactly how a word is to be pronounced. You'll turn to this tool when speech-to-text can't get the word correct even with the other SSML; if it's a foreign word; or if it's a proper name.

This power brings along complexity, because you will also need to know—or look up—specialized phonetic alphabets. The two that Alexa uses are the International Phonetic Alphabet (IPA) and the Extended Speech Assessment Methods Phonetic Alphabet (X-SAMPA). If you don't have an attachment to either, consider going with IPA. X-SAMPA was created to mimic IPA back when support for the specialized IPA characters on computers was nascent. As a result, becoming familiar with IPA will provide you with more benefits outside of programming, and looking up IPA for one-off adjustments will be easier. Conversely, if you plan to adjust the pronunciation often, typing X-SAMPA will be easier, because it uses the keys you have on your keyboard. You absolutely do not need to learn either in order to be successful building voice applications.

> **TIP**    If you decide to use IPA, the easiest approach is using an online IPA table where you can see or hear the corresponding sounds and copy the IPA characters. There are also interactive "keyboards" such as this one: http://westonruter .github.io/ipa-chart/keyboard/.

---

[11]  A full list can be found for each region at http://mng.bz/zMVg.

To use the phoneme tag, provide the alphabet and the phonetic pronunciation symbols (ph attribute). The word inside doesn't affect the pronunciation, but it will be important for you or anyone else who reads the code in order to understand what Alexa is going to say.

**Listing 7.14  Changing pronunciation with phonemes**

```
handlerInput
  .responseBuilder
  .speak(
    '<phoneme alphabet="ipa" ph="pəˈteɪtoʊ">Potato</phoneme>.' +
    '<phoneme alphabet="ipa" ph="pəˈtɑːtəʊ">Potato</phoneme>.' +
    '<phoneme alphabet="ipa" ph="təˈmeɪtoʊ">Tomato</phoneme>.' +
    '<phoneme alphabet="ipa" ph="təˈmɑːtəʊ">Tomato</phoneme>.' +
    "Let's call the whole thing off."
  ).getResponse();
```

Po-tay-to
Po-tah-to
To-may-to
To-mah-to

**NOTE**  Do not use the phoneme tag on actions on Google. Adding it to a response will skip the word inside it altogether.

The SSML tags do not have to be used in isolation. You will probably want to use multiple tags to get Alexa to speak in a more fluid way, especially for phrases that Alexa will say commonly. Do not worry if you have Alexa saying things, like search results, without using SSML to make adjustments. It's most important to focus on the areas where you can have the most impact.

## 7.3  *Embedding audio*

There's one more part to SSML that's different enough to warrant setting it off by itself, and that is *embedded audio*. Use embedded audio if you want to include a short music clip or a word or phrase in a different language, or if you want to control exactly how something is said and with which voices. (For an example of this last reason, check out the skill "The Wayne Investigation" by Warner Bros. Voice actors were hired to give the skill more life.)

Embedded audio can also set a skill apart through audio branding. This is a field that has grown increasingly in recent years and can make a significant impact for a brand by providing "a coherent voice across touchpoints, geographies, and product lifecycle… and [creating] brand value that grows over the years."[12]

Some developers even use audio as a way-finding technique, emitting a distinctive sound when the user can investigate further. In a cooking skill, the sound of a glass clinking might signal that the current recipe step is finished and that the user can move forward by asking for the next one; or audio can be used to "landmark" by playing a different sound for each frame, or section, to let users know they're in the right place.

---

[12] Laurence Minsky, Colleen Fahey, and Philip Kotler, *Audio Branding: Using Sound to Build Your Brand* (Kogan Page, 2017), p. 10.

The same cooking skill would have one sound after a recipe search, for example, and another for cooking tips.

If you have your Alexa skill on Lambda, the easiest place to store your sound files is on Amazon S3, but you can host them on any endpoint on HTTPS with an Amazon-approved SSL certificate (available at most hosting providers). There are a few other requirements, both documented and not. You can have at most five audio files for a total of 90 seconds of embedded audio in any Alexa response. The filenames can't have spaces, and they must be MP3 files with a bit rate of 48 kbps and a sample rate of 16,000 Hz. A program like FFMPEG or Audacity can convert your files if they aren't in the correct format.

Don't overdo it with the audio. Alexa won't speak over the audio, so you can't have background noise or music. Plus, adding superfluous sound effects will make you sound like a drive-time DJ. Finally, if you're including other recorded voices, don't jump straight from Alexa (or Google) to the recorded voices and back. This confuses people. Instead, have the default platform voice hand off control with a verbal acknowledgment, or with an extended pause.

> **NOTE**  Alexa won't speak over embedded audio, but Google Assistant has a nonstandard SSML tag, par, that can run audio in parallel.

You might decide to eschew the default voice altogether, either by hiring voice talent or by using another text-to-speech engine such as AWS Polly. This can have some big benefits. The default voice has its personality baked in before a user ever comes to your voice application. This comes from the voice, but also from what that voice is saying during interactions, which will be different on each platform and also for each user. Some people, for example, swear that Alexa has more "personality" than the voices on Google Assistant, and others believe the opposite. You may want complete control over the personality that comes through on your application.

You may also want to do this to set your skill apart from others, especially by hiring voice talent. "The Wayne Investigation," "Call of Duty," and "Comedy Central" are all Alexa skills that use a combination of the default and hired voices. They are also all skills backed by big brands. If you don't have that money behind you, you can still build engaging skills using the default voice. You also might use the default voice if your skill changes regularly—to avoid needing to re-engage a voice actor for each change—or if the skill includes significant variable information, such as data from an API.

But should skills with recorded voices eschew dynamic content altogether? Not at all. Most initial thoughts around the combination of text-to-speech and recorded speech conclude that it's a poor approach. But combining the two isn't impossible. Some research claims that users even prefer a combination of recorded and synthetic speech to synthetic speech on its own.[13] This research comes from 1999, and text-to-speech has progressed significantly since that time. Nonetheless, the finding is important in showing that users aren't turned off by having a recorded voice for static responses and a speech-to-text voice for dynamic information. Still, this mélange

---

[13]  Cohen, Giangola, and Balogh, *Voice User Interface Design*, p. 202.

requires some finesse. Don't jump straight from the recorded speech to the synthetic speech. Leave a pause between the two, as if the recorded speech is handing the conversation off to someone else.

In this chapter, we discussed the little words and phrases called discourse markers, which add meaning and flow in conversations. You also saw how to use SSML to transform how voice applications speak and pronounce the responses you craft in the fulfillment. These are tactics you can use to make your applications more understandable and more effective.

In the next chapter, we will look at how we can further enhance their effectiveness.

## Summary

- Discourse markers are short words or phrases that provide both conversation flow and meaning.
- SSML is the markup through which developers can change the pronunciation or prosody of speech.
- Embedded audio can allow for skill differentiation through sound clips or voices that diverge from the default Alexa voice.

# *Directing conversation flow*

**This chapter covers**

- Using questions and limiting choices to guide user interaction

- Creating a dialog with the dialog interface

- Confirming user input

- Handling errors

Ultimately, there is no user interface—on the web, mobile, voice, or anywhere else—that does not benefit from guiding users and helping them land where they want to go. This applies to voice more than other interfaces, because there is no persistent menu to help if a user gets lost, and there is no limit to user input. Compare that with a mobile app: a user can only tap on what's on the phone, and well-established UI patterns show the user what can be used and what can't.

Previously, we've looked at providing user guidance on what actions are available. In this chapter we'll build a new skill to see how you can encourage users to give responses the skill can handle once the interaction has already started.

## 8.1    *Guiding user interaction*

Imagine a web page that only has an input box and a Submit button. The user would have no idea what to do. Users need guidance in what they can, or should, do. Even the famously minimalist Google home page's button says "Google Search." Older versions of the Google page, before Google became so well known, had more information with a guidance of "Search the Web with Google." This is one of the benefits of web pages. They can add or hide additional information as necessary. Voice applications have similar mechanisms to guide users, such as through suggestive prompts.

Suggestive prompts are a useful approach to guiding a conversation. Suggestive questioning is generally frowned upon in day-to-day conversations. No one wants a coworker to ask, "Don't you think you could have done that presentation differently?" We can sense they have an agenda, and we want no part of it.

But the real problem is clumsily posed questions. After all, every parent has learned not to ask young children whether they want to do a chore. Instead, a better question is "Do you want to brush your teeth before or after you make your bed?" This question has a clear agenda (you aren't getting out of brushing your teeth or making your bed) and it probably wouldn't work on a peer level, but it does provide a proper amount of guidance. That's sometimes what is needed when building a computer–human skill interaction.

Look at the extreme: a skill that only says "What do you want to do?" Where would you start? There's too much open space. This *may* work for the overall device, once users learn what can be done. Device manufacturers take care to train users on what they can do with their gear. Take a new Echo device from the box, and you'll see that Amazon provides a glossy onboarding, teaching users what's possible.

There isn't an equivalent introduction for your skill. This is why Alexa requires three example interaction phrases before a developer can publish a skill. Don't forget this once a user is inside the skill. The question, "Tell me about movies," shouldn't be greeted with a broad response, but instead with something that guides, like "I can purchase movie tickets or look up details. Start off by telling me the name of a movie." This is one way to guide users down a path.

Another way, particularly in situations where a lot of information is necessary, is to get the information from the user in smaller pieces, through a dialog.

## 8.2    *Dialog interface*

The other day I went to the movies—I wanted to see an old John Wayne movie at the theater down the street. I walked up to the ticket booth and said, "I'd like a couple of tickets to 'Red River' at 8:40, please." Money provided, tickets bought. That's not the only way it could have gone, though.

How inconceivable is the following conversation?

> *DUSTIN: I'd like two tickets for "Red River."*
> *TICKET SELLER: Which showing?*
> *DUSTIN: The one at 8:40.*

> *TICKET SELLER: Alright, two for 8:40. Oh yeah, do you have any discounts? Are you a student or a member of our film club?*
>
> *DUSTIN: Nope!*
>
> *TICKET SELLER: In that case, I've got two tickets for "Red River" at 8:40 and it'll cost $16.50.*

This type of conversation, or *dialog*, happens every day. We have a back and forth, where the information dribbles out, whether because we forget or don't know necessary bits of information, or because saying it all at once would be too much. Beyond that, we want to confirm, for certain actions, that we understand what the person on the other side wants. It's no different in human–computer conversations. Indeed, because computers have a more difficult time understanding speech correctly than people do, this volleying and confirming proves more useful.

In chapter 5, you learned about maintaining state and using it to direct conversational flow. That same technique could be used in this situation. A user who provides all of the information up front is shuffled directly to the ALL_INFORMATION_COLLECTED state; otherwise, the skill heads to COLLECTION_IN_PROGRESS instead. To confirm information, there could be a CONFIRMATION_IN_PROGRESS state, with an attribute stored in the database indicating which information needs to be confirmed. You could do this with the level of knowledge you already have.

Amazon has provided another way to go about creating the same conversational flow, called the *dialog interface*. This interface is unique because it requires an extra model, in addition to the interaction model, that specifies which slots are required, when to ask for or "elicit" slots, how to ask for the slots, how the user can provide the slot values, when to ask for confirmation, and how to ask for it. These actions fall into three types:

- *Slot elicitation*—Asks for a slot value
- *Slot confirmation*—Confirms a slot value
- *Intent confirmation*—Confirms intent

Slot elicitation is asking for a slot value. In the movie ticket example, this is the same as the cashier asking "Which showing?" My response of "The one at 8:40" would then contribute the time into a possible ShowTime slot value. If that's all the information that was needed, that's great—the skill can continue. If there are other slots that need to be filled (like AvailableDiscount for students and film club members), Alexa can elicit those in turn.

Slot confirmation has Alexa ask the user to confirm the just-provided slot value. Alexa can ask a simple question ("Are you sure?") or use the provided value ("Okay, two for 8:40. Is that right?"), to give the user an opportunity to confirm or deny that Alexa has heard the correct value. Alexa then sends on to the fulfillment whether the user has confirmed the value or not. If the user says Alexa doesn't have it right twice, the session comes to a close.

Intent confirmation is different than slot confirmation in that it confirms the entirety of the user's intent, including all of the slot values. If the cashier had followed "I've got two tickets for 'Red River' at 8:40" by asking me if she had it right, that would have mirrored a skill's intent confirmation. Just like with slot confirmation, the intent confirmation can use the slot values to assemble the request. Using them is a best practice, because asking a user "Do I have everything right?" without saying *what* Alexa has heard isn't helpful.

> **TIP** You don't want to confirm *everything*. Confirming every spoken phrase works well for pilots when they're about to take off, but less so in everyday conversations. Why one and not the other? If one pilot misunderstands the other, a catastrophic failure might occur. If you misunderstand your friend's food request, she might end up with nachos instead of tacos—not the worst thing to happen. Take the latter approach with your skills. Ask yourself which actions are destructive or difficult to walk back, and make sure you confirm those. For all others, make your skill more forgiving and allow users a way to say, "I want to go back" or "I want to start over."

Throughout the entire process, the data continues to flow between the user and the fulfillment via the device and the Alexa service. Multiple steps, however, pass before the intent is completely fulfilled.

In figure 8.1, we see that even as the data goes through the full flow, with multiple questions to the user and new information being filled through spoken responses, the intent continues to be `BuyTicketsIntent`. The handler continues to be `BuyTicketsIntentHandler`.

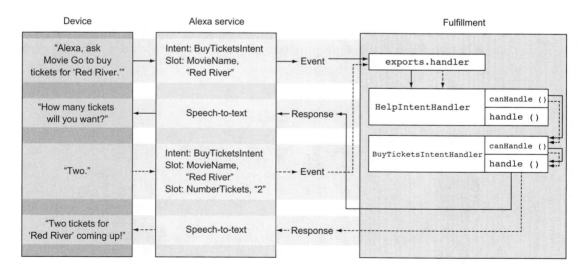

**Figure 8.1   Flow of data in the dialog model**

Whether a slot is elicited or confirmed, or an intent is confirmed, must be defined in the dialog model. The give and take that sees these steps through, however, can be handled in a few different ways. Alexa can handle the steps, or the fulfillment can, or both can in the same flow. The underlying principle of voice applications passing information back and forth between user and services remains, with potentially more round trips to gather the information and complete the user's request.

We can let Alexa handle the dialog because at each step in the dialog, Alexa sends the fulfillment an intent request that also contains a property named dialogState. In figure 8.2, you see the dialogState change as the dialog moves forward. Until every slot is filled and all information is confirmed, dialogState will have a value other than COMPLETED. The intent can check for the presence of this value and pass back control to Alexa if it's not present. Alexa will use responses defined in the dialog model to speak to the user.

Conversely, the fulfillment can handle this flow itself. This is not as taxing for the developer as using a developer-defined state would be, because the fulfillment continues to rely on dialogState and stays within a single intent. At each turn, the code determines if there's a need to elicit a slot, ask for confirmation, or continue with the response. In this scenario the developer has more control, but it comes with the trade-off of more code. For example, Alexa will not use any of the responses defined in the dialog model, expecting the fulfillment to send them instead.

You could also use a combination of the two, handing control back to Alexa unless the fulfillment needs to take it on. Maybe the theater only shows a single film at a single price before noon on Saturdays, and you want to branch off in a different direction if you know that's what a user wants.

The skill we'll build in this chapter will mirror the movie-purchasing interaction. It will begin by letting Alexa have control, but the fulfillment will take final control. Of course, our skill won't be able to purchase tickets in the end, but the only part we'll

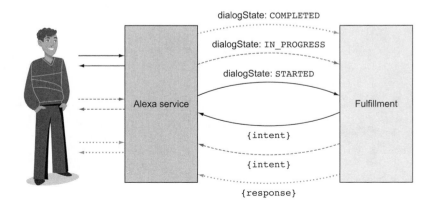

**Figure 8.2   The states of a dialog**

leave out is the final API call to a service that could. In the process, we'll implement the dialog interface and work with eliciting and confirming the necessary information.

### 8.2.1 Creating the skill

To get started, create a new skill titled "Movie Go" and deploy it immediately.

> **Listing 8.1 Creating the new skill**

```
$ ask new -n movie-go          ◄──────────
New project for Alexa skill created.
                                        │ Creates the skill

$ cd movie-go          ┌── Deploys the skill
$ ask deploy     ◄─────┘
------------------- Create Skill Project -------------------
Profile for the deployment: [default]
Skill Id: amzn1.ask.skill.0a00000a-d00a-977a-35db-44097acdc890
Skill deployment finished.
Model deployment finished.
Lambda deployment finished.
Your skill is now deployed and enabled in the development stage.
Try invoking the skill by saying "Alexa, open {your_skill_invocation_name}"
    or simulate an invocation via the `ask simulate` command.
```

Creating and deploying the skill is the first step. Next we need to set up the dialog model.

### 8.2.2 Setting up the dialog model

Our Movie Go skill will have an invocation name of movie go, with four intents (we'll only focus on BuyTicketsIntent, as the others are standard intents you've seen before). What information would a user need to proffer when buying movie tickets? I've never heard of anyone playing movie roulette and asking the box office to choose the movie, so we can start with the movie name. The showtime, how many tickets, and which theater come next.

> ### Creating a dialog model in the console or through the CLI
>
> Most resources on creating a dialog model recommend setting it up through the web console. This is understandable, because the GUI provides an easier way of viewing the relationship between slots and their elicitations or confirmations, and between intents and intent confirmations.
>
> For developers, especially those working with the CLI, this creates difficulties in keeping a consistent interaction model. For this reason (and because web interfaces change regularly, and I want this book to be useful for a long time), I will show you how to create the dialog model without going to the website.

**Table 8.1    The skill interaction model**

| Attribute | Value |
|---|---|
| Skill name | Movie Go |
| Invocation | movie go |
| Intent | `BuyTicketsIntent` |
| Slot | `MovieName (AMAZON.Movie)` |
| Slot | `MovieTheater(AMAZON.MovieTheater)` |
| Slot | `MovieTime (AMAZON.TIME)` |
| Slot | `TicketsNumber(AMAZON.NUMBER)` |

Because the interaction model is going to get long, we'll take it piece by piece. We'll start off by looking at the skill configuration in table 8.1, and the associated utterances in listing 8.2.

**Listing 8.2    Some utterances for `BuyTicketsIntent`**

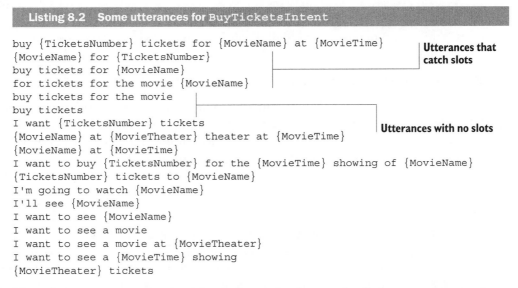

```
buy {TicketsNumber} tickets for {MovieName} at {MovieTime}
{MovieName} for {TicketsNumber}
buy tickets for {MovieName}
for tickets for the movie {MovieName}
buy tickets for the movie
buy tickets
I want {TicketsNumber} tickets
{MovieName} at {MovieTheater} theater at {MovieTime}
{MovieName} at {MovieTime}
I want to buy {TicketsNumber} for the {MovieTime} showing of {MovieName}
{TicketsNumber} tickets to {MovieName}
I'm going to watch {MovieName}
I'll see {MovieName}
I want to see {MovieName}
I want to see a movie
I want to see a movie at {MovieTheater}
I want to see a {MovieTime} showing
{MovieTheater} tickets
```

Utterances that catch slots

Utterances with no slots

Note there are utterances in this small sample that catch all slots, no slots, and any combination of slots. There's nothing new here, but it sets the groundwork for what's coming next. Some slots will be required and others will be elicited if the user doesn't offer them up independently.

Setting the groundwork for the elicitation requires a new addition to the interaction model, outlining the dialog.

**Listing 8.3  A `dialog` object in the interaction model (./models/en-US.json)**

```
{
  "interactionModel": {
    "languageModel": {
      ...
    },
    "dialog": {                         A new object to hold the dialog model
      "intents": [
        {
          "name": "BuyTicketsIntent",
          "slots": []
        }
      ]
    },
    "prompts": []
  }
}
```

The fundamental idea to know about the dialog model is that it is connected to intents and implemented through *prompts*. The prompts either elicit or confirm, and the prompts can come from the Alexa service, or they can come from the skill fulfillment. They can come from both, even.

To come from the Alexa service, the prompts must appear in the interaction model, both for elicitation and confirmation. The four entities of the BuyTicketsIntent each have their own rules concerning these two parts of the dialog, outlined in table 8.2.

**Table 8.2  The slot configuration**

| Name | Type | Confirm? | Required? |
|------|------|----------|-----------|
| MovieName | AMAZON.Movie | No | Yes |
| MovieTheater | AMAZON.MovieTheater | No | Yes |
| MovieTime | AMAZON.TIME | Yes | Yes |
| TicketsNumber | AMAZON.NUMBER | No | No |

### 8.2.3  Slot filling

Through the prompts, the dialog model can fill in individual slots, which means that users will say something just to fill a slot. The Alexa service needs to prepare for what users might say to each prompt, just like it's prepared for what users will say to trigger intents. For intent triggering, we provided samples to Alexa. For slot filling, we provide the same.

#### MOVIENAME

First up is MovieName. If the user speaks to the skill without specifying a movie—for example, with "I want to see a movie"—the skill will ask for a name. This introduces the idea of *slot sample utterances*. Much like intent sample utterances, those for slots train the Alexa NLU in how a user might fill slot values. In every set of slot sample utterances, you want to have a sample containing only the current slot, to account for terseness. But you'll also want to account for people being proactive and filling out multiple values at once, such as the name, time, and number of tickets. If people are proactive, Alexa will return those values, even if they aren't for the currently elicited slot.

**Listing 8.4   Slot-filling samples (./models/en-US.json)**

```
{
  "interactionModel": {
    "languageModel": {
      ...
      "intents": [
        {
          "name": "BuyTicketsIntent",
          "slots": [
            {
              "name": "MovieName",
              "type": "AMAZON.Movie",
              "samples": [
                "{TicketsNumber} for {MovieName} at {MovieTime}",
                "buy {TicketsNumber} tickets for {MovieName}",
                "{TicketsNumber} for {MovieName}",
                "for {TicketsNumber} for {MovieName}",
                "the {MovieTime} showing of {MovieName}",
                "{MovieName} at {MovieTime}",
                "{TicketsNumber} tickets to {MovieName}",
                "I'm going to watch {MovieName}",
                "I'll see {MovieName}",
                "I want to see {MovieName}",
                "{MovieName}"
              ]
            },
            ...
          ],
          ...
        }
      ]
    }
  }
}
```

> Slot samples represent how a user might fill a specific slot.

The samples alone are not enough to create the dialog. That also requires configuration inside the interaction model, outlining which slots or intents need confirmation or elicitation. That's shown in the following listing.

**Listing 8.5   Configuring the dialog for the `MovieName` slot (./models/en-US.json)**

```
{
  "interactionModel": {
    "dialog": {
      "intents": [
        {
```

```
      "name": "BuyTicketsIntent",
      "slots": [
        {
          "name": "MovieName",                  Does not require confirmation
          "type": "AMAZON.Movie",
          "confirmationRequired": false,  ◀──    Requires elicitation
          "elicitationRequired": true,  ◀──
          "prompts": {
            "elicitation": "Elicit.Slot.BuyTicketsIntent.
            ➥IntentSlot-MovieName"  ◀──     Elicitation prompts are
          }                                 identified with a unique ID.
        }
      ]
    }
  ]
  }
  }
}
```

In the preceding code, we are specifying that we do not want to confirm the `MovieName` slot, but we do want to elicit a value if the user hasn't already provided it. This is all connected via slot name (naturally) and intent, so a slot can require elicitation or confirmation in one intent, while eschewing that requirement in another intent. The intent connects to prompts through the use of an ID. I use descriptive prompts to make my life easier, but if you were to create all of this in the Developer Console, Amazon would create random IDs to make the connections.

The order of the objects in the dialog model's slots array determines the order of the elicitation. In the open-ended "want to see a movie" utterance, no information is provided for any of the slots. In this case, it's best to start with the most central piece of information. Deciding which slot to fill first isn't always easy, as multiple slots can vie for alpha status. For movie purchasing, the movie itself is probably most important, as users generally don't know exact showtimes and are often willing to choose between multiple theaters (at least in a dense city).

The dialog can also take place entirely via the Alexa service, but for that to happen, we need to tell Alexa what to say, through prompts.

**Listing 8.6  How Alexa can prompt to elicit the slot (./models/en-US.json)**

```
{
  "interactionModel": {                   The prompt ID applies to
    ...                                  different prompt variations.
    "prompts": [
      {
        "id": "Elicit.Slot.BuyTicketsIntent.IntentSlot-MovieName",
        "variations": [
          {
            "type": "PlainText",
            "value": "What movie do you have your eye on?"
          },
          {
            "type": "PlainText",
```

```
              "value": "Okay, which movie will you be watching?"
            },
            {
              "type": "PlainText",
              "value": "Great, what movie do you want to see?"
            }
          ]
        }
      ]
    }
  }
}
```

**The prompt ID applies to different prompt variations.**

`MovieName` connects to the prompts through an ID, with a different ID for elicitation and for confirmation. Notice the use of discourse markers such as "okay" and "great," which mark understanding and continue the flow of the dialog, plus the multiple prompt variations. Alexa will cycle through the variations whenever a user returns.

### MovieTheater

Next up is the movie theater slot. Again, this one needs filling, but without confirmation. Because this is an early item in the dialog, the samples need to account for proactive slot filling.

---

**Listing 8.7   Utterances to fill the `MovieTheater` slot**

```
I'll be going to {MovieTheater}
I'm seeing it at {MovieTheater}
{MovieTheater} for the {MovieTime} showing
{MovieTheater} at {MovieTime}
{MovieTheater} for {TicketsNumber} person
{MovieTheater} for {TicketsNumber} people
{MovieTheater} for {TicketsNumber} at {MovieTime}
I want to go to {MovieTheater}
{MovieTheater}
```

**Includes prompts that receive just the MovieTheater slot or also other slots**

Once more, we're allowing for proactive filling, and for slot-only terseness. Notice that we aren't accounting for the `MovieName` slot, because we expect that it will have already been filled—the slots are elicited in the order they appear in the interaction model.

The following listing requires elicitation of the `MovieTheater` slot.

---

**Listing 8.8   Requiring slot elicitation (./models/en-US.json)**

```
{
  "interactionModel": {
    ...
    "dialog": {
      "intents": [
        {
          "name": "BuyTicketsIntent",
          "slots": [
            ...
            {
              "name": "MovieTheater",
              "type": "AMAZON.MovieTheater",
              "confirmationRequired": false,
```

**Requires no confirmation**

```
                "elicitationRequired": true,
                "prompts": {
                  "elicitation": "Elicit.Slot.BuyTicketsIntent.
                  ➦IntentSlot-MovieTheater"
                }
              }
            ]
          }
        ]
      }
    }
  }
}
```

**Requires elicitation**

**The ID of the elicitation prompt**

We then fill out the elicitation prompts and connect them through the prompt ID (`Elicit.Slot.BuyTicketsIntent.IntentSlot-MovieTheater`). In them we see a twist of what we saw before.

**Listing 8.9** `MovieTheater` **elicitation prompts (./models/en-US.json)**

```
{
  "interactionModel": {
    ...
    "prompts": [
      ...
      {
        "id": "Elicit.Slot.BuyTicketsIntent.IntentSlot-MovieTheater",
        "variations": [
          {
            "type": "PlainText",
            "value": "You wanna see {MovieName}, got it. Which theater?"
          },
          {
            "type": "PlainText",
            "value":
              "You wanna see {MovieName}? I've heard good things. Which
              ➦theater?"
          },
          {
            "type": "PlainText",
            "value": "Where do you wanna see {MovieName}?"
          }
        ]
      }
    ]
  }
}
```

**Previously gathered slot values are inserted via curly braces.**

The prompts here not only ask for the theater, but also implicitly confirm that Alexa heard the movie's name correctly by repeating it, inserted through the use of the slot name in curly braces. This isn't an explicit confirmation, because that would be too much confirmation. It does, though, provide feedback to the user.

Of course, feedback without the opportunity to correct a misunderstanding is worse than a misunderstanding on its own and will only frustrate the user. The user needs to be able to correct mistakes and say, "That is not what I meant at all." A user following up with a correction continues the flow and the move theater elicitation, because the movie is filled out, not the theater.

This illustrates the necessity of testing and for and addressing shortcomings in the platform itself. A natural way of correcting a misunderstanding is "No, I meant to say…" but Alexa would not understand. This happens.

Sometimes your only option is to limit the functionality of the skill to what can be shown to work reliably. Eric Olson, developer of popular Alexa skills Complibot, Insultibot, and others, spoke on a Voicebot podcast about his desire to add "meta intents" to tell users exactly what they could do within the skill. In the end, this led to too many collisions with the primary intents, and he had to remove them.[1]

Later on in this chapter, we'll look at implicitly limiting input options for users, in order to match what the skill and Alexa can handle or expect. Covertly training the user helps to do this. Alexa may not understand "I meant to say," but "I want to see" works fine. With this knowledge, each of the prompts can include that phrasing. The prompts don't explicitly say how to respond, but people tend to use the vocabulary of their conversation partners. In other words, the "system should always use a consistent set of its own preferred terms."[2]

## MOVIETIME

Finally comes the `MovieTime`. This slot has both elicitation and confirmation. Try putting together samples and prompts for the elicitation yourself, using the previous ones for guidance. As you do so, think about when in the dialog the movie-time elicitation should come. Is there prior information that needs to be implicitly confirmed? Are there discourse markers you should use to demonstrate forward movement and the near-arrival of the end of the dialog?

We've already seen that confirmation should be used judiciously, so why does the time require confirmation? Times and numbers are commonly difficult to understand for both humans and computers. Many numbers sound alike, and there generally aren't many words to pull from. A "nine" could sound like a "five," and "nine ten" is similar to "nineteen." This kind of situation calls for explicit confirmation, with a similar interaction model for configuration as with elicitation.

> **Listing 8.10   Requiring confirmation for `MovieTime` (./models/en-US.json)**

```
"dialog": {
  "intents": [
    {
      "slots": [
        ...
        {
          "name": "MovieTime",
```

---

[1]  "Alexa Developer Panel with Octavio Menocal and Eric Olson," Voicebot podcast episode 39, http://mng.bz/Wa90.

[2]  See the "Stealth Training" section in chapter 13 of Randy Allen Harris, *Voice Interaction Design: Crafting the New Conversational Speech Systems* (Morgan Kaufmann, 2004).

```
        ...
        "confirmationRequired": true,        ◄─────┐ Requires confirmation
        "prompts": {                               └
          ...
          "confirmation": "Confirm.Slot.BuyTicketsIntent.
          ➡ IntentSlot-MovieTime"          ◄─────┐ The ID of the confirmation prompt
        }                                         └
      }
    ]
  }
 ]
}
```

The confirmation, like the elicitation, is specified inside the dialog configuration in the interaction model. It's also connected to prompts in a similar way, through an ID.

Listing 8.11 Confirmation prompts for `MovieTime` (./models/en-US.json)

```
"prompts": [
  ...
  {                                          The ID of the prompt │
    "id": "Confirm.Slot.BuyTicketsIntent.IntentSlot-MovieTime",  ◄──
    "variations": [                    What Alexa will say, with space for │
      {                                      a slot value in curly braces │
        "type": "PlainText",
        "value": "Did I hear you right, that was the {MovieTime} showing?"  ◄──
      },
      {
        "type": "PlainText",
        "value": "I got the {MovieTime} showing, is that right?"
      }
    ]
  }
]
```

When confirming a slot, that slot's value *must be in the prompt*. Without that, what's the point? "Did I hear you right?" Well, that question is impossible to answer, but thanks for asking anyway. Instead, we put the value we are trying to confirm in the prompt itself.

### 8.2.4 *Intent confirmation*

At this point, all of the slot elicitations and the movie time confirmation are in place. But there's still one thing missing. If this skill went to its logical end and connected to an outside service, the point would be to buy tickets, which means charging a credit card, which means spending money.

I had a boss once, who always drilled into me that I could make mistakes on some parts of the product, but not on anything having to do with money. This applies doubly for voice interactions. Even if Alexa heard everything correctly and the fulfillment handled everything correctly, the user might not have said everything correctly.

In his book *Voice Interaction Design* (Morgan Kaufmann, 2004), Randy Allen Harris refers to *grounding*—the process between conversational parties through which they come to an understanding. He refers to conversations where that back and forth is important as conversations with *high grounding criteria.* Any action from which recovery is difficult, such as spending money or deleting an account, has high grounding criteria and lends itself to explicit confirmation. Conversations where the work required to confirm information does not significantly outstrip the benefit, meanwhile, has *low grounding criteria.* Grounding criteria, then, is how much of a conversation is necessary to achieve understanding.

Purchasing movie tickets is an action where recovery is difficult, so it necessitates confirmation. In the Alexa lexicon, confirming the entire intent is called *intent confirmation,* and it has its own prompt.

---

**Listing 8.12    Requiring intent confirmation (./models/en-US.json)**

```
"dialog": {
  "intents": [
    {
      "name": "BuyTicketsIntent",
      "confirmationRequired": true,          ◄──  Confirmation is required
      "prompts": {                                directly on intent.
        "confirmation": "Confirm.Intent.BuyTicketsIntent"   ◄──
      },                                            Confirmation prompt ID
      "slots": [
        ...
      ]
    }
  ]
}
```

Finally, the confirmation connects to the prompts through an ID.

---

**Listing 8.13    Prompt for intent confirmation (./models/en-US.json)**

```
"prompts": [
  ...
  {
    "id": "Confirm.Intent.BuyTicketsIntent",
    "variations": [
      {
        "type": "PlainText",
        "value": "Okay. So, {TicketsNumber} for {MovieName} at
    {MovieTheater}, for the {MovieTime} showing. If that all sounds good,
    I'll charge your credit card. Do you want to continue?"   ◄──
      }                                        Includes all relevant slot values
    ]
  }
]
```

This is the ultimate confirmation. Alexa reads out all of the most relevant details, and the user has the opportunity to correct them. Pay attention to the formulation and how it directs the user with a "yes" or "no" question. The interaction model definitely needs to handle a user going "off-road" and responding with "I want three tickets" to correct a misunderstanding on how many tickets are needed, but it also needs to let the user indicate that everything is good and that the flow should continue.

If you expect people to come back to your skill often (and I hope you do), consider multiple prompts that Alexa can cycle through. Do not take the single prompt in this example as anything but an opportunity for you to express your creativity in your own intent confirmation prompts.

> **WARNING** Did you get an error when you tried to deploy this confirmation? That's because you also need to specify the slots in the dialog model. The number of tickets (`TicketsNumber`) hasn't been added to the dialog model yet, so you'll need to add it along with the others. You don't have to add `confirmationRequired`, `elicitationRequired`, or `prompts`. They're unnecessary. Remember, you can find the entirety of the code at www.manning .com/books/voice-applications-for-alexa-and-google-assistant or on GitHub at https://github.com/dustincoates/voice-applications.

In formulating the confirmation prompt, you need to consider the grounding criteria and how they impact how you confirm information. Harris groups confirmation prompts (he refers to them as "feedback") into five descending levels: explicit, implicit, inferential, open, and no confirmation. These are also shown in table 8.3.

Explicit confirmation is exactly what it sounds like, repeating the words to the user, or asking for direct confirmation of an action. Implicit confirmation uses the information gathered from the user to tell the user that an action is going to happen. For example, "I am going to buy two tickets for you to 'Red River.'" With inferential confirmation, the response includes the user's request in some way, such as "The *Houston Astros* won last night against the Texas Rangers, 12 to 0." Open feedback doesn't use the information at all, but instead acknowledges receipt by saying something like "got it" or "alright." Finally, no feedback in itself can provide feedback, as it implies that everything is going well.

As grounding the conversation becomes more important, the confirmation level grows, too. Confirmations need to be more explicit, and more immediate. The intent confirmation has high grounding criteria because it has the capacity to charge money, theoretically at least. As a result, the confirmation level is explicit, and we confirm immediately when there's enough information to do so.

Now let's look at how the dialog model configuration connects to the skill fulfillment.

**Table 8.3  Levels of confirmation prompts**

| Level | Criteria |
| --- | --- |
| Explicit | "I heard you say you wanted the lights blue, is that right?" |
| Implicit | "I'll now turn the lights blue." |
| Inferential | "Look how nice the lights are when blue." |
| Open | "Done and done." |
| None | Lights turn blue, but nothing is said. |

### 8.2.5  *Dialog model fulfillment*

When Alexa handles most or all of the elicitation and confirmation, the fulfillment still has two tasks. The first is to delegate control back to Alexa if the dialog isn't complete—if not all of the slots that need further action are complete. If all of the elicitation and confirmation *is* complete, the second task is to provide Alexa with the speech it will use to respond.

> **Listing 8.14  The handler for the `BuyTicketsIntent` (./lambda/custom/index.js)**

```
...
const BuyTicketsIntentHandler = {
  ...
  handle(handlerInput) {
    const dialogComplete = "COMPLETED";
    const dialogStarted = "STARTED";
    const intent = handlerInput.requestEnvelope.request.intent;
    const ticketPrice = 10;

    if (handlerInput.requestEnvelope.request.dialogState !== dialogComplete) {

      if (handlerInput.requestEnvelope.request.dialogState === dialogStarted) {
        intent.slots.TicketsNumber.value = intent.slots.TicketsNumber.value
      || 1;
      }
    } else {
      const movieName = intent.slots.MovieName.value;
      const movieTime = intent.slots.MovieTime.value;
      let ticketsNumber = intent.slots.TicketsNumber.value;

      if (ticketsNumber) {
        ticketsNumber = parseInt(ticketsNumber);
      } else {
        ticketsNumber = 1;
      }

      const price = ticketsNumber * ticketPrice;

      const speech = `Alright <break strength="strong" /> ${ticketsNumber} ` +
                     `for ${movieName}. Total cost, $${price}, and the movie
      ➡ ` +
                     `starts at ${movieTime}.`;
      return handlerInput.responseBuilder
        .speak(speech)
        .getResponse();
    }
  }
};
...
```

At each step of the dialog, the inbound request specifies whether the dialog is complete.

Initializes the number of tickets when the dialog starts

Provides the final response

The dialog model introduces a new information flow concept. The flow is similar to the back and forth between user and fulfillment via the Alexa service that you've seen since chapter 1. What's new is that while *that* flow had a new intent request every time (the user might have asked for the same intent twice in a row, but it was a new request), this flow stays within the same intent request. Once it hits the fulfillment it must go through the flow of checking each handler object to find the one responsible, but it is still within the same intent request and can be thought of as a sub-request.

As you can see in the preceding code, the handling of this sub-request is the developer's responsibility. The dialog goes back and forth between the user and Alexa, and between Alexa and the fulfillment, with a dialog state that goes from STARTING to COMPLETED.

The Alexa service provides the state of the dialog, and we can perform different behaviors based on what that state is. For example, if the dialog state is COMPLETED, we can respond back to the user the final response for this intent, just as in all of the intents we've seen previously.

We can also check to see if the dialog had just begun. This is useful if we're seeding data at the very beginning. We don't ask users for the number of tickets in the dialog, and we seed the value as 1, assuming that a person who hasn't said otherwise will buy just a single ticket.

The dialog flow doesn't store the data about the flow anywhere, and for that reason the fulfillment provides the intent back to Alexa when delegating, with the updated slot values.

> **Listing 8.15  Returning intent to Alexa (./lambda/custom/index.js)**

```
const BuyTicketsIntentHandler = {
  ...
  handle(handlerInput) {
    ...
    if (handlerInput.requestEnvelope.request.dialogState !== dialogComplete)
    {
      ...
      return handlerInput.responseBuilder
        .addDelegateDirective(intent)          ⟵ If the dialog isn't complete, pass back
        .getResponse();                             control with the current intent to Alexa.
    } else {
      ...
    }
  }
};
```

We use the addDelegateDirective method to hand control back to Alexa. We are, in fact, *delegating* control to Alexa. Through this delegation, we are saying that Alexa should use the prompts we outlined in the interaction model to complete the next step of elicitation or confirmation.

Take a moment and try testing the skill in the testing console or on a device, and see how it goes. Where does it succeed and where does it fail? You should find that the conversation is successful in determining what the user wants and completing the action.

Functionally, the skill does what the user expects. Further, the responses use discourse markers, such as "and" and "okay now," and they subtly train the user in the preferred nomenclature ("showing") and implicitly confirm the movie. Nonetheless, there are two clear areas where the dialog doesn't work well.

First is the confirmation. If the user explicitly stated a desire for a number of tickets, the confirmation works. Without that number, though, the skill assumes a solo viewer. That assumption needs to be in the confirmation. True, this is a situation where the user can correct the error easily by invoking the skill again and purchasing more tickets, but that does not assist the user in successfully fulfilling the goal.

The other issue is even more maladroit. Very few people in this locale—everyday American English—will speak the time like a 24-hour digital clock: "twenty one fifteen." Instead it's "nine fifteen P.M." or "a quarter after nine."

Your first inclination might be to reach for SSML. There is indeed an `interpret-as` value for `time`. This, however, is for translating "2'13"" to "two minutes thirteen seconds." We're going to have to handle this on our own, in the code. The secret to doing so is that, while Alexa is handling the dialog and eliciting slots, the fulfillment can fill and manipulate slot values on its own. By checking to see if `MovieTime` has a value, and overwriting it with a more friendly value, we can improve the dialog.

Try your hand at creating a function called `friendlyTime` that transforms the time format from what looks natural to a computer or on a bedside clock into something that Alexa would say. These small touches make the difference between a weekend project and a skill that users will feel comfortable using.

Next we need to tell Alexa to use this new "friendly time."

---

**Listing 8.16   Resetting the `MovieTime` value (./lambda/custom/index.js)**

```
const BuyTicketsIntentHandler = {
  ...
  handle(handlerInput) {
    ...

    if (handlerInput.requestEnvelope.request.dialogState !== dialogComplete)
    {
      ...

      if(
        intent.slots.MovieTime.value &&
        intent.slots.MovieTime.confirmationStatus !== "CONFIRMED"
      ) {
        let movieTime = intent.slots.MovieTime.value;
        movieTime = friendlyTime(intent.slots.MovieTime.value);

        intent.slots.MovieTime.value = movieTime;
      }

    return handlerInput.responseBuilder
```

*Checks that the MovieTime slot has a value to manipulate and transform, and makes sure the status is not confirmed*

*Assigns the new value to the slot value on the inbound intent object*

```
        .addDelegateDirective(intent)
        .getResponse();                    ◀─────┐  **Provides the updated value to Alexa**
    } else {
      ...
    }
  }
};
```

We want to get at the `MovieTime` value after the user has provided it, but before confirmation. We're providing our own value, which Alexa is going to use in the prompt—we inserted the slot value in the confirmation prompts through the curly braces.

The takeaway here is the same as what you've seen since the beginning: the table-tennis interaction of Alexa passing data to the fulfillment and the fulfillment passing data back to Alexa. The fulfillment can step in at any time to update slot values, setting value defaults or short-circuiting the elicitation process. In the end, we're handing most of the dialog off to Alexa, but we still maintain some control.

The skill is getting there, but it still places too much responsibility on the user to know which showtimes are available for a movie.

### ELICITING SLOTS

Relying on Alexa to elicit the showtime slot requires hand-waving because Alexa needs a predefined response, with only already-provided slot values as variable information. The user hasn't asked for a showtime, and likely won't even know which showtimes are available. Instead, the fulfillment needs to proactively elicit the showtime value by providing the user with choices in the prompt.

**Listing 8.17  Faking movie times (./lambda/custom/index.js)**

```
const nowPlaying = {
  "river oaks": {              ◀───┐ The theater                    Movie and showtimes
    "red river": ["12:15", "15:30", "18:05"],  ◀────┐
    "wizard of oz": ["09:30"],
    "the godfather": ["20:45"]
  }
};
```

Instead of putting together an API call, we'll instead use a stand-in object with movies and times. We'll then grab the times when the user asks for a movie.

This opens up the question of how a user will know which movies are available. As is common for voice applications, the answer is situation-dependent. A theater showing first-run movies may not need to give any initial prodding to the user, who may know what movies are currently out. The application could then provide progressive guidance if the user is unsure or if they ask for an unavailable movie. A theater showing old movies, on the other hand, might provide the information up front. Because the Movie Go skill mimics a service that knows about all theaters, we can assume that the user knows the movies.

We want to elicit the user's desired showtime when they have already selected a movie and a theater, but not selected a time.

**Listing 8.18   Confirming slot presence (./lambda/custom/index.js)**

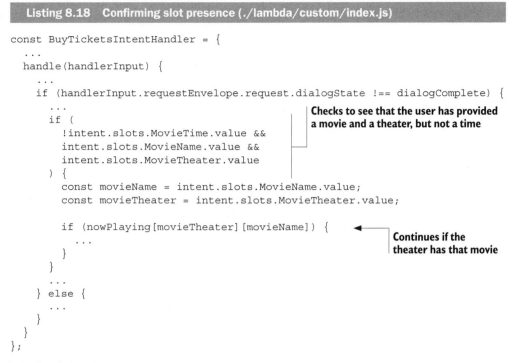

```
const BuyTicketsIntentHandler = {
  ...
  handle(handlerInput) {
    ...
    if (handlerInput.requestEnvelope.request.dialogState !== dialogComplete) {
      ...
      if (
        !intent.slots.MovieTime.value &&
        intent.slots.MovieName.value &&
        intent.slots.MovieTheater.value
      ) {
        const movieName = intent.slots.MovieName.value;
        const movieTheater = intent.slots.MovieTheater.value;

        if (nowPlaying[movieTheater][movieName]) {
          ...
        }
      }
      ...
    } else {
      ...
    }
  }
};
```

Checks to see that the user has provided a movie and a theater, but not a time

Continues if the theater has that movie

We check for the presence or absence of the movie time, movie name, and movie theater slots, and then we check to see if the user's theater is showing the user's movie.

**Listing 8.19   Providing showtimes for the movie choice (./lambda/custom/index.js)**

```
if (nowPlaying[movieTheater][movieName]) {
  const movieTimes = nowPlaying[movieTheater][movieName];
  let prompt = `${intent.slots.MovieName.value} is playing at `;

  movieTimes.forEach((time, index) => {
    prompt += friendlyTime(time) + ", ";
    if (movieTimes.length - 2 === index) {
      prompt += "and ";
    }
  });

  prompt += "which showing do you want?";

  const reprompt = "When do you wanna see the movie?";

  return handlerInput.responseBuilder
    .speak(prompt)
    .reprompt(reprompt)
    .addElicitSlotDirective(intent.slots.MovieTime.name)
    .getResponse();
}
```

Builds a response listing all of the available times, including "and" before the last one, to read like a real sentence

Prompts for the movie time

In this code, the fulfillment wrests control of the dialog flow, at least for one round, from Alexa. Building a prompt that lists the showtimes for the day, we provide guidance to the user and do so in a way that's natural.

The easy way is to list the times one after another. But that sounds unnatural and places the cognitive load on the user, who must ask the question "Is this the last showtime?" Even a moment of distraction is cause enough to take on that responsibility. What we'll do instead is insert "and" before the last one, just like humans do. This tells the user, "Hey, we're almost done, have you made your choice?"

Notice as well the prompt and the reprompt. Alexa is asking the user a question and expecting an answer, so if the user doesn't respond, Alexa asks again. We also need to let Alexa know which slot we're eliciting, by providing its name.

> **TIP** If the user asks for a movie and theater pairing that doesn't exist, we should let the user know and ask for another choice. We probably even want to track whether the user asks next for the same movie or the same theater. If the user asks for the same movie twice in a row, but neither theater is showing it, we can offer up theaters that are. If they ask for the same theater twice, we can offer the currently shown movies.

Through all of that, there's still one giant bug in this flow. Have you spotted it? Try this conversation:

> *USER: Ask Movie Go to buy three tickets for "Red River."*
>
> *ALEXA: You wanna see "Red River," got it. Which theater?*
>
> *USER: River Oaks*
>
> *ALEXA: "Red River" is playing at a quarter after twelve P.M., three-thirty P.M., and six-oh-five P.M.; which showing do you want?*
>
> *USER: Three-thirty P.M.*
>
> *ALEXA: Did I hear you right—that was the three-thirty P.M. showing?*
>
> *USER: Yeah.*
>
> *ALEXA: Okay. So, three for "Red River" at three-thirty P.M., at River Oaks. If that all sounds good, I'll charge your credit card. Do you want to continue?*
>
> *USER: No.*
>
> *ALEXA: Alright, three for "Red River." Total cost, thirty dollars, and the movie starts at three-thirty P.M.*

What just happened there? The user has denied the intent confirmation, but the fulfillment and Alexa's response continue as if nothing has changed. Let's look at the code again and see if we can guess why.

**Listing 8.20  Confirming dialog completion (./lambda/custom/index.js)**

```
const BuyTicketsIntentHandler = {
  canHandle(handlerInput) {
    ...
  },
```

```
handle(handlerInput) {
  const dialogComplete = "COMPLETED";
  const dialogStarted = "STARTED";
  const intent = handlerInput.requestEnvelope.request.intent;
  const ticketPrice = 10;

  if (handlerInput.requestEnvelope.request.dialogState !== dialogComplete)
  {
    ...
  } else {
    ...
    return handlerInput.responseBuilder
      .speak(speech)
      .getResponse();
  }
}
};
```

In the BuyTicketsIntent, we're checking to see if the dialog state is COMPLETED or not, but that's it. When a user refuses to confirm an intent, that doesn't mean the dialog is no longer complete. In fact, what happens is the opposite. The dialog is now complete, but the confirmationStatus is DENIED. Alternatively, affirmatively confirming the intent leads to a status of CONFIRMED. We should, instead, alter the response depending on the confirmation of the intent.

**Listing 8.21   Handling an intent confirmation denial (./lambda/custom/index.js)**

```
const BuyTicketsIntentHandler = {
  canHandle(handlerInput) {
    ...
  },
  handle(handlerInput) {
    const intentConfirmed = "CONFIRMED";          ◄──   The confirmation status is either
    ...                                                 CONFIRMED or DENIED for the intent.

    if (handlerInput.requestEnvelope.request.dialogState !== dialogComplete)
    {
      ...                                               If the user confirmed, continue as before.
    } else if (
      handlerInput.requestEnvelope.request.dialogState === dialogComplete &&
      intent.confirmationStatus === intentConfirmed
    ) {
      ...
    } else {
      const speech = "Sorry, can we try again? What movie do you wanna see?";
      const reprompt = "Tell me which movie you want to see.";

      return handlerInput.responseBuilder
        .speak(speech)
        .reprompt(reprompt)
        .getResponse();
    }
  }
};
```

Otherwise, let the user correct the error.

By checking whether the user has confirmed the intent, we can change our response to the user. If we find out that the user has chosen not to confirm—either the user misspoke or Alexa misheard—we want to add a prompt to start again. What we don't want to do is say we'll proceed unabated or just close off the conversation.

## 8.3 Handling errors

By confirming a slot or an intent, we've seen one type of error handling, which is using confirmations to ensure that the fulfillment has the right information from the user. There are others, and taking a look at the different types of errors is useful, because it informs us what to guard against.

There are errors caused by the user and errors caused by the computer. Errors caused by the user generally involve them doing something that the skill cannot handle. This is why anticipating what users will say, and subtly training them, is vital for a good voice experience.

Errors caused by the computer are broader. The speech-to-text can misunderstand what the user said, the intent parser can incorrectly categorize what the user wants to do, the creator of the interaction model can fail to anticipate another way of speaking to the skill, and, of course, the skill developer can introduce a bug. The problem is that, in the fulfillment, there's little way to know what type of error it is. This means that a user needs to be able to correct an error when the error is costly in time, money, or effort. Also, when a clear error occurs, it needs to be handled smoothly without the developer or the code necessarily knowing the root cause. This requires some guesswork, some creative flowing, and some dialog that will help the user without placing blame.

One error where the cause is limited to just two options is the Unhandled handler. This handler will handle any intents that the fulfillment does not handle already, meaning either the developer didn't anticipate the need, or the user is trying to do something that isn't supported.

When Unhandled is invoked, users don't know the internal flow of the fulfillment. They are trying to achieve their goals, not think about intent flow, so they're unaware that what they want to do is not handled by the code. The first thing to do is to take care of the error, never blaming the user but also not being overly apologetic. (In fact, that's true of all errors.) Tell the user what is possible without going into too much detail. If you've put in some time thinking about the possible interaction needs, the best path is to tell the user that the requested intent isn't supported, and then turn to restate what *is* possible. "Hmm, I don't think I can do that yet. Would you like to know the score of last night's game instead?"

One of Grice's maxims that we discussed in chapter 3 was the maxim of quantity, which states that each conversation partner should say enough to move the conversation on, without saying too much. This maxim shouldn't go out the window when we're handling an error. When thinking about how to respond, try to figure out the smallest response you can have Alexa give that will re-orient most people. The brief response won't prevent all users from ending up at an unhandled intent again. Users who continue to run into the same error shouldn't get the same message back each time—if it didn't put them on the right path the first time, why should it work the second or third time? (You're unlikely to get someone making the same mistake more than three times, simply because they'll stop trying.) Change the responses based on how often a user has arrived at the error, increasing in specificity, as shown in figure 8.3. The first response should be simple and restart the flow quickly; the second response can provide more information about the possible actions; and the third response can go into much more depth as a final effort to keep the user from giving up. For example, start with, "I can't do that right now. Which movie do you want to buy tickets for?" before moving to "Start by telling me the name of a movie. You can also ask for help at any time to get a full list of what you can do."

In this escalation, we first have Alexa guide the user to what is possible: buying tickets for a specific movie. When the user comes back with another unsupported intent, our response gets more specific. Now we tell the user the exact piece of information we need, while pointing out that there is a help intent that goes even more in-depth with guidance. (Movie Go doesn't have a help intent now, but you should always have one for skills you're releasing publicly.) Each subsequent roadblock provides more insight into successful paths.

To make this happen, the skill needs to keep track of how often the user has run into an error. In chapter 5 you saw how to store session and user data, and it's the same thing here.

There should be separate counters, and separate responses, for the different places where a user can get to an error state. How users recover from an unhandled intent error will be different from how they recover if Alexa has heard a faulty slot value.

This approach is also relevant when the user is looking for data that isn't present or is out of bounds. For example, if the theater only shows westerns, but the slot value maps to "Dude, Where's My Car?" the first error message might say "We don't have that movie." Subsequent responses can point out that the theater only has western movies. Then, if the list of available movies is short, it could list exactly which are currently showing.

We also know that speech-to-text isn't perfect. Perhaps the most common error in voice applications is out-of-bounds slot values. Guiding users by implicitly limiting what's available will help cut down on these errors by reducing the chance that they'll ask for something that's unsupported. For example, we ask users which theater they want to buy tickets for so they understand that the skill doesn't traffic in rentals. Properly training the NLU with a tightly defined list of possible inputs helps, too, by limiting the likelihood

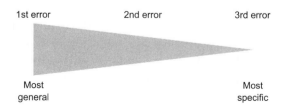

**Figure 8.3   Guidance becomes more specific as the user makes more errors.**

of a misunderstood value. Nonetheless, mistakes will happen. We saw in chapter 4 how entity resolution can help cover up slot value misunderstanding errors by adding synonyms for values that the text-to-speech commonly misunderstands.

Finally, a user who doesn't have the information you need can introduce another error. We know that "I don't know" is not a movie, but the slot elicitation can easily mistake that as a movie name. Especially when asking users to provide specific information, such as an ID number or even exactly which movie they want to see, consider ways to account for the user not knowing these details. How could Movie Go handle a user who says, "I don't know?" One approach would be to move to the question of *where* to see the movie, and then return with the movies at that theater.

If you build a skill that guides a user along the interaction and doesn't place too much on their shoulders, you should have a skill that performs well and that has users delighted to come back. However, errors do still happen. Expect the best case (so as not to burden your users with too much prompting), but be ready to catch anything less.

## Summary

- The limitations of voice first necessitate adding bumpers and constraints to the VUI, including using leading questions, limiting possible inputs, and chunking information gathering.
- The dialog model for Alexa allows developers to hand control for slot elicitation, slot confirmation, and intent confirmation to Alexa, and then respond once the dialog is finished.
- Errors should be handled smoothly, by re-orienting the user toward what is possible.
- Error responses can be escalated to give users the right amount of information to proceed without bogging them down.

# Building for
# Google Assistant

9

**This chapter covers**

- Examining Google Assistant and how it differs from other platforms

- Learning the difference between the Actions SDK and Dialogflow

- Building an interaction model in Dialogflow

- Creating a Dialogflow-powered action

Already you've seen the basics of a good VUI and how to build an Alexa skill. Alexa, though, is not the only major voice-first platform. Nearly as prominent is Google, with Google Assistant coming on the Google Home and third-party devices. Although it was released after Alexa, Google has taken hold in the market, and may have even caught up to Amazon in the number of devices sold by the time you read this. As I write this, in 2019, Google has been consistently growing faster than Amazon in putting smart speakers in homes.

Developers have been building for the Assistant platform from the beginning, creating what Google calls *actions*, which extend the platform with custom interactions. Google is further trying to expand Assistant by playing to the search engine's strengths, creating tools for website creators and Android developers so they can create actions based on what they've already built. Developers can also create new actions that are untied to anything but Assistant.

> **NOTE** A quick word about nomenclature. When Google talks about voice experiences, it often talks about *actions* and *apps*, sometimes seemingly interchangeably. An *action* is a combination of intent—what the user wants to do—and fulfillment of that intent. An *app* is a combination of actions. I'll primarily refer to what we build as apps, and they can be considered to be equivalent in concept to Alexa skills.

Users interact with actions through Google Assistant. Assistant is on both stand-alone devices such as Google Home and Android phones, but the massive size of the Android user base means Assistant is a *voice added* interaction as often as it is *voice first* or *voice only*. How users interact with an app when there is only voice will differ from when there's a touchscreen at hand, and the way the app responds should reflect that. We'll look at how to handle these different modes in chapter 12, but we'll start with the voice-only interaction paradigm.

Another difference between Alexa and Google Assistant is that Google Assistant apps are not necessarily tied to a specific natural language understanding platform. Instead, the developer can choose whichever platform they wish. The recommended—and easiest—natural language understanding platform to integrate into Assistant apps is Dialogflow (formerly API.AI). The vast majority of developers will stick with Dialogflow, only bringing in another NLU if they have specialized needs or an existing system in place. Building without Dialogflow is often referred to by Google as building with the Actions SDK.

We'll build an app using the Actions SDK in chapter 12; in this chapter we'll build on top of Dialogflow. Using Dialogflow requires less tooling, and you'll see what Dialogflow provides once we strip it away in chapter 12.

We can later build an app without relying on Dialogflow because of one significant manner in which building for Assistant differs from building for Alexa—Google provides the text of what users say to developers. This is useful when we want to analyze the utterance in any way we choose, and we can also use it for logging and analytics to further improve the user experience. We could alternatively ignore it altogether, relying only on Dialogflow for the NLU and handling of the interaction model. That's what we'll do in our first application.

## 9.1 Setting up the application

Let's build something to impress your colleagues (or, if you work for yourself or you're a student, your housemates). We'll build an application that provides information about your company's office.

We'll start by setting up the application. Google has provided a console where you can specify the application's metadata: https://console.actions.google.com/.

You can guess what to do first: add a project. Name it whatever you want, so long as it's descriptive (I'll name mine "Office Guide"), and select the language and region (I chose English and United States). Then wait patiently as Google creates the application.

The next screen will ask you to categorize what you're building. This matters, and it doesn't. Largely, these options are there to guide you through setup, and there's a large difference between the choices at the bottom. A Templates action uses Google spreadsheets, whereas Device Registration is for hardware applications. We won't build with either of these. In this chapter we will build a Conversational application, so select that one. (We'll build with the Actions SDK in chapter 12.)

This takes you to the next screen, where you'll see the options to set up the application. You can fill out the application description and image later. We'll start with the user interaction. In the menu, you'll see an option for Actions, which will present you with a screen where you can select Add Your First Action.

One important feature of the Google Assistant platform is that users can implicitly invoke actions. That's why Google wants developers to specify actions in the Assistant configuration settings *and* in Dialogflow. If Google later determines that one of your actions can handle a user's request, it will send traffic your way, without the user needing to enable anything. For example, if you build an application that provides business hours, and a user asks "What time does the Sushi Wa on 6th Street open?" without providing an invocation name, Google might determine there's a question-and-answer match and send them to your app.

When you click to add an action, you will see a bunch of options for *intents*. This may seem odd, because you just selected actions. But remember that an *action* is *an intent plus the application's response.* Google needs to first know what intents the application will handle. It might then, for those implicit invocations, route the request for the application to handle. Voilà! Intent plus fulfillment equals action.

Again Google is working to make your work easy for the general cases, and it's providing preseeded intents that represent common user requests. There are situations that many applications might handle, like checking the weather or a bank account. Ours is not a general case. We are special. We'll select Custom Intent and make our own.

Most of the interaction model, including the intent, lives within Dialogflow, which is where Google will take you next.

## 9.2    *Building the interaction model*

Dialogflow is going to house the entire interaction model inside what it calls an *agent.* The agent will map what the user wants to do with what the user is saying. How this happens is easier to understand when you see the different paths an interaction can take from the user and back, as shown in figure 9.1. Once again, Google provides different options. You can even let Dialogflow build the response entirely on its own.

What the user says is in fact sent directly to Dialogflow, and Dialogflow can respond with a fully formed phrase. Dialogflow needs to know *where* to respond, and that is specified by linking an agent with an Assistant application. Google does this automatically if you go from the Assistant console and you click Create on the agent creation screen.

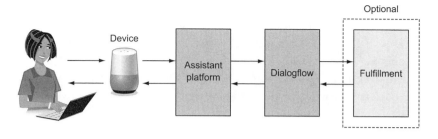

**Figure 9.1  Flow of data in a request when using Dialogflow**

**NOTE**  Dialogflow offers prebuilt agents, as well. These are already trained for common requests, such as searching for events or asking for jokes. They come with intents and entities already prepared, but they require custom responses.

Once you arrive in Dialogflow, you'll see a screen with two intents that Dialogflow already offers. If you click through to the default welcome intent, you will see that a trove of configuration awaits. There's the intent name, which describes what the intent does and provides a hook that you can use later inside your code. You will also see something intriguing—a space for *events*. With Dialogflow, Assistant can send an event name that doesn't necessarily correspond to something the user said, and Dialogflow will match it to the intent.

For the welcome intent, when a user launches an action without specifying anything else (for example, "Hey Google, speak to Voice Tips."), Assistant sends the `Welcome` event, and Dialogflow matches that to the welcome intent. Absent an event, Dialogflow will match based on what the user says, which you can see in figure 9.2, noted as *training phrases*.

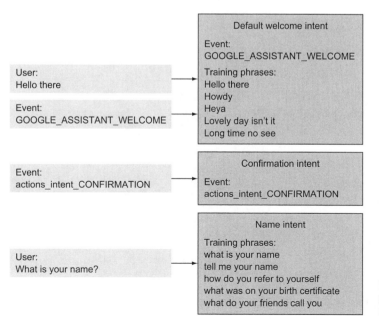

**Figure 9.2  Intent-matching on events and user utterances**

If a user were to say, "Hey," "Hi there," or even "Lovely day isn't it," Dialogflow will match the request to the welcome intent, because Dialogflow starts out with these pre-added phrases in English. We could, of course, remove any of them or even add our own, like "engage" or "start up": "Hey Google, tell Office Guide to engage."

If you head over to the fallback intent, you won't see any training phrases. Dialogflow hits the fallback intent when it can't match what the user said to anything else, as in figure 9.3.

You can think of the fallback intent as a backstop that catches any balls that fly past the catcher. It is similar to the built-in Alexa fallback intent, but it's importantly unlike the `Unhandled` handler we added to Alexa skills. The `Unhandled` handler will craft a response when there's a matched intent without a handler in the fulfillment. The fallback intents occur when there's no matched intent.

Both the fallback and welcome intents already have responses set up. The fallback intent lets the user know that Dialogflow didn't understand, whereas the welcome intent asks the user what to do next. Really, the welcome intent responses don't work very well. As we've already seen, voice applications need to aid in discoverability, and a response such as "Greetings! How can I assist?" doesn't get the user any closer to knowing what is possible. Once we build out our application and add more functionality, you may want to come back here and give the user a hint on what to do.

Let's apply what you've just learned digging through Dialogflow and create an intent.

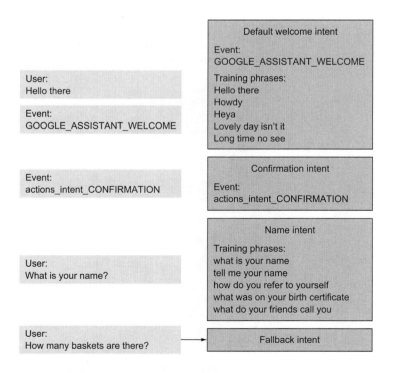

**Figure 9.3   When Dialogflow can't match, it sends the request to the fallback intent.**

### 9.2.1 Building an intent

Because our application is all about providing information about an office, why not start with an intent where people can ask exactly *whose* office it is? We could call it `office_info` and provide that name on the intent configuration screen.

As usual, to figure out what users might say, we'll start speaking some phrases out loud and write them down after. If you came to this chapter first, you can see tips on building good voice responses throughout the book, but chapter 3 is a good place to start.

When users interact with Assistant applications through Google Home or other voice-first devices, there's no significant difference in how an application should respond compared to other platforms, such as Alexa. Remember, though, that Assistant isn't only triggered by voice. People can also communicate with it through their phone and the phone's keyboard. For Assistant, the phrases we expect to tie to an intent always need to include how people might type the request. Users will communicate through the keyboard less than voice, so place more focus on spoken requests, but don't ignore the written ones completely.

Try doing the exercise yourself. How would you ask a Google Home for the definition of a voice application? How might users ask their phones when typing out the question? Here are some I came up with.

---

**Listing 9.1    Training phrases**

```
whose office is this
what company is this
where am i
tell me whose office this is
tell me about this office
give me info about this office
show me where i am
```

> These phrases represent the fact that the user will be commanding Assistant to do something.

These phrases represent what the user will say (or type) to Assistant. In the reverse direction is what Assistant will respond to the user. Dialogflow again differentiates itself here, because these responses can live in the Dialogflow platform, with no need for code. Dialogflow responds back directly, as in figure 9.4. You might put responses inside Dialogflow directly when there's no logic behind them. What Assistant will say to the current intent—asking for general information about the office—won't need to differ based on the time of day, whether a user is new or returning, or anything else. (We probably do want even static responses to vary to provide some variety, which is done simply through adding multiple responses. Dialogflow will then choose a response on each turn.)

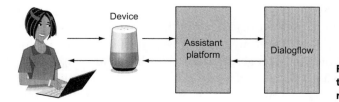

**Figure 9.4    Dialogflow can be the terminus for requests, building the response itself.**

The same VUI principles apply to a static response as to one we handle in the code It should answer the user's question, do it efficiently, and do it with the right manner. It should also look good on the screen.

Let's play "bad response, good response" to a user's question of "Whose office is this?" and let's consider especially how we could support both screen and spoken responses. We'll look later at how to target responses based on the device type, but we'll start by supporting both.

Consider this response:

*"It belongs to the company who pays rent here."*

Alright, we started off with a purposely really bad one. It's bad because the response fails on a few levels. First, the response isn't nearly complete. The statement is true, but it omits much of what the user actually wants to know. Another spot for improvement is that there's no implicit confirmation that the app correctly understood the user. This isn't as much of a problem with a typed request, because users will generally assume that what they see on the screen is "visible" to Assistant unless a response is far enough afield to dispel that assumption. The implicit confirmation is more important for the voice-first side, where a number of misunderstandings could happen between the user's request and the ultimate response.

Here's another:

*"This is the office of Foo Corporation. There are sixteen meeting rooms spread out across three floors. Furthermore, the closest restrooms are to the right, and the kitchen may be found one floor up. The Foo Corporation makes widgets and other business products."*

Another response with a couple of problems. This response answers the question well, but maybe too well. Recall that spoken interactions move in one direction—forward—in constant time. Your users probably don't want to wait through this long response. (There are certainly voice applications where users are looking for longer responses, such as audiobooks or news reports. But it's not clear that this is such an app—you should assume that it isn't until you establish that it is.) This would work much better on the phone, because a display gives users the chance to scan information quickly. Another problem with this response is the language it uses. It is, again, apparently geared toward written communication. Be aware of the language you're using, and lean toward words and phrases that work well both in writing and speaking.

*"You're in the offices of Foo Corporation."*

Or,

*"This is the office of Foo Corporation. Go to the front desk to check in."*

These are both good responses. They are both succinct, relevant to the question, and use language that works in both settings. They both start out by implicitly confirming the request, and they end with a meaty portion of the response. Our replies in conversation generally follow this approach, ending with what's most important. We want people to remember what's key, and that's no different in voice applications. Both of these responses could work well, as could many others I'm sure you can create.

**NOTE** Because Dialogflow can handle the NLU for many different platforms, it can also send different responses to each platform. That's why you'll see a tab for Assistant responses and one for the default, which is the fallback if there are no platform-specific responses.

When we add the responses to the intent configuration screen, the final option that Dialogflow provides is whether the response ends the conversation or not. If you select this, Assistant won't wait for the user to say something else after sending the response. Leave it unselected, and the user has a chance to follow up. We aren't asking the user for a follow-up in this case, so you can set the intent as the end of the conversation.

You're probably eager to test the application. The quickest way to do that is in the simulator.

### 9.2.2  Testing with the simulator

One thing you'll need to get used to when building for Assistant is the separation of the different parts of the application. Unlike Alexa, where everything lives either in the Alexa console, locally, or deployed in the fulfillment, the modularity of Assistant introduces a separate section for the NLU. This is a nice benefit, because it lets you use your own NLU, but it might take a while in the beginning for you to remember where everything is.

If you look for the simulator inside Dialogflow, you won't find it, as you can see in figure 9.5. The simulator is a part of Assistant and is in the Assistant console.

> **Necessary Google account settings for simulator testing**
>
> To test the app using the simulator, you'll need to turn on some settings for your Google account:
>
> - Web & App Activity
> - Device Information
> - Voice & Audio Activity
>
> These are the permissions Google requires for all users of the Assistant, which includes the simulator.

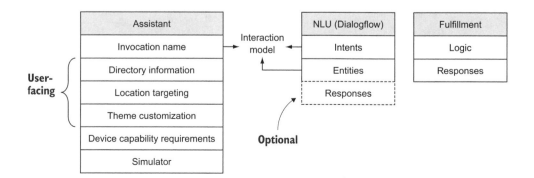

**Figure 9.5  Google Assistant is a highly modular platform.**

The easiest way to begin is with the phrase, "Talk to My Test App." (It's "test app" because we haven't provided an invocation name yet.) You'll hear something like this: "Alright. Getting the test version of my test app. Greetings! How can I assist?"

Where's that coming from? The first part of the response is what the simulator says when testing a test app—the user wouldn't hear that in the end. The second part comes from one of the responses built into the default welcome intent from Dialogflow.

"Whose office is this?" we say back.

"You're in the offices of Foo Corporation."

It looks like everything's working. We can now add another intent that handles parameters.

### 9.2.3   *Parameters and entities*

Parameters are variable pieces of information that a user can specify while triggering an intent. They are similar to query parameters in a URL or input fields in a web form, as in figure 9.6.

The fields in a form explicitly state the information the user can provide and which are required or optional. They can often specify the format or values accepted, too. It may be a phone number or an email address.

A select field, meanwhile, limits users to a set number of choices. You could think of this as a sign-up intent with five different entities.

Figure 9.7 shows a phrase someone could say to achieve the same goal as figure 9.6, mapped on top of the sign-up form. "My name is {FirstName} {LastName} and I go by {Username}@gmail.com with password {Password}. Again, that's {Confirmation}." This

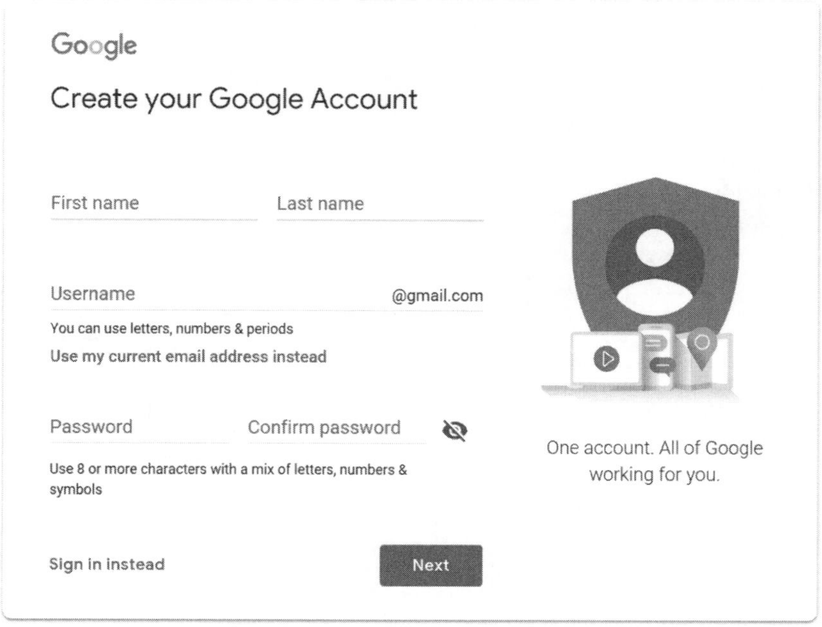

**Figure 9.6   Google's sign-up form**

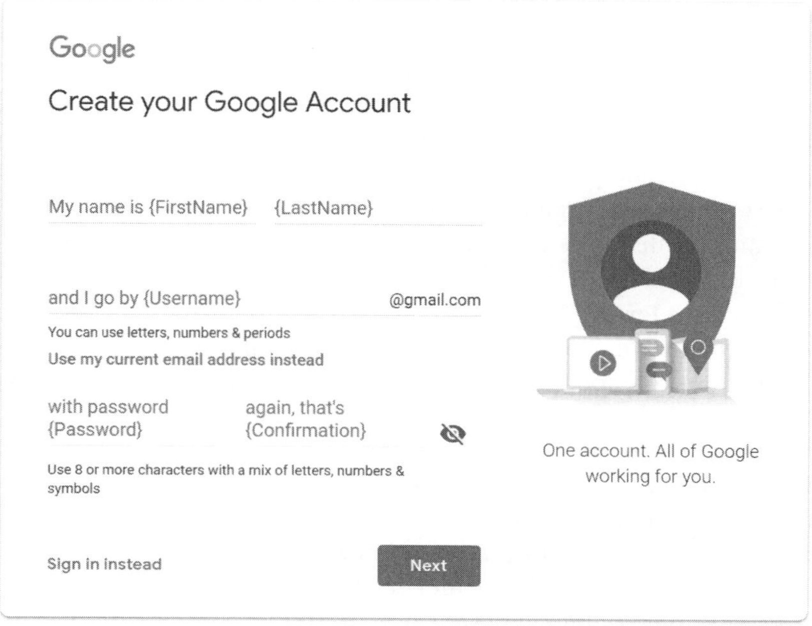

**Figure 9.7    Google's sign-up form imagined conversationally**

more clearly shows the relationship between the entities and how they relate to variable information.

This is how it works inside Assistant, too. You specify the type of each parameter, where you expect the user will provide the values, and which values you expect. From there, Assistant will send them back to you, along with the intent.

To continue exploring parameters and entities, we need to create another intent that maps to a user asking for information about locations inside the office. I'd call it the office_locations intent. Users will ask how to get to the kitchen or bathroom, and it might sound something like, "How do you get to the kitchen from here?" or "How do you get to the supply closet from here?"

With just these two phrases, we already have some duplication. Not only duplication, but the phrases are completely the same except for one small variable piece. When you see a phrase duplicated several times with only a single item changing, that's a sign you should reach for parameters and entities.

### 9.2.4   Adding entities

An entity represents a variable piece of information within a user-spoken phrase. That phrase will map to an intent, which is what a user wants to do. The user wants to perform that behavior *with* or *to* something—the *entity*. In our previous example, the user wants to find the location of a room. That room could be the kitchen, the supply closet, or somewhere else.

We can train Dialogflow on which values a user might provide, but users are *not* limited to what we provide. This is a good thing, because we don't want to have to list every possible value, and the user doesn't want to be limited to the values we provide.

The grouping of values that a user might provide is known as an *entity*. The exact value that a user then provides is known as a *parameter*. Each parameter will have an associated entity, and an entity can lend itself to multiple parameters. If we think back to our experience with Alexa, a parameter is equivalent to a slot and an entity is similar to a slot type. You can provide values to the entities within Dialogflow. All that's needed is the name of the entity (such as "room") and the values that go toward training it.

The parameters for our intent will cover the different rooms in the office. These rooms might be the "meeting room," "kitchen," "supply closet," and others. Dialogflow accepts synonyms, too. A user might ask for a "broom closet" instead of a "supply closet," or "conference room" or "meeting space" for "meeting room."

You can go to the Entities section and create a new entity, which you could call anything descriptive. I'll call it "room" and fill out the values.

When creating parameters, your goal is to capture the primary ways that a user will ask for information, similar to training phrases. You do not need to be exhaustive. Throwing values in there just in case they're needed might even hurt the NLU. Putting "room closet" in there because a user might conceivably use that in place of "broom closet" could harm the understanding.

Do, though, use synonyms extensively. Not only do they help in organization, they'll be easier to handle in the code inside the fulfillment. If you had to worry about "broom closet" *and* "supply closet" individually, the code would be a lot messier and more brittle. The code would need to change each time the list of parameters did. Instead, by using synonyms, the code can check on only the canonical value.

Dialogflow also provides an option called *automatic expansion*. This option takes all of the entity values that you provide and extrapolates from there, so that Dialogflow will still capture a parameter value if the user provides something that's related but not in the list you've set up. For example, maybe the user asks for the location of the server room. That's not in the original list, but it *is* related to the other values. The thing about automatic expansion is that you need to provide a lot of initial values for the extrapolation to work well. All the more reason to spend significant time considering how your users will speak to your app.

Upon saving, you can use the parameters inside the intent, via the training phrases.

### 9.2.5   *Using parameters in intents*

We're inside the `office_locations` intent and we looked at a few ways a user might invoke it. "How do you get to the kitchen from here," "Get to the kitchen from here," and "Find the kitchen" are a few, and I'm sure you can come up with others.

When adding these phrases, we need to specify where we expect the parameters, too. The nice thing about Dialogflow is that it will generally do this for us. It looks at the training phrases and matches the words inside them with entity values. (Sometimes, even too strongly, as you'll see if you add the phrase "First of all, where is the kitchen?"—Dialogflow assumes the word "first" is an entity of the type `@sys.ordinal`.)

Now, when a user says "How do you get to the kitchen from here?" we will have access to the intent (`office_locations`) and the parameter value (`kitchen`). We'll be able to use this value in the code, but we can also use it directly inside of Dialogflow in the responses.

Inside Dialogflow, you can access the value with the parameter name prefaced with a dollar sign. In our case, Dialogflow assumed we wanted the parameter name `room` to match with the entity name, and we can access the value in the responses with `$room`. Ultimately, you'll have a response that looks something like "The $room is somewhere in this office."

Except that's really underwhelming. A user is going to ask how to get somewhere and hear that the room is here… somewhere. Obviously it is! This response flouts Grice's maxim of quantity, because it doesn't fully answer the question. But there's no logic inside of Dialogflow for the responses, and no way to choose a response based on the parameter value.

To implement custom logic, we need to turn to the fulfillment.

## 9.3    *Fulfillment*

So far, the flow of information goes from the user to the device, from the device to the Assistant platform, and then from the platform to Dialogflow. It then returns to the same user in the same order, reversed. For situations where the interaction calls for any sort of logic to build the response, however, at least one more piece needs to be added: the fulfillment.

The fulfillment step comes after Dialogflow and takes the intent and entities that Dialogflow offers. As you'll see, there is then a flow within the fulfillment itself.

First, we'll use Cloud Functions for Firebase to host the code. Cloud Functions for Firebase is built on Firebase, which is Google's platform for mobile and serverless applications. It includes tools to run code in one-off situations, data stores, logging, and other features. Cloud Functions is similar to AWS Lambda, which we used to build Alexa skills.

You do not have to use Cloud Functions to build for Assistant. You can host the fulfillment on AWS Lambda, Azure, or *any* secure server where you can receive the requests. We'll use Cloud Functions because it's the simplest way to get started, especially as we can also bring in the Cloud Functions library to ease handling the requests.

> **TIP** Firebase doesn't allow for network calls outside of Google services on its free plan. The apps we'll be building won't need a paid plan, and the pay-as-you-go plan has limits that likely won't be hit by your application. Nonetheless, keep this in mind for your future apps.

**Developing locally without deploying**

You can also use localtunnel, ngrok, or another similar tool to develop locally without deploying to Cloud Functions each time. You'll use `firebase serve --only functions` and then provide that to the outside world via a URL from one of the aforementioned tools.

You can see instructions on how to set this up in Silvano Luciani's blog post, "Deploy your Assistant app fulfillment webhook using Cloud Functions for Firebase," http://mng.bz/ 8JdP. If you do that, you can skip down to section 9.3.1.

To create and deploy the fulfillment, you'll need the Firebase CLI.

**Listing 9.2   Setting up the Firebase CLI**

```
$ npm install -g firebase-tools
$ firebase login          ◄──────────── Log in with your Google account.
$ mkdir office-guide && cd office-guide
$ firebase init           ◄──────────── When prompted, choose only "functions."
```

These steps set up the Firebase CLI and then create the project structure. In particular, `firebase init` will run through specific choices to get you started, including connecting the project with your Google Action (choose the name you provided in the Assistant console) and other project-specific settings. You need to choose only functions when it asks which Firebase CLI features you want, connect the local project to the correct Google Action, and then choose as you wish. (My choices were to go with JavaScript over TypeScript, to use ESLint, and to install the dependencies. Choose these if you want to follow along as closely as possible.)

That's it for the Firebase portion for now.

**TIP**  You may need to answer different questions based on the version of Firebase tools you have.

As you might guess, Google provides tooling for handling the data from Dialogflow. We'll be using the Actions on Google Node.js library, which wraps the handling of Dialogflow's response in an easier-to-use package.

**NOTE**  The Actions on Google Node.js library also offers tooling for building Actions SDK applications.

As always, there's a little bit of housekeeping to build the fulfillment. Don't worry; this will be quick. We need to install that library now:

```
$ npm install --prefix ./functions actions-on-google --save   ◄─┐
                                          Saves the Actions on Google library │
                                            in the fulfillment directory │
```

For an action as straightforward as ours, we'll need just two packages. One is for Firebase (installed on setup) and the other is for Actions on Google. All of the fulfillment can live in a single file along with the necessary libraries. We'll write that file now.

### 9.3.1 The code

The way an action works is that a request will come in to the fulfillment, and the fulfillment, via the different libraries and your logic, will transform the request into a response, which is sent back to the requester.

Let's start at the beginning, with the request coming in to the index.js file.

**Listing 9.3   Initializing the app and opening it for requests (index.js)**

Imports the Dialogflow tooling

The library that handles requests on Cloud Functions for Firebase

The app creates the response and has optional logging for debugging.

```
const {dialogflow} = require("actions-on-google");
const functions = require("firebase-functions");

const app = dialogflow({debug: true});

exports.app = functions.https.onRequest(app);
```

Exports code to run on every inbound request

Here's how I like to think about this. Have you ever missed a package? You come home, and the carrier has left you a note saying that if you want the package, you have to go to a warehouse on the outskirts of town. The warehouse has a single entrance to go through, and you arrive at a desk. "I'm looking for a missed package notice for Dustin Coates," you say (presumably using your name instead of mine). The clerk takes your information, goes into the back to find the shelf with your package, and brings you the box and the receipt. There's a whole warehouse behind that desk that you can't see, and that you don't care about. All that matters to you is that you've brought the right information, and you receive the package in return.

It's the same with actions, as you can see in figure 9.8. There's a single entry and exit point (`exports.app`) and a single point of responsibility for unraveling and assembling everything (the app object itself). What's left is the unseen warehouse—the logic that will handle the intents. This code represents the edges of the application.

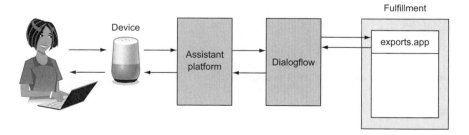

**Figure 9.8   There is one entry and exit point for the fulfillment.**

Listing 9.4   Handling the intent (index.js)

**Base responses for when users ask for**
**each different concept**

**Parameters come as an object with**
**parameter names as keys.**

```
    ...

app.intent("office_locations", (conv, {room}) => {
  const responses = {
    kitchen: "take a left and then the first right",
    "supply closet": "go to the other side of the floor, next to the devs",
    "meeting room": "it's just on your right"
  };
  const response = `To find the ${room}, ${responses[room]}`;

  conv.close(response);
});
```

**Sends the response and doesn't**
**listen for follow-up**

**Builds the response based on the parameter**

In the preceding code, `app.intent` is doing two jobs. It registers the intent handler by intent name, and then it calls the handler when the intent comes in. When a request arrives, the app object looks through all of the registered intents to find one that matches. In figure 9.9, the matching intent is `intent_3`.

Once it finds a matching intent, it calls a handler that creates the response. The handler for the `office_locations` intent receives a conversation object (as `conv`) that contains most of the helpers you'll use in the fulfillment. The conversation object is to the handlers what `app` is to the overall application. The handler then crafts the response by calling `conv.close`, which also indicates that the conversation is over and shouldn't listen for a follow-up from the user.

Now you're probably eager to start interacting with the app.

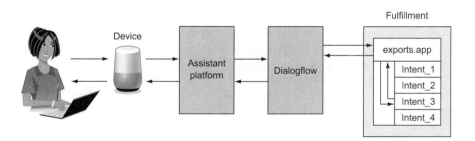

**Figure 9.9   Information flows within the fulfillment, too.**

## 9.3.2   *Deployment*

To deploy the app to Cloud Functions, we'll use the Firebase CLI again.

**Listing 9.5  Deploying the function**

```
$ firebase deploy --only functions
=== Deploying to 'office-guide'...

i  deploying functions
i  functions: ensuring necessary APIs are enabled...
✔  functions: all necessary APIs are enabled
i  functions: preparing functions directory for uploading...
i  functions: packaged functions (40.61 KB) for uploading
✔  functions: functions folder uploaded successfully
i  functions: creating function app...
✔  functions[app]: Successful create operation.
Function URL (app): https://us-central1-project.cloudfunctions.net/app

✔  Deploy complete!

Project Console: https://console.firebase.google.com/project/project/overview
```

**Your URL will be different; note it.**

**The online console for checking the status and logs of the function**

The preceding command packages the code, deploys it to Cloud Functions, and, importantly, provides the URL where it lives. This is the URL you'll need to provide to Dialogflow to complete the application. If you deploy again and maintain the same object reference (exports.app), the URL will stay the same and the newer code will be live online.

Go into the Dialogflow console where you added the intents and entities. There you'll see a section for Fulfillment. Enable the webhook, and provide the URL.

If you were to test this in the Assistant simulator now, you would see the same response we had before: The kitchen is somewhere in this office. Dialogflow is still handling the responses.

You can tell Dialogflow to let your code handle the fulfillment by going back to the office_locations intent and selecting Enable Webhook Call for This Intent in the Fulfillment section. Now, for this intent, the code will build the response instead of Dialogflow, which is still doing the intent and entity detection.

You could now go in and say, "Talk to my test app" and follow the conversation through to its conclusion. The "my test app" wording sticks out, though. How can we fix it?

### 9.3.3  *Changing the invocation name*

Google creates all applications with the "my test app" invocation name, which is nice for getting started quickly. Soon, though, you'll want your own invocation name. You might think it's best to save it for the end, but moving quickly to a real-world setting is important here, just as developing a website with an environment similar to production is important. For voice development, it's not catching bugs that's important, it's putting yourself in the same context as your users. You might find that certain phrases flow with your invocation name but don't with "my text app," and vice versa. The invocation name can inform your overall interaction planning.

Google hosts the invocation name inside the Assistant console. (You can find it under Invocation in the sidebar.) This is the one piece of the interaction model that lives within Assistant, as was shown in figure 9.5.

This is understandable, because to route a request to an NLU, Google needs to know which application is handling the request. It determines this by looking at the invocation name. Unlike some other platforms, the domain name metaphor holds up well with Assistant, because Google doesn't allow reuse of invocation names (although we aren't yet seeing high-priced secondary markets for invocation names!).

I'll use the name "Office Guide" for my application. It's pretty generic, which would generally be a negative, but it's easy to remember. Plus, it's short to type and to say, reducing the bar for usage a little bit more.

With the invocation name, the interaction model, and the deployment set up, we've got a working app, but there's more we can do. In the next chapter, we'll build it up.

## Summary

- A Google Assistant application contains actions, which map intents to fulfillment.
- The Actions SDK is available for developers who want to use their own NLU tool.
- Dialogflow is Google's preferred NLU tool for creating Assistant applications.
- Information flows from the user through Assistant, to Dialogflow, and to the fulfillment, before a response is sent back to the user in the reverse order.

# Going multimodal

**This chapter covers**

- Extending voice applications beyond voice
- Balancing spoken requests with screens
- Choosing when to use other modes
- Adding display interactions to Assistant applications

Something key to voice applications that we've left until now is that there are three ways of interacting with them: voice only, voice first, and voice added. Voice only is what it sounds like: voice and nothing else. Voice first uses voice as the primary interaction method, but it has other input or output. Voice added adds voice to an existing experience to enhance, but not supplant, what the user can do. In figure 10.1, you can see that voice will take a larger or smaller role in the user interaction.

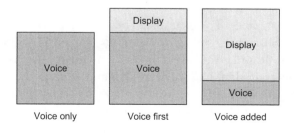

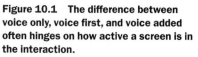

Figure 10.1 The difference between voice only, voice first, and voice added often hinges on how active a screen is in the interaction.

The different input and output mechanisms are called *modes*. You could, for example, have a voice mode, a display mode, or a physical input mode (such as the Alexa buttons). Developers can combine modes to create *multimodal* applications. In this chapter, we are going to extend the application from chapter 9 to add multimodal capabilities.

## 10.1  *Introducing multimodal*

The primary multimodal systems that people think of are devices with displays, like the Google Home Hub. These are voice-first devices because voice is the primary input and output mode, but the display is available when it's helpful. Alternatively, you might consider the Google Home to be a singly modal experience because there's only voice input and output. Think for a moment, though, and ask yourself if that's really true. Does the Google Home device only have a single mode?

A Google Home has, in fact, multiple modes. Voice is the primary one by a large measure, but the device also has lights on the top that display information. You, the Assistant application developer, don't have access to these lights, but thinking about them as an output mode may make you think of other ways that people might communicate with voice devices, beyond the voice back-and-forth. This perspective is especially important when building for Google Assistant, because the Assistant is often paired with a screen on phones.

Different modes can serve different purposes, and that's true for both input and output. We've discussed what voice is good for several times, and that doesn't change when extra modes are introduced. Voice is useful for returning smaller pieces of information that don't require large amounts of precision. These are interactions like turning on or off lights or rolling a virtual die. Voice is not the mode of choice for situations involving larger amounts of information or more precision, such as providing a password or credit card number, or returning a list of the 12 people who have walked on the moon. In those situations, a display is more useful.

> **NOTE**  Over on the Alexa side, there are Alexa gadgets, such as buttons, that most often serve as input for group games. This illustrates how different modes can make up for the shortcomings of voice. Voice recognition is still nascent, and it's even more limited if multiple people are shouting out for an answer. Thus, buttons come to the rescue, much like on television game shows, to clearly mark which player was the first with an answer.

By thinking creatively about different modes, developers and designers have expanded how users can interact through voice. For example, The Food Network's Alexa skill ties into what the user is likely watching on their televisions (surreptitiously) by tying into the network's show schedule and giving users the ability to ask for the recipe that's currently showing. On the gaming side, *Call of Duty: WWII* and *Destiny 2* both tap into the user's behavior in the game. *Call of Duty* uses the player's performance as a type of input, and becomes a coach to help the player improve. Meanwhile, *Destiny 2* uses voice as an input and the in-game Ghost as the output.

**TIP** Even smart-home devices could be thought of as another mode. When a voice-first device turns off the lights, the change in illumination provides its own feedback.

An action doesn't *need* multiple modes. Many actions will never go beyond voice, and developers need to accept that users may not use all of the modes they have available. In the case of display-added experiences, consider that many people interacting with an action may not have a voice-first device with a display or are not in a context in which they can view or interact with the display. A father cooking dinner for his children could have his back to the display, and a woman driving won't be able to safely look at the console. But some experiences can benefit by having an extra mode, particularly a display. The goal is to build an experience that works well when navigating only through voice and that is enhanced by the display.

**NOTE** In a multimodal application where a non-voice mode is used for input, building an action that works without that non-voice mode is more difficult, as the input is often more fundamental to the experience. Even in this case, though, there are often ways to fall back to voice only.

Because Google Assistant lives on phones, speakers, and smart displays, it is well suited for multiple modes and provides developers multiple ways to display information and handle screen input.

## 10.2 Multimodal in actions

On phones, the responses from actions live within the Assistant app, so Google gives developers several display options that handle a multitude of different situations, such as

- Simple responses
- Rich responses
- List responses
- Suggestion chips

This limits the developer's options, but it also reduces the developer's work. Instead of building something from scratch, developers only need to provide the content and specify the structure they require. Everything on the display is paired with a spoken response, but the content for the voice and display do not need to be the same.

Let's look at each of these display options in turn.

### 10.2.1 Simple responses

The default display is a simple response. This is just a chat bubble that displays text along with the application icon, and it's the easiest to send. In fact, we've been sending them already.

But recall our efforts to find responses that worked well for both reading and listening. We might instead want to send one response for Assistant to speak and another for it to display on the screen. All we need to do is to use the `SimpleResponse` helper. Assistant provides a number of these helpers for creating the proper response arguments.

**Listing 10.1   Using the `SimpleResponse` helper (index.js)**

```
const {dialogflow, SimpleResponse} = require("actions-on-google");
...
```

◄─── Imports SimpleResponse helper

```
app.intent("office_locations", (conv, {room}) => {
  ...
```

Specifies the responses we'll display on the screen

```
  const displayTexts = {
    kitchen: "The kitchen is to your left and then a right. " +
             "Grab a snack or a drink, on the house.",
    "supply closet": "For the supply closet, you'll go all the way around " +
                     "until you reach the developers. " +
                     "Find the cleaning supplies, paper, and paper clips.",
    "meeting room": "Look to your right and you'll see the meeting room. " +
                    "This meeting room seats six people and you can " +
                    "book it online."
  };
  const displayText = displayTexts[room];
```

◄─── The chosen response for the currently requested concept

```
  conv.close(new SimpleResponse({
    speech: response,
    text: displayText
  }));
});
```

Sends both speech and text

I recommend not using the same message for two modes. Most often, the text response will be wordier and with more information than the spoken response.

That doesn't mean that the text is a superset of the spoken response. Indeed, you will often have something in the spoken response that's *not* in the text, as shown in figure 10.2. Often this will be words or a phrase that makes the speech more conversational. The Food Network discovered that, when testing its voice application, people will actually become more impatient if they have a screen in front of them in addition to voice, so you will want to tailor your responses.[1] (If you doubt this, think about presentations where the speaker reads everything from the slides.) Generally, a best practice for text responses is elaborating on the points and providing more information, but not overloading the user with information. Again, this is a conversational interaction, and part of being a good conversational partner is not hogging the attention too much.

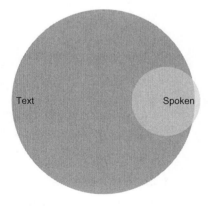

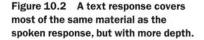

**Figure 10.2   A text response covers most of the same material as the spoken response, but with more depth.**

---

[1]  "Tim McElreath of Scripps/Food Network Talks Multimodal Design," Voicebot podcast episode 28, 34:13.

Text on the screen is useful, but it doesn't truly take advantage of what a screen offers. Assistant specifically offers more than that, through *rich responses.*

### 10.2.2 *Rich responses*

Google Assistant offers an array of different formats for displaying information on a screen, but these are truly just options. You can't, for example, display an arbitrary layout on the screen, but most of what you'll want to do is accounted for. These rich responses range from a card to embedded media. They also include touchable interactions that can send a request back to the application. Rich responses work well with actions that involve large amounts of information or media, like an image or a video that makes the response more full-fledged. Lists often work well, such as sports standings.

I think we've exhausted what we can do with the `office_locations` intent for now, so let's explore rich responses with a new intent. The events and meetups that this fictional office hosts will provide a list we can work with, so let's build a `get_events` intent that users can ask for this information. We'll want to provide training phrases that represent how people will speak to the application, as usual, but we won't need any parameters because this intent won't have any variable information. So go ahead, add phrases like "What events are coming up?" or "What's the next event in the office?"

> **TIP** Don't forget to mark the fulfillment as Enable Webhook Call for This Intent in Dialogflow.

The various types of rich responses differ in how they present information, how much information they present, and the interaction options they offer to users. For example, a *card* is the simplest kind of rich response. It can contain only formatted text, only an image, or a combination of the two. Moreover, it can contain a title, a subtitle, and a link out to a web page.

A card is useful when you want to present text that you *expect* the user to read. Most often, this will be when a user asks a question that most fully can be answered by reading. Don't take this to mean that you shouldn't answer the question in the spoken response! Remember the Venn diagram of responses—figure 10.3 shows what it looks like for a card.

As with a simple response, though, you should not rely on the text to answer the question. It can answer the question more *fully*, but the spoken response should suffice on its own, as in the following listing.

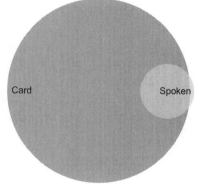

**Figure 10.3 A card can provide even more information than a simple response.**

---

**Listing 10.2   Adding a basic card (index.js)**

```
const {dialogflow, SimpleResponse, BasicCard} = require("actions-on-google");
...

app.intent("get_events", (conv) => {
  const title = "Upcoming Events in the Office";
  const subtitle = "Meetups and gatherings for the tech community";
  const text = "Our next events are:  \n" +
               "- JS Ninjas  \n- NLP Study Group  \n- Voice-First Devs";
  const card = new BasicCard({title, subtitle, text});

  conv.close("We have upcoming events for JavaScript and voice-first dev.");
  conv.close(card);
});
```

Imports the BasicCard class

Note the two spaces before the \n, required for the new line.

Provides text for the spoken response

Creates a card object

Once again, we're using a helper from the Actions library to create the response. The BasicCard class will assemble the JSON that the fulfillment sends back to the Assistant platform. Recall that the interaction between the user and the Assistant is a round trip of data, and the fulfillment is but one part of that.

We shouldn't hog the conversation, providing too much information in the spoken response or on the screen, but we should fully take advantage of the screen's capabilities. A screen, especially on a mobile phone, provides users with the opportunity to read and scan through longer pieces of information, for when they want to go into some depth. We can provide a link out via a button.

---

**Listing 10.3   Adding a button to the basic card (index.js)**

```
const {
  dialogflow,
  SimpleResponse,
  BasicCard,
  Button
} = require("actions-on-google");

...

app.intent("get_events", (conv) => {
  ...

  const button = new Button({
    title: "See all upcoming events",
    url: "https://www.example.com/upcoming-events"
  });
  const card = new BasicCard({title, subtitle, text, buttons: button});

  ...
});
```

Imports the Button class

Creates a button with text and the destination

Adds the button directly on the card

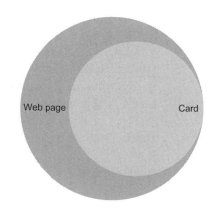

**Figure 10.5  A web page will almost always provide more information than a card.**

**Figure 10.4  A card with a button, from the simulator**

The button adds a small link to the web on the bottom of the card, as you can see in figure 10.4. Users can click it and see all the details about upcoming events.

With the link out to the web, we introduce a new information difference between the spoken response and the written one. The web link offers a breadth of information that users can drill into deeply if they wish. In figure 10.5, you can see that the web page offers potentially much more information than the card. This further extends the multimodal nature of the app, enabling users to rely on the mode that they feel is most useful. That enablement should be at the core of all multimodal applications. If a voice application's central role is to help users complete their goals more efficiently, it should also let them move away from voice when voice isn't the fullest or most efficient mode.

What we're currently displaying on the screen is a list of sorts, but it's pretty limited. Limited in size—around 15 lines if there's not an image—and limited in functionality. If we want to give users the ability to ask about a specific entity, there's a better rich response that provides more interaction ability: a list.

### 10.2.3  List responses

A list is useful when you need to provide a number of different options to a user, and events certainly fall within this bucket. A list is also useful when the options are similar and you need users to choose one. For example, if a user were to ask for "events for developers," you might list events for voice developers, for backend developers, and so on. In terms of the information balance between spoken and displayed responses, a list further grows the on-display information.

A list on the display is a good example of the two modes offering their own strengths. Spoken responses are characteristically bad at providing multiple options, especially those with ambiguity. In contrast, lists aren't the best way of quickly completing tasks. Like a pool and a hot tub, they serve different, and complementary, purposes.

The following code for sending a list is similar to what you've seen before, with another built-in helper.

**Listing 10.4   Sending a list of events (index.js)**

```
const {
   ...
   List                   Imports the List class
} = require("actions-on-google");

                           An object of list items
...
                                              A value that the Assistant will provide to the
                                              fulfillment when the user presses the item
const upcomingEvents = {
   "JS Ninjas": {                             Other ways for users to reference the item
     synonyms: [
       "JavaScript ninjas",
       "JavaScript devs"
     ],                                       The display properties for the item
     title: "JS Ninjas Over Lunch",
     description: "Friday at noon"
   },
   ...
};

app.intent("get_events", (conv) => {         The display title for the entire list
   const list = new List({
     title: "Upcoming Events",
     items: upcomingEvents
   });

   conv.close("We have upcoming events for JavaScript and voice-first dev.");
   conv.close(list);
});
```

What we do here is provide a list of options and what we want to display on the screen, as in figure 10.6. We send it back to the Assistant platform along with the speech to be spoken out loud.

Once again, the list isn't the entire response—it provides *extra* information, including text for disambiguation or secondary options.

And, of course, we provide the list items and ways for the user to select an item. The ability for users to make selections shows that we should only use lists when we want it to continue the conversation, and that we need to handle the selections.

### LIST OPTION SELECTION

So far we've used voice as the input mechanism, with the screen as output. But that's not the only possibility—the screen can certainly be used for input too. Users can type their requests to Assistant, and they can tap the screen when the application provides options, such as with a list.

I want to reiterate the central tenet of multimodal experiences, which is that developers should only introduce a mode if it makes the application easier to use. If an application has multiple modes, the developer's responsibility is to handle the interactions that arise as first-class citizens.

> **TIP** There may be situations where you don't want any interaction beyond the list, and there's no reasonable follow-up. In this case, you can't respond with, "Sorry, I only used a list for display." Instead, choose the right display for the interaction, which would be a table card.

For the list, we can make the selection an equal part of the application by giving the user more information about the events.

Office Guide ✕

Alright. Let's get the test version of Office Guide. We have upcoming events for JavaScript and voice-first dev.

## Upcoming Events

JS Ninjas Over Lunch
Friday at noon

Natural Language Processing
Study Group
Monday evenint

**Figure 10.6   A list, from the simulator**

---

**Listing 10.5   Handling option selection (index.js)**

```
const upcomingEventsSelect = {
    "JS Ninjas": "JS Ninjas is a monthly lunch gathering of JavaScript devs " +
                 "who come together to discuss best practices.",
    ...
};
```

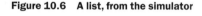
Handles an event-driven action

```
app.intent("actions.intent.OPTION", (conv, params, option) => {
    const response = upcomingEventsSelect[option];

    conv.close(response);
});
```

This code introduces a slight change to how we perceive handlers. We're now handling an event-driven, rather than a speech-driven, intent. An event-driven intent occurs without a user saying anything. This is, in fact, not the first time you've seen an event-driven intent. The welcome intent in chapter 9 happens via an event as well. Of course, we handled that event directly within Dialogflow, but we could have handled it in the fulfillment, too.

If you were to deploy this now, it wouldn't work. Whenever you selected an option (within the simulator or on a phone), you wouldn't get the response you'd expect. You might troubleshoot this by changing the event name or adding a `console.log` call and checking the Firebase function logs. Neither of those approaches will work, and the reason is due to the flow of data within the application (see figure 10.7).

As you saw in chapter 9, user interactions go through Dialogflow before reaching the fulfillment. Dialogflow doesn't know how to handle the option selection event, so it will use the Default Fallback Intent, which responds directly from Dialogflow without hitting the fulfillment. If we don't want the fallback intent to respond (and we don't), then we need to tell Dialogflow what to do with the incoming event.

> **NOTE**   If you want to know whether a request has an error due to the fulfillment, Actions, or Dialogflow, you can generally see by the error message that comes back. This is especially true when using the Assistant simulator. For example, "Webhook error" shows clearly that the error is in the fulfillment. Inbound requests going through Dialogflow also appear in the History section, which will log requests and show which ones didn't match any intents.

To do this we need to create an intent in Dialogflow like normal, and give it a name that matches up with the handler (`actions.intent.OPTION`). The difference between the intents inside Dialogflow that you saw before and this new intent illustrates the difference between an intent and an event. With a normal intent, we provide training phrases. With an event, we provide the name of that event instead. In this case, it's `actions_intent_OPTION`.

> **NOTE**   As always, if you don't select Enable Webhook Call for This Intent in the Fulfillment section, Dialogflow will respond and not send the request to your code.

A list is a perfect example of how different modes can interact together. You can see that a user could interact with the application entirely through voice, or entirely through the screen. The list provides information and lets a user follow up on it.

The display can also help direct engagement in a way that voice alone cannot, such as with suggestion chips.

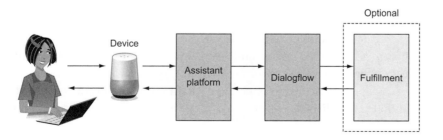

**Figure 10.7   The request goes to Dialogflow before the fulfillment.**

### 10.2.4 *Suggestion chips*

Suggestion chips increase the size of the information on the screen, usually without a corresponding decrease in the information of the spoken response. Indeed, even within the context of the screen, the chips should be additive and not a replacement for information or selections in other contexts, like lists.

To see why suggestion chips are interesting, think about some of the voice challenges we have already encountered. For example, you know that guiding the conversation is one of the challenges that anyone building for voice needs to take on. One of the heavier approaches is prompting the user with examples:

*"Which do you want? You can, for example, choose a hamburger, a hot dog, or a salad."*

The problem with this prompt is that it goes against the guideline that says to have the most important part of the response at the end. By the time the user has heard the possible options, the question is long in the past. Most of the time, this will be a marginal problem, but it is still a less-than-ideal user experience. We can instead elongate the response to move the question to the end:

*"Now is the time to choose. You can have, for example, a hot dog, hamburger, or salad. Which do you want?"*

This runs afoul of Grice's maxim of quantity. We're providing, arguably, too much information. There are, of course, times when we want to go this much in depth. For example, the escalating help when the user couldn't get to a workable intent several times in a row ended up with a very explicit prompt for the next utterance. Still, that's an extreme case, and not one we want to go to right away. A screen, though, with its broader real estate is an ideal place to put these nudges. Assistant offers that functionality through suggestion chips.

Suggestion chips increase the size of the information on the screen, usually without a corresponding decrease in the information of the spoken response. Indeed, even within the context of the screen, the chips should be additive and not a replacement for information or selections in other contexts, like lists.

There are two kinds of suggestion chips: those that come back to the conversation, and those that link out to a URL.

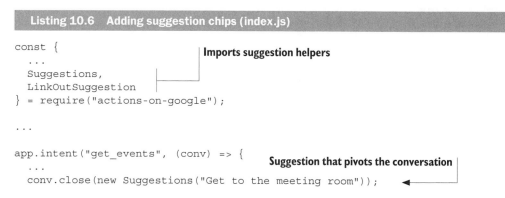

Listing 10.6  Adding suggestion chips (index.js)

```
const {                              Imports suggestion helpers
  ...
  Suggestions,
  LinkOutSuggestion
} = require("actions-on-google");

...

app.intent("get_events", (conv) => {      Suggestion that pivots the conversation
  ...
  conv.close(new Suggestions("Get to the meeting room"));
```

```
conv.close(new LinkOutSuggestion({
  name: "View All",
  url:  "https://www.example.com/upcoming-events"
}));
  ...
});
```

**Suggestion that links out**

Here we've provided both types of suggestions. One links to the web page that displays all of the Dialogflow system entities. The other keeps the conversation going and pivots it to a discussion of how to add a parameter. This shows how different the Assistant on a phone can be, and how many different modes it can handle.

The conversation can rely only on voice, only on the keyboard, only on touch, or a combination of the different modes. The user can also decide at any point to move between the available modes, maybe starting with voice, moving to touch, and then back. What we need to do is support the different options but not push users to a specific one.

Some modes of interaction are only available on certain devices, however, and we need to account for that.

## 10.3   *Surface capabilities*

As we've discussed, applications should handle multiple modes, but not all devices have all modes, or *surface capabilities*. A Google Home Mini won't have a screen, and a Google Home Hub won't have a browser. (A browser isn't actually a mode, but Google does consider it a *surface*.) The application's support of multiple modes doesn't—and shouldn't—mean that the application responds the same way for every device, independent of the available surfaces.

For example, think about our previous discussion of hot dogs, hamburgers, and salads. When we provide options in the spoken response, we break Grice's maxim of quantity. This is especially true when the user has a display surface, because that display can hold a list, suggestion chips, or other indications of the user's options. For a device that doesn't have a display, we might want to have Assistant speak those options out loud if they aren't commonly known. For example, major league baseball teams wouldn't necessitate hints, but upcoming events would, even if it means a longer response.

> **NOTE**   Another reason to provide different responses based on surface capabilities is that Google will reject the application if it leaves the connection open without asking a question. A list or suggestion chip will always leave the connection open, which isn't desirable if they can't be displayed.

To conditionally set responses based on surface capabilities, we need to reach into the request. The Actions on Google library makes this possible, as with so much else, on the conversation object passed to the intent handler.

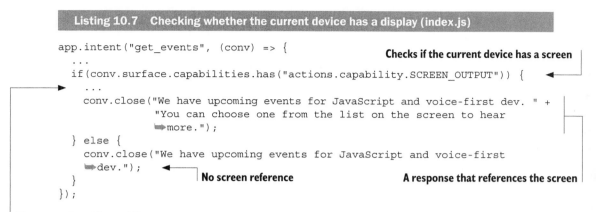

Listing 10.7   Checking whether the current device has a display (index.js)

```
app.intent("get_events", (conv) => {
    ...
    if(conv.surface.capabilities.has("actions.capability.SCREEN_OUTPUT")) {
        ...
        conv.close("We have upcoming events for JavaScript and voice-first dev. " +
                "You can choose one from the list on the screen to hear
                ➥more.");
    } else {
        conv.close("We have upcoming events for JavaScript and voice-first
        ➥dev.");
    }
});
```

Checks if the current device has a screen

No screen reference

A response that references the screen

The suggestion chips and list

In this code, the conditional statement checks if the current device (the *surface*) has a screen output. If it does, the response will include a list and a different spoken output than if it doesn't.

Beyond conditional responses in the fulfillment, Dialogflow can map intents based on actions or spoken phrases. It can also take into account *input contexts*, which are strings that an application sends to help the intent routing.

Assistant and Dialogflow can work together to use surface capabilities for intent mapping. If you add `actions_capability_audio_output`, `actions_capability_screen _output`, `actions_capability_media_response_audio`, or `actions_capability _web_browser` to the Contexts section of the intent configuration in Dialogflow, only the requests with the specified surface capability will be eligible for mapping to that intent. You can use this when you don't want to reach an intent on certain devices. Of course, you will generally serve your users better if you provide conditional responses to let them know *why* they can't get the full experience, or ask them to move to another device that can support the response.

## 10.4   Multisurface conversations

People often describe their enchantment with voice applications as arising from the sci-fi nature of speaking to a computer naturally. Me, I was never really into sci-fi, and speaking to a computer naturally was just a major quality-of-life improvement that portended what could reasonably happen with new technology. But still, the ability to speak to a computer, which can then hand off the conversation to another device, *does* feel pretty sci-fi to me. Because people use the same Google account across multiple devices, Assistant has just that power.

Handing off a conversation from one surface to another (read: from one device to another) is known as a *multisurface conversation*. It requires the developer to check whether the user has the surface or surface capability (such as a web browser) on any device, and then request permission to move the conversation.

**Listing 10.8   Requesting a surface handoff (index.js)**

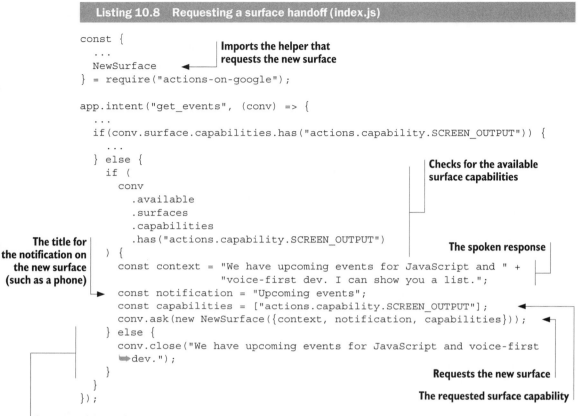

```
const {
   ...
   NewSurface          ◄──┐  Imports the helper that
} = require("actions-on-google");    requests the new surface

app.intent("get_events", (conv) => {
   ...
   if(conv.surface.capabilities.has("actions.capability.SCREEN_OUTPUT")) {
      ...
   } else {
      if (
         conv
            .available
            .surfaces
            .capabilities
            .has("actions.capability.SCREEN_OUTPUT")
      ) {
         const context = "We have upcoming events for JavaScript and " +
                         "voice-first dev. I can show you a list.";
         const notification = "Upcoming events";
         const capabilities = ["actions.capability.SCREEN_OUTPUT"];
         conv.ask(new NewSurface({context, notification, capabilities}));
      } else {
         conv.close("We have upcoming events for JavaScript and voice-first
         ➥dev.");
      }
   }
});
```

Checks for the available surface capabilities

The title for the notification on the new surface (such as a phone)

The spoken response

Requests the new surface

The requested surface capability

Response if the surface capability isn't available

In this code, if the current surface doesn't have a screen, we'll check to see if the *user* has a device with a screen. If they don't, we'll respond with just a spoken request. If they do, we'll ask the user if we can hand the conversation off to the device.

You can understand why Google would want us to ask the user for permission. This request adds an extra permission request, but it prevents the developer from treating the surface handoff like a backdoor notification system, always pushing the handoff, even when it's unnecessary. (This does require the user to have close access to the phone. This includes you when you're testing this code.)

The code also needs to handle the user's response to that request.

**Listing 10.9   Handling the user's response to the handoff request (index.js)**

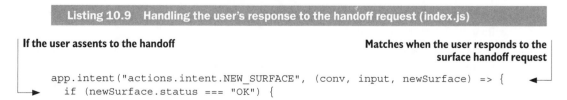

If the user assents to the handoff

Matches when the user responds to the surface handoff request

```
app.intent("actions.intent.NEW_SURFACE", (conv, input, newSurface) => {
   if (newSurface.status === "OK") {
```

```
const list = new List({
  title: "Upcoming Events",
  items: upcomingEvents
});

conv.close(new Suggestions("Get to the meeting room"));
conv.close(new LinkOutSuggestion({
  name: "View All",
  url:  "https://www.example.com/upcoming-events"
}));
conv.close(list);
conv.close("Alright, here's your list of upcoming events. " +
           "You can choose one on the screen to hear more.");
} else {
conv.close("All good. Let me know if you want to see a list or hear
more.");
}
});
```

**The response on the new surface**

**If the user rejects the handoff**

This handler responds to the user's response to the handoff request, both in the affirmative and the negative. If the user has declined the request, Assistant makes a simple spoken acknowledgment. If the user has responded favorably, Assistant displays a list. This is the same list we would show if the user uses a display from the beginning, so we could probably pull that away into some shared code. The spoken response, however, is not the same, because this is no longer a response directly to the request for events, but rather one for a list displayed on a screen, and the response needs to be relevant to *that* request.

As before, with Dialogflow sitting between the request and the fulfillment, the action needs the intent registered in Dialogflow with the actions_intent_NEW_SURFACE event. If it isn't, Dialogflow will send the request to the fallback intent.

Assistant doesn't expect (or allow) the developer to handle the request entirely. Depending on the locale, you'll see Assistant step in with an addition to the spoken response like, "Is it okay if I send that to your phone?" Assistant then follows it with "OK, go ahead and check. And I'll talk to you there."

> **TIP** To fully test the handoff, you need two things. First, you need to test in the simulator or on a device in voice-only mode. You can switch the simulator between surfaces, and select the speaker to test voice-only. The second thing you need is a phone that's connected to the same Google account as the one on which you're building the action.

We've now continued the conversation on the new surface, meeting the user in the right place for that request. Sometimes, though, we need to meet the user not at the right place, but at the *right time*. That may happen even before the user speaks to Assistant. We'll see in the next chapter how a voice application can be proactive instead.

## *Summary*

- Multimodal applications combine voice with other inputs and outputs, like a display.
- A response on a display is generally more in-depth than a spoken response.
- A spoken response and a visual response will have overlap, but the spoken response will be tailored to listening.
- Assistant has the capability to hand off a conversation between surfaces.

# Push interactions

## *11*

We've looked at interaction models where the user kicks off the discussion and Assistant reacts accordingly. The assumption is always that the user is the one who should start a conversation. The slowness of the major voice platforms to add push interactions is understandable. People have needed to trust that voice first wouldn't go the way of mobile, with an overwhelming proliferation of notifications calling out for the user's attention. Indeed, it's easy to see the link between the growth of voice and the population's growing enmity toward attention-seeking mobile phones.

Let's return to our central idea that voice needs to help users efficiently accomplish a given action. A requirement that users must *always* be the party that initiates the interaction contravenes this goal. There are certainly situations where the

187

computer can more efficiently achieve something without waiting for the user. A notification that a favorite team's game is about to start can help a baseball fan watch a game without having to ask repeatedly. Updating of the number of training miles for the day can help a backpacker train for an upcoming hike. In each of these situations, the computer is taking the mental load from the user, freeing that person from having to remember an interaction with the device.

Assistant provides a handful of ways to proactively interact with users. With *routine suggestions*, developers can suggest that users add an action to a routine they are already using with Assistant, like waking up or leaving the house. (This would have been useful in the sleep-tracking skill we built chapters back.) *Daily updates* will do just what it sounds, which is send users a notification every day at a set time. *Notifications*, meanwhile, happen whenever there's relevant information to send the user.

**NOTE**   Alexa also supports push interactions, through what it calls *proactive events.*

## 11.1   *Routine suggestions*

Assistant has a user-facing feature called *routines*. Users set this up to perform specific actions when they say a specific trigger to Assistant. Indeed, as shown in figure 11.1, these actions can span multiple applications. A user can say a phrase such as "Okay Google, good morning," and Assistant will perform the actions that the user has specified within the Assistant app ahead of time. Perhaps the user wants Assistant to turn on the lights, say the weather, give a voice UI tip, and then play music.

The developer doesn't need to know what is happening within the routine. The developer just needs to provide an action that Assistant can trigger on its own. This means that the action needs to be what's called a "one-shot" intent, or an intent that doesn't need any extra information or interaction from the user.

If we take a look at the Actions on Google application we've been building so far, we can use the one-shot intent about which rooms are in the office. We can think of it as a "getting to know the office" routine. Rooms won't change often, and we wouldn't want to repeat them every day or the user would get bored. Let's cycle through the rooms.

If we go with that approach, we'll need to advance to the next room each time the routine runs. We'll start out with the first room before moving to the second, then on to the third, and beyond. You might be seeing a new requirement here. We will need to keep track of which room the user last heard about. We'll need to store information about the user.

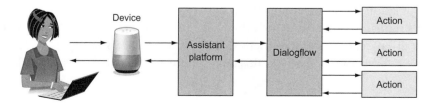

**Figure 11.1   A routine invokes multiple actions in multiple applications.**

### 11.1.1 Storing user data

There are three types of user data based on its lifetime:

- *Request data*—Information relevant to the current request
- *Conversation data*—Information relevant to the current conversation
- *Long-term storage*—Information relevant to the overall lifetime of a user's repeated interaction with the application, also known as *user storage*

As shown in figure 11.2, these different blocks of data can overlap with each other, as there can be many requests within a single conversation and many conversations within the lifetime of the user.

We keep track of the information for the current request through the local variables we've already been working with. Because it's only for the request, the information is sent back to the user through the Assistant as soon as that request is answered, and the information can be discarded.

The current conversation data, meanwhile, needs to potentially persist through a series of back-and-forth requests. An example of this information could be which question a user is answering in a trivia game. You saw another example in chapter 8, where the application provided progressive assistance, with the help becoming more explicit the more often the user hit a dead end.

This information is tracked in the flow of information back and forth between the Assistant platform and the fulfillment, with the request and response objects as couriers.

What happens is that, at the beginning of the conversation, the platform initializes a *conversation token* that will represent all of the data the developer wants to remember related to the user and sets it to an empty string. It includes the token along with the user's request. The fulfillment then adds its own data to the string, deserializing the string at the beginning of the request, and stringifying the data object again. The fulfillment then sends the string back to the platform as part of the response. The platform doesn't change it at all, but includes it in the next part of the conversation.

If you use the Assistant client library, you don't need to worry about deserializing or stringifying the data. Instead, the library adds a helper, as it usually does, on the conversation object.

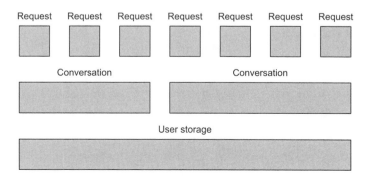

**Figure 11.2   Data has three different lifespans depending on its purpose: request, conversation, and long-term.**

**Listing 11.1   Storing data for the current conversation**

```
app.intent("user_assistance", conv => {
  conv.data.timesSeen = conv.data.timesSeen ? conv.data.timesSeen + 1 : 1;
  ...

  conv.close(response);
});
```

Increments or initializes the "times seen" tracker

By the time the fulfillment arrives at the intent handler, it has already deserialized the conversation token and made it available on `conv.data`. From there, we can store how many times the user has seen the `user_assistance` intent, and use it to tailor our responses.

> **TIP** You would probably want to use a less generic descriptor than `timesSeen`, because the conversation token is for the entire conversation. If you wanted to keep track of how often the user has seen multiple intents, you don't want to have collisions with each incrementing the same `timesSeen` variable. (Unless, of course, you're trying to keep track of how many turns the conversation has taken.)

In previous chapters, you've seen that requests go through Dialogflow when passing between the Assistant platform and the fulfillment. You might wonder how the conversation token impacts this flow.

Dialogflow has a functionality called *contexts*. Their primary use is to trigger specific intents based on information about the user or the interaction. For example, Dialogflow could have different intents for a new user versus an existing one, and Dialogflow could decide which to choose by looking at the user's request ("What can I do?") with the context from the fulfillment (such as a context of `existing_user`). The Node.js client library uses `conv.contexts.set` and `conv.contexts.get` to set and retrieve the current contexts. You can see this in figure 11.3.

These contexts will have a default lifespan of either 5 turns or 20 minutes, or whatever the fulfillment sets to override the default. They can also store parameters that include information. You may see where this is going.

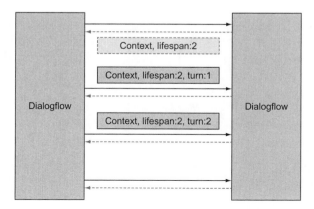

Figure 11.3   Dialogflow passes context between its platform and the fulfillment.

The client library sends the conversation data as a context parameter with a lifespan of 99 each time the conversation passes through Dialogflow. With this "trick," Dialogflow becomes a waypoint for the conversation data as it moves between the platform and the fulfillment, much as the reception desk of an office is a waypoint for lunch between the delivery person and the hungry software developer. Because the lifespan resets to 99 each time, conversation data will continue to be available to the fulfillment for as long as the conversation continues.

The conversation data (`conv.data`) is not a good fit for information that the fulfillment needs in the long term, because it's passed between the fulfillment and the platform and is lost when the conversation ends. There's a different way to store data across conversations.

**LONG-TERM DATA STORAGE**

Unlike what you saw with Alexa, the Assistant platform has a built-in way to store data across conversations without you needing to set up a data store and handle permissions. The platform has user storage available, as long as the data stays below 10 KB.

User storage is useful for tracking information across conversations, such as how often a user has used the application or user preferences. Or, for our application, which items a user last viewed.

If we are going to have `office_locations` as a one-shot intent, we also need to make sure that a user *can* invoke the intent without providing a room. Right now the only training phrases we've provided include space for a parameter (such as "How do you get to the *kitchen* from"), so we'll only match the intent if the user includes one. You'd also want to add training phrases that are more general and don't include a parameter, such as "What are the rooms in the office?" Otherwise, you'd have an unreachable feature in the code.

We can then use the user storage and memory about the rooms a user has encountered to make sure we provide information about all of the rooms.

Listing 11.2 Tracking last-viewed location (index.js)

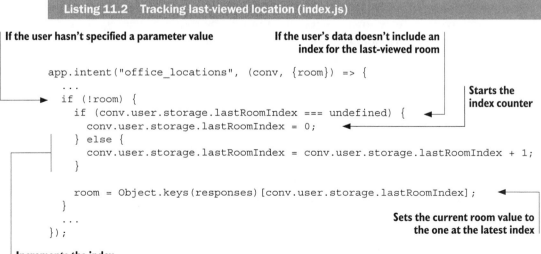

If the user hasn't specified a parameter value

If the user's data doesn't include an index for the last-viewed room

Starts the index counter

Sets the current room value to the one at the latest index

Increments the index

```
app.intent("office_locations", (conv, {room}) => {
  ...
  if (!room) {
    if (conv.user.storage.lastRoomIndex === undefined) {
      conv.user.storage.lastRoomIndex = 0;
    } else {
      conv.user.storage.lastRoomIndex = conv.user.storage.lastRoomIndex + 1;
    }

    room = Object.keys(responses)[conv.user.storage.lastRoomIndex];
  }
  ...
});
```

We're looking here to see whether the user has provided a value to the room parameter or invoked the intent as a one-shot intent. If there's no parameter value, we want to choose a room on the user's behalf, cycling through them in order. We *could* shuffle them, but there are two potential problems with that. If we shuffle the rooms each time, we might possibly get the same room twice in a row. Not good. We could instead shuffle on the first go, and keep track of which rooms the user has heard, but with user storage capped at 10 KB, we'd eat up a lot of that space. Instead, we'll go more light-weight and cycle through them in order.

> **TIP**    We don't have the code in here, but we would also want logic inside the handler to start over at the beginning once the user has reached the final room.

Once the user can invoke this intent in a one-shot manner, so can Assistant on the user's behalf. It's ready to be a suggestion for a routine.

### 11.1.2  *Action suggestion for a routine*

Google provides two ways to suggest an action for a user to add to a routine. One way is simple, but hands the control to Assistant. The other way requires code, but hands the control to the developer.

The simpler, Assistant-controlled way takes place in the Actions Console (https://console.actions.google.com/). Inside a specific project (such as Office Guide), and within the actions section (Build, and then Actions), you'll see a list of actions that Google knows about. The list is probably incomplete so far, because we've been using Dialogflow and, as you've seen, Dialogflow is handling the intent trafficking. For Assistant to know about intents to suggest that the user add them to a routine, Dialogflow needs to first reveal them to Assistant. You can connect the two through the Integrations section of Dialogflow, and then the Integration Settings for Assistant.

From this pop-up, you could specify which intents users to reveal to Assistant. You *could* add all of your intents, but choose the ones that are most relevant to people who want to invoke the application as a routine or a notification, or—as we'll see later—who might ask Assistant a general question and be routed to your application instead. (Of course, you're not choosing any follow-up intents or option or surface selection, either.)

In our application, we have multiple actions that would be routine-worthy. From the perspective of information that's useful to hear every day, the best intent would be get_events, because that could have new information every day. To explore this feature, though, we'll work with the office_locations intent. It's not currently as complex as get_events and it will let us focus on routines. Let's imagine that our users are dying to hear about all of the rooms in the office.

To set this all up, you need to select the office_locations intent within the actions pop-up, and Dialogflow then shares it with Google Assistant. From there, you would go back into the Assistant console for the application, go to the Actions section, and see the shared intents. Clicking on one will provide the Would You Like to Let Users Add This Action to Google Assistant Routines? option. Select it and add a description (for example, "Office Guide"), and Assistant will suggest to users that they add the intent to their routines.

That's simple. With the action added to the user's routine, every time they trigger the routine, the action will trigger too. A user may want to run many actions every day on request. For actions that run daily without a request, there are daily updates.

## 11.2 Daily updates

Daily updates are ideal if a user wants a reminder each day, or if there is fresh information to share. A silly, but spot-on, example is cat facts. A user will never reach the end of new cat-related facts, and for cat fans, a new fact each day will be a welcome daily moment. Another daily update could aggregate the day's news, or report on the closing price of a stock. More personally, a daily update could report on how many steps the person walked the previous day, and offer encouragement for the day to come.

> ### Phone-based testing
>
> Unlike routines, which users can invoke on any device, users can only receive daily updates on Android phones. If you don't have an Android phone, feel free to continue with this section, but you won't be able to test daily updates. This also means that if you want to test out whether the update flow works, you won't be able to do it in the Simulator. You would need to get your device and try it there.
>
> You have two options when you need to move to on-device testing. You can develop ahead of time a set phrase, or a set number of phrases, to trigger whatever action you want. Maybe you have it written down in front of you, and you go full-throttle into testing. Or you can go as you may and say phrases as you think of them. The first approach will be much more efficient. With the second, you will be more likely to spot Assistant misunderstanding what you're saying, or discover a gap in your training phrases list that you should fill. Because if you're using phrases that suddenly come to you, surely the users will too.
>
> There's space for each approach, but you probably know which one I'd suggest most of the time. Put in the extra work, do not work off a script, and take the load off the users.

As with actions, developers can hand off control of opting in to the Assistant platform. The steps are the same as for actions (inside the Actions console, go to Build, then Actions, and choose the intent), except at the end, when you need to select Would You Like to Offer Daily Updates to Users? from the User Engagement section of the intent.

As with routine suggestions, however, the developer can decide to handle the opting in to daily updates instead.

### 11.2.1 Developer control of daily updates

Developers can control the user opt-in process for adding an action as a daily update. This offers the developer all of the control, and it's useful if you feel that Assistant is too eager or too reticent to make a suggestion on your behalf (or, if you're simply a person who likes to know exactly what's happening when). Let's consider how we might build the logic, focusing again on `office_locations` to more easily see what we're adding.

> **NOTE** You still need to specify in the Actions console that daily updates are available for the individual actions, like you did when you let Assistant handle the opt-in.

Has the user already added the `office_locations` intent as an update? If so, we don't want to suggest it to them *again*. Of the users who haven't already added the suggestion, we have the question of how often we should show the suggestion.

**Listing 11.3  Providing a daily update suggestion (index.js)**

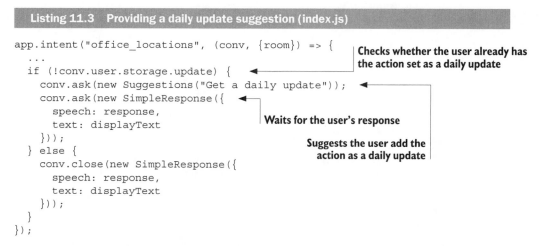

```
app.intent("office_locations", (conv, {room}) => {
  ...
  if (!conv.user.storage.update) {
    conv.ask(new Suggestions("Get a daily update"));
    conv.ask(new SimpleResponse({
      speech: response,
      text: displayText
    }));
  } else {
    conv.close(new SimpleResponse({
      speech: response,
      text: displayText
    }));
  }
});
```

Checks whether the user already has the action set as a daily update

Waits for the user's response

Suggests the user add the action as a daily update

Here we display a suggestion chip that gives the user a way to add the action as a daily update. This doesn't yet add the daily update—it merely provides the first step in the process. We don't want to nag (how annoying is that in human-to-human conversations?), so we only show the chip to users who haven't already accepted the suggestion.

> **NOTE** We didn't build that frequency logic into this example—we'll show the tip every time until the user adds the update—but it's something you'd want to consider, especially because the suggestion chip takes up a lot of space on the display.

More accurately, we limit the suggestion to users for whom we have not *recorded* acceptance of the suggestion. This is a slight difference, but it's important. For example, it shows that we need to store that information ourselves, and we will once users express a desire to add the daily update by tapping the suggestion chip. (The user can also say "Get a daily update" aloud to start the registration process.)

> **TIP** If you plan on publishing this action, you should either suggest a daily update only if the current surface is a screen or end the spoken response for the nonsubscriber with a call to action to request daily updates. The current flow leaves the microphone open to listen for a response, and Google rejects actions that do that without there being a clear expectation of a user response.

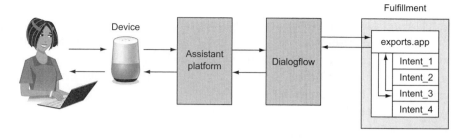

**Figure 11.4  Data flows between user and fulfillment, with several steps in between.**

As you've seen several times before and you can see again in figure 11.4, the request and response loop goes from user to fulfillment and back, passing through the Assistant platform and Dialogflow on its way. And like before, we'll need to add an intent to Dialogflow if we want the request to end up at the fulfillment properly. The question is how to specify that the intent is for the daily update suggestion.

Assistant sends the suggestion chip text as the utterance to Dialogflow, so we can add that to the training phrases for the intent (which we could call `daily_registration`). Then we can let the webhook handle the fulfillment.

If you've read the previous chapters, you know at least part of the next step. We need to handle the intent we just added to Dialogflow, because it's going to end up at the fulfillment.

**Listing 11.4  Handing the update registration flow back to Assistant (index.js)**

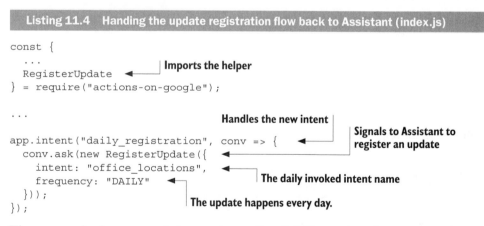

The new code does some deft turnabout. Our fulfillment has the opportunity to perform any necessary business logic, but it ultimately hands control back to Assistant to register the daily update. All we've got to do is tell Assistant that that's what we want, and for which intent and how often. In this example we only ever register a daily update for the `office_locations` action, but we could have multiple choices. A flow to do this would store the most recent intent in the user data (`conv.data`) and pass that along with the registration.

> **NOTE** You can also request that Assistant invoke an action with parameter values. The only requirement is you need to specify the parameter value at registration time, and that will always be the parameter value.

With this configuration, we tell Assistant to register the update, which includes asking the user what time each day the update should arrive.

But how does Assistant know what to bring back to the fulfillment? That magic is hidden away in the `RegisterUpdate` helper, so we could get by without really thinking about what's happening. Still, I feel that if we understand what the entire flow is doing, we'll build better voice applications.

What we need to know is that there are two types of intent behaviors. As developers we can either fulfill an intent that Assistant sends to our code, or we can request that Assistant fulfill an intent. The `RegisterUpdate` helper does just that—asks Assistant to handle the fulfillment of registering an update, instead of requiring the developer to take in the time of day and pass that back to the Assistant platform.

You can see the flow in figure 11.5. After Assistant registers the update, it will pass control back to the fulfillment, matching to an intent in Dialogflow through the `actions_intent_REGISTER_UPDATE` event. (Meaning, add `actions_intent_REGISTER_UPDATE` as the event name when you create the intent in Dialogflow.)

The fulfillment is then responsible for letting the user know whether the registration succeeded or failed.

> **Listing 11.5   Responding after Assistant handles the daily update registration (index.js)**

**The intent name from Dialogflow**

```
app.intent("daily_registration_completion", (conv, params, registered) => {
  if (registered && registered.status === "OK") {
    conv.user.storage.update = true;
    conv.close("Ok, starting tomorrow you'll get daily updates.");
  } else {
    conv.close("Alright, I won't be sending you updates each day after all.");
  }
});
```

**If the user completed the daily update registration, note and respond.**

**Otherwise, still respond.**

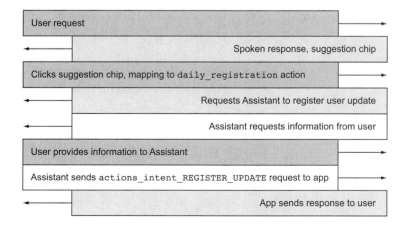

Figure 11.5   We provide control to Assistant for part of the daily update registration flow.

Once the Assistant platform completes the daily update registration flow, it hands control back to the fulfillment. This process is understandable. There's little need for the developer to handle the actual registration when it's a standard procedure, but what happens next can be different from app to app. Perhaps users pick up where they left off, or maybe there's nothing more to do.

In our example, we will track that the user has registered a daily update and close off the conversation.

> **NOTE** Developers also have manual control over routine suggestions. The frequency is simply ROUTINES rather than DAILY.

> **TIP** If you want to know whether the invocation for an intent came from a routine or a daily update, you can create separate intents for these two purposes. Your intents would perform the same actions but log out the detail that they're not invoked in the usual way—the only difference would be internal, like two turnstiles leading to the same stadium. Because these specially logging intents are not the same as the directly invoked intents, this would be a situation where you could not leave the opt-in to Assistant. Assistant only suggests the intents that a user invokes directly.[1]

There is some information that the user can't wait a day to find out. Some information is timely. Some information calls for push notifications.

## 11.3 Push notifications

Developers can use push notifications to send information to their users as it becomes available, or at a scheduled frequency that doesn't fit in with daily updates. This isn't a free-for-all. Developers are limited to 1 notification a minute or 10 per day at most, and users still need to opt in to push notifications. Plus, notifications aren't available on speaker devices. Still, push notifications are a useful way to continue the conversation, with Assistant taking the proactive role.

> **NOTE** The Alexa platform has a different way of handling push notifications. It doesn't have the deep integration into phones that Assistant does, especially on Android, but it does allow developers to send notifications directly to standalone devices.

We need to expand our view of the information flow for notifications. Figure 11.6 shows that Assistant will register the user for notifications, and figure 11.7 shows that the notifications themselves will come from another script that we will need to create.

---

[1] Credit for this idea goes to Allen Firstenberg, an active Actions on Google Developer, who sums it up pithily with "Intents represent what the user does, not what your action does."

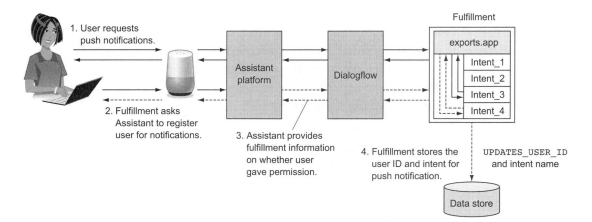

Figure 11.6   **The notification registration flow requires handoff to Assistant.**

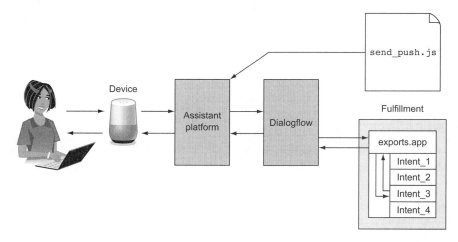

Figure 11.7   **A script kicks off the flow by sending a push notification, and a user triggers an action when interacting with the notification.**

The user continues to have a conversation with the fulfillment and the Assistant platform to opt in to notifications. However, there is another actor that comes in to start the conversation. Once the user notices and interacts with the notification, Assistant triggers the intent that the fulfillment registered back when the user opted in.

The steps for setting up the opt-in are the same for notifications as they are for daily updates, so I won't repeat them here. Instead we'll move straight on to the fulfillment, which is similar to the fulfillment for daily updates but with a couple of differences.

**TIP**   If you see that the request is making its way to the fulfillment, but you still receive "My test app isn't responding right now. Try again soon." from Assistant, confirm that you specified in the console that the office_locations action will send push notifications. If you rush to do that now and discover the action still doesn't work, get up, get a snack, and then come back. This change will take a little bit longer to propagate than you'll think it should.

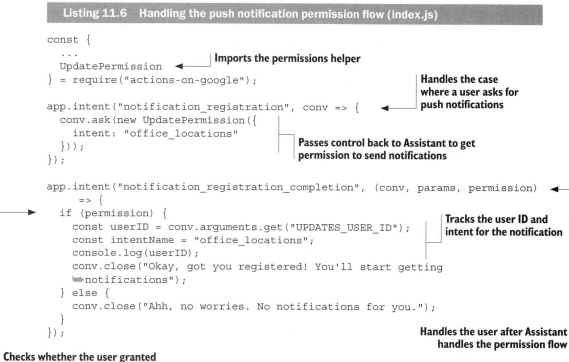

**Listing 11.6  Handling the push notification permission flow (index.js)**

```
const {
  ...
  UpdatePermission          ◄──────┤ Imports the permissions helper
} = require("actions-on-google");
                                              Handles the case
                                              where a user asks for
app.intent("notification_registration", conv => {   ◄──┘ push notifications
  conv.ask(new UpdatePermission({
    intent: "office_locations"
  }));                              Passes control back to Assistant to get
});                                 permission to send notifications


app.intent("notification_registration_completion", (conv, params, permission)   ◄──┐
    => {
  if (permission) {                               Tracks the user ID and
    const userID = conv.arguments.get("UPDATES_USER_ID");   intent for the notification
    const intentName = "office_locations";
    console.log(userID);
    conv.close("Okay, got you registered! You'll start getting
    ➥notifications");
  } else {
    conv.close("Ahh, no worries. No notifications for you.");
  }                                              Handles the user after Assistant
});                                              handles the permission flow
```

**Checks whether the user granted
permission for notifications**

In the fulfillment, we're once again turning to the intent handlers. The first intent handler (for the notification_registration intent) will be for when the user asks for push notifications. This would map to training phrases such as "Send me the latest tips" or suggestion chips that say the same. The second intent handler (notification _registration_completion) comes about after our fulfillment has handed control to Assistant to get permission to send push notifications, and Assistant has sent control back, along with the Dialogflow event actions_intent_PERMISSION. At this second intent handler, the user has either affirmed or rejected push notifications, and Assistant lets us know which.

We need to remember that ultimately what Assistant does with push notifications is send a notification to the user's phone and then trigger an action when the user opens the notification. Assistant needs to know three things then: which intent, which user, and which application.

We don't have code for it here, but you'll need to store the user ID and the intent name somewhere that an external script can reach—it can't be within the user storage. In the preceding code, we're instead just logging out the user ID. If you're running a local tunnel, you can find the user ID logged to the terminal. Otherwise, you could see it from within the Firebase function logs. Either way, you would need it in order to send the notification.

The third piece of information that Assistant needs is which application is sending the notification. We've largely avoided tedious account setup when working with Assistant, but we need to take a couple of minutes to put things in order. The push notification needs to come from a script that runs on its own, and that script needs a level of authorization to communicate with the Assistant API. You'll need to follow these steps to make that happen:

1 Go to the Actions console and look for the project settings (likely behind a cog icon).

2 Note the project ID (likely `voice-tips`).

3 Visit the Actions API dashboard at https://console.developers.google.com/apis/api/actions.googleapis.com/overview?project=voice-tips (replacing "voice-tips" at the end if you have a different project ID), and click Enable if you see the option.

4 Visit the credentials page at https://console.developers.google.com/apis/credentials?project=voice-tips (again replacing the project if necessary).

5 Select Create Credentials and then Service Account Key.

6 Select New Service Account, give it a name of your choosing (such as "push-notifications"), and choose the Project Owner role before creating the credentials.

7 Download the JSON file and store it somewhere safe.

These steps create credentials that will allow you to communicate with the Google Assistant API from outside of the fulfillment. You can send push notifications from any script using those credentials: a script, like this script, that starts with authorization.

#### Listing 11.7  Authorizing with Google to send a notification (send_push.js)

```
const {google} = require("googleapis");
const request = require("request");
const util = require("util");                    The location of the credential
const key = require("<PATH TO CREDS FILE>");      file you downloaded

const endpoint = "https://www.googleapis.com/auth/actions.fulfillment.send
➥conversation";
const jwtClient = new google.auth.JWT(
  key.client_email, null, key.private_key, [endpoint], null
);

jwtClient.authorize()          Gets a one-off JSON web token
  .then(tokens => {
    console.log(tokens);                Initializes an authorization client
  })
  .catch(console.error);
```

You don't need to fully understand everything that's happening in this code. Just be aware that `googleapis` has tooling to authenticate and receive a JSON web token (JWT), which we need to use for subsequent requests when we actually send the push notifications to the Assistant platform in the next listing.

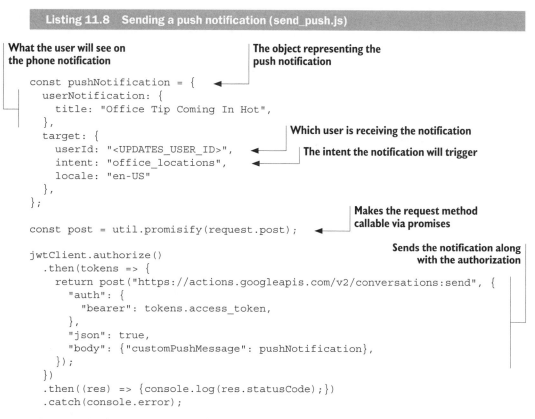

**Listing 11.8  Sending a push notification (send_push.js)**

```
const pushNotification = {
  userNotification: {
    title: "Office Tip Coming In Hot",
  },
  target: {
    userId: "<UPDATES_USER_ID>",
    intent: "office_locations",
    locale: "en-US"
  },
};

const post = util.promisify(request.post);

jwtClient.authorize()
  .then(tokens => {
    return post("https://actions.googleapis.com/v2/conversations:send", {
      "auth": {
        "bearer": tokens.access_token,
      },
      "json": true,
      "body": {"customPushMessage": pushNotification},
    });
  })
  .then((res) => {console.log(res.statusCode);})
  .catch(console.error);
```

This code is the final piece of the push notification flow. It's what starts the interaction anew and sends the push notification to the Assistant platform, which then sends it along to the user, who interacts with it and triggers the action.

The script needs to live somewhere that allows it to run on a regular basis. You can deploy it to AWS or Heroku or set an alarm clock on your phone that reminds you to walk to your computer to run the script. It doesn't matter, so long as you realize that you aren't deploying this with your application code.

> **NOTE**  It's not *necessary* to promisify the request library's post method. I did so to make the code more readable.

All of this behavior is purposeful. A user has to request push notifications and has to interact with them when they arrive. The user has to know the application ahead of time. Often, though, a user just wants information and doesn't care who sends it along. This is why Google introduced *implicit invocation*.

## 11.4  Implicit invocation

So far in this chapter we've talked about new ways for users to interact with your Assistant application that involve either Assistant proactively interacting with the user (daily updates and notifications), or the user interacting with Assistant. All these interactions require that the user knows about the application, has interacted with it previously, and explicitly opts in to future interactions. But there's another method of interaction where the user has Assistant invoke the application, but the user doesn't need to know about the application. Instead, the user only needs to have a specific goal in mind.

This is *implicit invocation*, where a developer tells Assistant about the actions inside their applications, and Assistant chooses the action from all applications that can best complete a request.

Think about the way that Assistant normally routes a request. All applications on the Assistant platform are unique, so when a user asks for "VUI Tips," only one application can complete that request. Assistant knows exactly where to route that request.

The goal for Google (and all the other voice-first platforms) is to reduce the friction involved in getting an answer. Years ago, if you typed "weather" into a browser's address bar, the browser wouldn't have known how to route that request, or would have tried to send the user to weather.com. Increasingly, though, browsers send such requests to a search engine, so users can choose the site they want to visit. The difference between the web and voice is that voice can't easily present a list of choices to the user.

With this limitation in mind, Google selects what it thinks is the best application and sends the user's request off directly. Assistant then signals that it has a possible application, and asks the user for permission to make the handoff. For example, "For that, you might like VUI Tips. Want to give it a try?"

Google doesn't reveal what goes into the algorithm for routing implicit invocations any more than it reveals the makeup of its core search engine. Nonetheless, we know that the similarity of the user's request to an action's training phrase has a positive impact. We can also imagine that user behavior, such as how often a user signals dissatisfaction with an application, would be seen as a negative signal.

> **NOTE** The Alexa platform has a similar feature for developers to use, called `canFulfillIntent`. This requires the fulfillment to let the platform know whether it can handle the user's request (or even if it "maybe" can) in real time before Alexa decides which skill gets the user's attention.

If you want to add an action for implicit invocation, you would need to, as you saw before, tell the Actions platform which intents are available within Dialogflow. You can set this up within the Integrations section of Dialogflow, further navigating to Google Assistant.

> **NOTE** Google mixes the terms a bit here, implying that "explicit invocation" is only for times when a user asks for the app by name and doesn't say anything else (for example, "Okay Google, talk to VUI Tips."), whereas "implicit invocation" represents everything else ("Okay Google, talk to VUI Tips about system entities."). Google's other documentation uses implicit invocation in the manner we've been talking about it, to represent requests without an invocation name, and that's the way we'll continue to use it.

The intents that you need for routine suggestions, notifications, or daily updates will be available for implicit invocation if you let Assistant handle the user opt-in for these features. But you can choose other intents, too, such as one-shot intents that don't need the user to have already used the application.

Further, the response in the intents should directly answer the question, and so should be closely tailored to what the user is requesting. Remember that the user will be coming into the app completely fresh and not have any background.

Users will be able to invoke the application without requesting it directly, leading to more app usage. When working with Assistant, most of my app usage has indeed come from implicit invocation.

In this chapter, we looked at ways that Assistant goes beyond the user-device conversation paradigm. In the next chapter, we'll shed something we've used since the beginning: the Dialogflow NLU. Instead, we'll build an application using the Actions SDK.

## Summary

- Routine suggestions are a way to have a user trigger an action alongside others, often at the same time each day.
- Notifications and daily updates communicate with users proactively, and trigger an action in a one-shot mechanism.
- Implicit invocation lets users invoke an action without specifying its invocation name.
- Google determines the action best equipped to serve a user's request based on a list of actions provided by developers.

# Building for actions on Google with the Actions SDK

## This chapter covers

- Differences between Dialogflow and Actions SDK actions

- The Actions SDK action package

- Analyzing text with regular expressions

- Using the Actions CLI

- Action deployment

Often in the book, we have examined the flow of information throughout the conversation. I've focused so much on this concept because I believe that by looking at this we can start to understand the system, understand what we can do, and understand where things might go wrong. In this chapter, we upend it—a bit.

## 12.1 Dialogflow and the Actions SDK

Let's look again at the information flow in the Actions on Google app we built in the previous chapters, shown in figure 12.1. And look at the flow of a representative Alexa skill, shown in figure 12.2.

In both flows, among everything else, there is an NLU service. It's very clear and discrete in the case of the Actions on Google app—the NLU is Dialogflow. The Alexa NLU is bundled up with everything else on the Alexa platform, but it's still there.

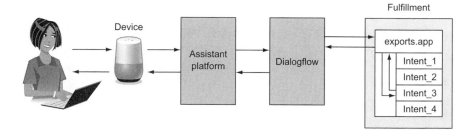

**Figure 12.1   Data flows between user and fulfillment, with several steps in between.**

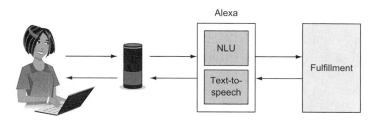

**Figure 12.2   Data flow in an Alexa skill**

That separateness on the part of the Actions on Google app opens up a question. Although there needs to be some level of NLU no matter what (no NLU, no conversational interface), can't the developer own that? That's what the Actions SDK provides, as you can see in figure 12.3.

Indeed, this is one of the confusing aspects for beginners when they build for Assistant. What's the difference between a Dialogflow app and an Actions SDK app? A Dialogflow app uses Dialogflow for the NLU, whereas Actions SDK comes with no NLU platform.

When we build with the Actions SDK, we'll have a few benefits beyond learning how it's done. We'll get a deeper appreciation for what Dialogflow does, once we take it away. On top of that, we will have the chance to do our own "natural language processing," which will give us a shallow insight into what an NLU platform might do.

We'll do something fun with this project and build an assistant inside the Assistant. Users will be able to speak to the app, asking it to connect them to other "apps" (which are, in fact, simple objects inside the fulfillment) that will then handle their commands. We'll call it "Exhibit Engine." Along the way, we'll look at how regular expressions might match inbound natural language to complete a task.

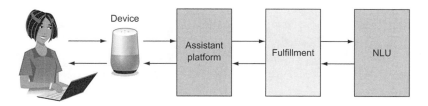

**Figure 12.3   Data flow in an Actions SDK app**

## 12.2   App planning

We've decided conceptually what the app will do, so now we can sketch out how the interaction might go with the user. This will inform the query patterns that trigger specific intents and the behavior of the fulfillment—especially which patterns to match and how to respond.

For an app that contains smaller apps, we can surmise that a user will invoke the app, specify the sub-app, and then say what to do with the sub-app. This might look like, "Hey Google, tell Exhibit Engine to…" followed by what the user wants to do. In this case, "Hey Google, tell" is the trigger, "Exhibit Engine" is the invocation name, and "to" is a bridge that indicates that an intent phrase is coming.

The simplest intent phrase a user can say is none at all: "Hey Google, talk to Exhibit Engine." The second simplest is a one-off phrase that doesn't contain any variable information. An example of this type of phrase is asking for help. The user might say "Help," "Give me assistance," or "Tell me what I can do," but variable information is unlikely. Finally come phrases that can have variable information. In chapter 2, these were phrases such as "I will sleep for six hours" where "six" was the slot value corresponding to a number of hours. You've seen all this in Alexa skills and in actions with Dialogflow.

With those applications, it was the NLU platform that processed the text and matched to an intent. You'll soon see that there's some basic matching of user utterance to intent, but the NLU responsibility primarily falls to the fulfillment. This works because Google provides the text representation of what the user said to the fulfillment.

> **NOTE**   Apps built on Dialogflow and the Actions SDK both receive what the user says, but that text of course isn't needed by the developer building an app on Dialogflow.

Getting back to how the user will interact with the app, we first need to handle the simple cases of launching the app or asking for help. These functions will be similar in our app, but there is nonetheless a small difference.

A user launching the app needs information about how to use the app, but the response is also there to welcome the user and set the ground for what comes next. The assistance is secondary to moving the user forward.

The help action's primary goal is giving help. Due to the nature of the app we're building, giving users the proper guidance will be key. One of the most important jobs for a voice application developer is guiding the user in just what's possible:

> *"Hey Google, talk to Exhibit Engine."*
>
> *"Hey there! With Exhibit Engine, you can talk to other apps. Just say 'engage' and then what you wanna do. Like… engage calculator to add one plus one."*
>
> *"Hey Google, ask Exhibit Engine for help."*
>
> *"Help is what I'm here for. Exhibit Engine has a couple apps. Calculator will calculate two numbers. Echo will repeat what you say. You can try it by saying something like, 'Engage echo to repeat well, that just beats all.'"*

Grice's maxim of quantity says that in a good conversation, the response should have just enough content to answer, but not more. The response to the request for help is long, but it doesn't provide extraneous information. It tells users what is possible and then turns back control.

How will users interact with the meat of the app? There needs to be a way to specify which sub-app the user wants, and what the user wants to do. An ideal method of doing this is the same as for all voice apps! A trigger gives way to an invocation, then a bridge, and finally an utterance. The only difference needs to be in the trigger. Using the same triggers as Assistant apps causes problems—there needs to be a way to differentiate between the Exhibit Engine trigger and the sub-app trigger. A good trigger that indicates action but isn't already ruled out is "engage." As a nice bonus, it also gives a mid-twentieth-century sci-fi feel:

> *"Hey Google, ask Exhibit Engine to engage calculator to add 1 + 1."*

> *"Hey Google, ask Exhibit Engine to engage Echo for repeating hello world."*

Going through this exercise, we can see that users will use different bridge words. "To," "and," "for," and "with" are all words that could tie the sub-app's invocation and utterance together. We'll use the trigger and the bridge as waypoints that indicate the location of the invocation name and the intent.

Despite most of the NLU happening within the fulfillment, we still need to let Assistant know how users might interact with the actions. We can do this through the action package.

## 12.3 The action package

Building a Google Assistant app with the Actions SDK necessitates using both the online Actions on Google Developer Console *and* a local command-line tool. The developer console is where you start and finish, creating the project and then submitting it to Google for publishing. The command-line tool is where the code deployment happens.

To get everything set up, go into the Developer Console (https://console.actions .google.com/), select the option to add a project, and name it "Exhibit Engine." You can then skip the next screen and move to the Google Actions (gactions) CLI tool.

The gactions CLI is an executable that you must download directly from Google (https://developers.google.com/actions/tools/gactions-cli). Download the executable in any directory you desire, so long as you won't accidentally delete it down the line. (For that reason, the downloads directory is probably not the best choice.)

> **WARNING** Mac and Linux users will need to make the file executable by running `chmod +x gactions` from the directory where gactions lives. You can also update your PATH to include gactions and avoid referencing the entire file path each time you want to use the CLI tool. In the following examples, I will simply use `gactions`. You will either need to replace that with the location of your gactions executable or have it included in your PATH.

You can use the CLI to initialize the project:

```
$ mkdir exhibit-engine
$ cd exhibit-engine              References the location where you have
$ gactions init    ◄──────       the gactions executable
Action package file successfully created at action.json
```

The gactions CLI will create an action.json file with the `init` command. This file contains the configuration of the app, with the different actions and how to tie those actions to a fulfillment. It contains some sample values that you'll want to immediately replace with the values in the following listing.

**Listing 12.1   Defining actions in the action package (./action.json)**

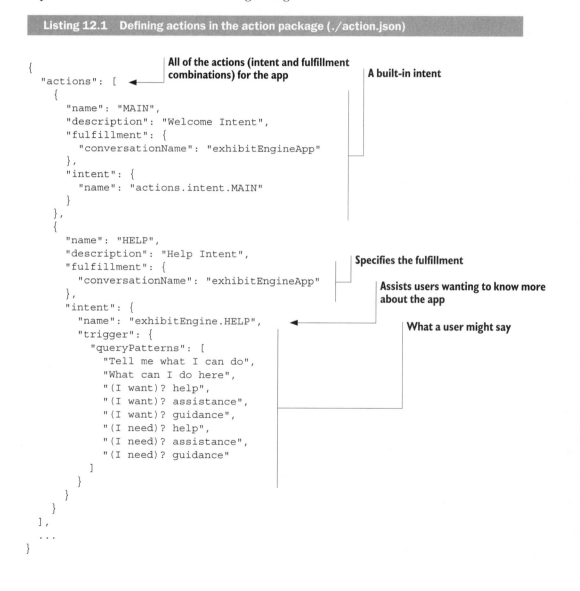

```
{                              All of the actions (intent and fulfillment
  "actions": [  ◄──────        combinations) for the app                    A built-in intent
    {
      "name": "MAIN",
      "description": "Welcome Intent",
      "fulfillment": {
        "conversationName": "exhibitEngineApp"
      },
      "intent": {
        "name": "actions.intent.MAIN"
      }
    },
    {
      "name": "HELP",
      "description": "Help Intent",
      "fulfillment": {                                  Specifies the fulfillment
        "conversationName": "exhibitEngineApp"
      },                                                Assists users wanting to know more
      "intent": {                                       about the app
        "name": "exhibitEngine.HELP",
        "trigger": {                                    What a user might say
          "queryPatterns": [
            "Tell me what I can do",
            "What can I do here",
            "(I want)? help",
            "(I want)? assistance",
            "(I want)? guidance",
            "(I need)? help",
            "(I need)? assistance",
            "(I need)? guidance"
          ]
        }
      }
    }
  ],
  ...
}
```

The action package outlines the intents that users can trigger and the metadata associated with each, coming together to create actions. (Remember, actions equal intents plus fulfillment.) Our action package has two intents, one built-in and one custom.

The built-in intent is the MAIN intent, which users trigger by asking for the application without specifying an intent. For example, "Hey Google, talk to Exhibit Engine" would trigger this intent.

We've also got the custom intent we created for when users want help. Because it's a custom intent, we need to tell Assistant how users will trigger it through the sample phrases they might say. They're not exactly sample phrases but *query patterns*. This terminology is enlightening. You can see not only the phrases and words that we are expecting from users, but also mark some as optional with the (phrase)? formulation.

---

**Query pattern arguments**

All of the query patterns in listing 12.1 are strings, but the action package also supports arguments, similar to Alexa's slots. An argument can either be a built-in type, which maps closely with Schema.org types, or a custom type:

- "My answer is $SchemaOrg_YesNo:answer"
- "Turn the lights color $SchemaOrg_Color:color"
- "Reserve the $RoomNames:room room"

In these three examples, the arguments would come through as answer, color, and room, respectively.

---

Finally, we specify for each action how the request will be fulfilled. We point to a fulfillment in the actions section, and provide the details further on in the action package as conversations.

**Listing 12.2    Defining the locale and fulfillment (./action.json)**

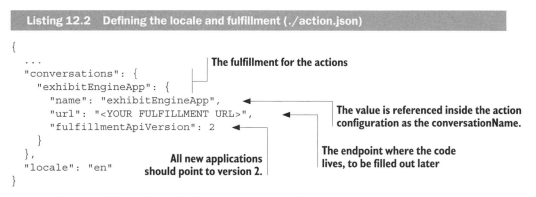

```
{
  ...
  "conversations": {                          The fulfillment for the actions
    "exhibitEngineApp": {
      "name": "exhibitEngineApp",             ◄
      "url": "<YOUR FULFILLMENT URL>",        ◄    The value is referenced inside the action
      "fulfillmentApiVersion": 2   ◄               configuration as the conversationName.
    }
  },                              All new applications      The endpoint where the code
  "locale": "en"                should point to version 2.  lives, to be filled out later
}
```

Here we're specifying where Assistant should send the request for fulfillment, and different intents can point to different endpoints. We're not doing that here, and such a configuration will likely be rare in practice, but it's possible. We connect the fulfillment to the intents through the conversation names.

You know from everything you've seen so far that the configuration is just one part of the overall application. There's also the business logic for the responses. That's the fulfillment.

## 12.4 The fulfillment

The fulfillment still contains a placeholder. Just as with the application we built with Dialogflow, we can host the fulfillment anywhere. But again, the close integration of Firebase makes for easier deployment.

> **NOTE** If you haven't already installed the Firebase CLI, do it now. It's a Node package (firebase-tools) that you install globally. Follow that up by running firebase login to log in to your Firebase (Google) account.

We need to initialize the Firebase project, which will hold the fulfillment code:

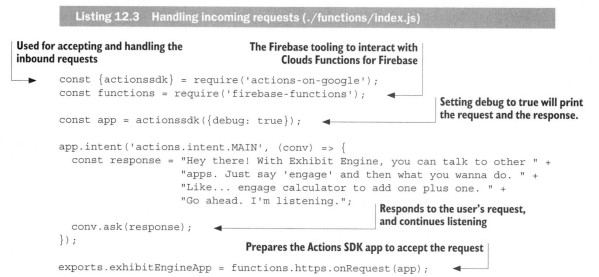

```
$ firebase init              ◄─────── Initializes the project        Adds the Actions on Google package
$ npm install actions-on-google --save --prefix functions/   ◄──────
```

> **TIP** When you run firebase init, select Functions as the only Firebase feature you want to use and Exhibit Engine as the Firebase project to associate with the directory. Choose JavaScript in order to follow along exactly, and choose linting as you wish before installing the dependencies.

Among other files, Firebase CLI will create a Functions directory with an index.js file that contains all of the fulfillment. Inside that file will be the code that handles inbound requests coming from Assistant.

> **Listing 12.3   Handling incoming requests (./functions/index.js)**

Used for accepting and handling the inbound requests

The Firebase tooling to interact with Clouds Functions for Firebase

```
const {actionssdk} = require('actions-on-google');
const functions = require('firebase-functions');   ◄──────

const app = actionssdk({debug: true});   ◄──────

app.intent('actions.intent.MAIN', (conv) => {
  const response = "Hey there! With Exhibit Engine, you can talk to other " +
                   "apps. Just say 'engage' and then what you wanna do. " +
                   "Like... engage calculator to add one plus one. " +
                   "Go ahead. I'm listening.";
  conv.ask(response);   ◄──────
});

exports.exhibitEngineApp = functions.https.onRequest(app);   ◄──────
```

Setting debug to true will print the request and the response.

Responds to the user's request, and continues listening

Prepares the Actions SDK app to accept the request

The preceding code prepares for any incoming request by specifying which intents the fulfillment will handle. Whenever a request comes in, the Actions SDK will go through the declared handlers, looking for one connected to the inbound request.

The handler will assemble the response—JSON to be sent back to the Assistant—while also specifying whether the Assistant should close the conversation (`conv.close`) or continue listening (`conv.ask`). The current functionality can't handle every possible request that a user might ask, like a real assistant such as the Google Assistant would, but it's a start.

> **NOTE** Come up with a handler for the custom help intent. How might we respond to users asking for help?

The code is now ready to deploy to Firebase.

**Listing 12.4   Deploying the fulfillment**

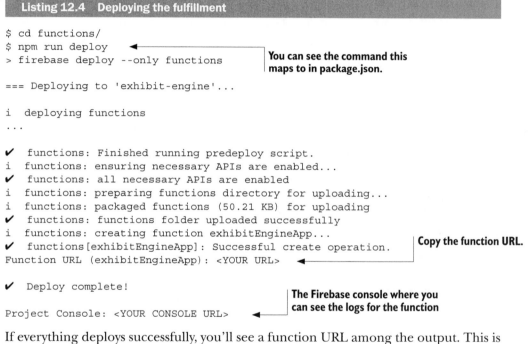

```
$ cd functions/
$ npm run deploy        ◄──────────────  You can see the command this
> firebase deploy --only functions       maps to in package.json.

=== Deploying to 'exhibit-engine'...

i  deploying functions
...

✔  functions: Finished running predeploy script.
i  functions: ensuring necessary APIs are enabled...
✔  functions: all necessary APIs are enabled
i  functions: preparing functions directory for uploading...
i  functions: packaged functions (50.21 KB) for uploading
✔  functions: functions folder uploaded successfully
i  functions: creating function exhibitEngineApp...
✔  functions[exhibitEngineApp]: Successful create operation.   Copy the function URL.
Function URL (exhibitEngineApp): <YOUR URL>   ◄────────

✔  Deploy complete!
                                           The Firebase console where you
                                           can see the logs for the function
Project Console: <YOUR CONSOLE URL>   ◄────
```

If everything deploys successfully, you'll see a function URL among the output. This is the URL that the Actions SDK will hit every time a user requests the app. You should add it to the action package, among the "conversations."

**Listing 12.5   Pointing to the deployed fulfillment (./action.json)**

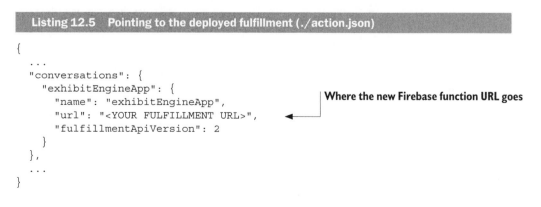

```
{
  ...
  "conversations": {
    "exhibitEngineApp": {
      "name": "exhibitEngineApp",
      "url": "<YOUR FULFILLMENT URL>",      Where the new Firebase function URL goes
      "fulfillmentApiVersion": 2   ◄────────
    }
  },
  ...
}
```

Next up is deploying the action package to Google. Google will train the Assistant's speech recognition with the query patterns in the action package and route requests to the fulfillment URL you just specified.

You now need to use the project ID that Assistant gave you when you created the project, and deploy the package. (If you left that page, you can get back to it in the project settings.)

```
$ cd ..
$ gactions update --project exhibit-engine --action_package action.json    ◀──  Updates the project details
$ gactions test --project exhibit-engine --action_package action.json    ◀──
```
**Sets up the action for testing in the simulator inside the Developer Console**

You can now test the app inside the simulator in the Actions on Google Developer Console. Talk directly to the app to get the MAIN intent, or ask for assistance to get the help intent. Just note that until you change the invocation name in the console, any testing will be done with the invocation name "my test app."

In testing, you'll quickly realize that the app, as currently built, can't do much. Indeed, you'll get an error if you even try to respond to the MAIN intent's request for a follow-up. It's time to build more. But first, a brief stop to look at regular expressions.

### 12.4.1  Parsing input with regular expressions

For the bulk of the app we're building, we're receiving—and responding based on—the raw text of the user's request. The app will need to perform specific actions based on different requests. The naïve, but simple way to do this is to check for each possible request.

> **Listing 12.6   Naïve user request matching**

```
input = input.toLowerCase();
                                              Matches these two general "turn on" phrases
if (input === "turn on lights" || input === "turn on the lights") {    ◀──
  turnOnHandler();
} else if (input === "turn off lights" || input === "turn off the lights") {
  turnOffHandler();
} else if (input === "turn on lamp" || input === "turn on the lamp") {    ◀──
  turnOnHandler("lamp");
                                      Matches these two phrases specific to a lamp
}
```
**Matches these two "turn off" phrases**

This is tedious, in constant need of updating, and unlikely to truly cover how people will actually make requests. It will, for example, miss "Turn off all the lights" or "Turn on my lights."

Better coverage will come through looking for specific key phrases within the input.

**Listing 12.7 Matching requests to behavior based on key phrases**

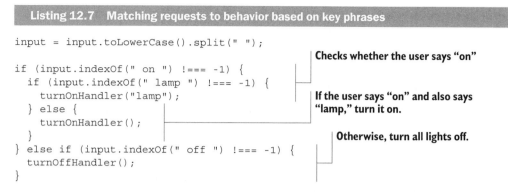

```
input = input.toLowerCase().split(" ");

if (input.indexOf(" on ") !== -1) {          Checks whether the user says "on"
  if (input.indexOf(" lamp ") !== -1) {
    turnOnHandler("lamp");                   If the user says "on" and also says
  } else {                                   "lamp," turn it on.
    turnOnHandler();
  }                                          Otherwise, turn all lights off.
} else if (input.indexOf(" off ") !== -1) {
  turnOffHandler();
}
```

This is better, but still a bit of a mess, especially when looking for arguments, such as "lamp." If you could be certain that the device would always appear in a specific place in the string, it would be easy—just look at the word in the, say, fourth position. But this ignores that sometimes people will say "Turn off the lamp" and other times "Turn off lamp." It further fails if the words we're looking for appear, but don't mean what we expect. For example, the phrase "Turn on all lights except the lamp" would lead to the opposite of what the user wanted.

Regular expressions can be useful. By using regular expressions, we can match patterns a lot more easily than by using a long list of nested conditionals.

**Listing 12.8 Matching requests with regular expressions**

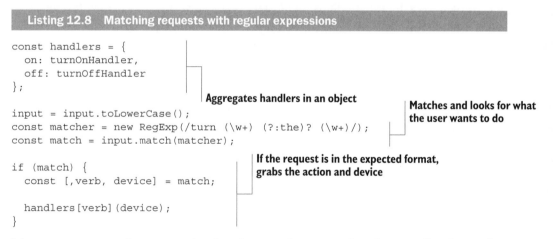

```
const handlers = {
  on: turnOnHandler,
  off: turnOffHandler
};
                                             Aggregates handlers in an object

input = input.toLowerCase();                                  Matches and looks for what
const matcher = new RegExp(/turn (\w+) (?:the)? (\w+)/);      the user wants to do
const match = input.match(matcher);

                                             If the request is in the expected format,
if (match) {                                 grabs the action and device
  const [,verb, device] = match;

  handlers[verb](device);
}
```

It's not necessary to know exactly what that regular expression does yet. Just know that it essentially matches each of the following:

- "Turn on the lights"
- "Turn off the lights"
- "Turn on the lamp"
- "Turn off the lamp"
- "Turn on lights"
- "Turn off lights"

- "Turn on lamp"
- "Turn off lamp"
- "Turn on the bathroom"
- "Turn off the bathroom"
- "Turn out the lights"

It also captures the values of certain parts of the phrases. Trying to approximate a friendlier representation of what we're matching, we could end up with this:

*"turn $verb (the)? $device"*

This looks very similar to the query patterns we built for the voice app, doesn't it?

The app's users will ask for a specific functionality by saying "engage," followed by the functionality name. That name is important, because it will determine how the fulfillment will handle the request. We need to capture that name.

**Listing 12.9    Capturing the functionality name (./functions/index.js)**

```
const functionalityMatcher = new RegExp(/engage (\w+)/);
```

**Any string with "engage" followed by a space and a single word**

This regular expression not only matches the "engage (functionality)" pattern, it also captures the functionality name. The regular expression will match "engage echo" and capture "echo" or "engage calculator" and capture "calculator." It will not match "go go echo" or "engage" on its own. When we compare the regular expression to the user request, we'll have the name regardless of where it appears in the string.

We also expect the name to precede a bridge word, like "to," "and," "for," and "with." These bridge words indicate the separation between the functionality name and what the user wants that functionality to do. The specific word is immaterial to what the functionality will do, so we don't need to capture it. Normally, to match *this* or *that* inside of a string, the best option is to use a capture group, using pipes.

**Listing 12.10    Matching the bridge word (./functions/index.js)**

```
const functionalityMatcher = new RegExp(/engage (\w+) (to|and|for|with)/);
```

**Pipes indicate the expression will match any of the words inside of the parentheses.**

The regular expression here will match "engage," followed by a functionality name, followed by any of the bridge words. The only small problem is that the parentheses we use to mark all the bridge words also form a capturing group that captures the expression and returns it as part of the match. This isn't a significant challenge, but if we have any other capture groups that follow (and we will), unnecessary captures will make keeping track of everything difficult.

This is easy to fix by prepending ?:, which turns a capture group to a group that doesn't capture.

**Listing 12.11  Doesn't capture bridge words (./functions/index.js)**

```
const functionalityMatcher = new RegExp(/engage (\w+) (?:to|and|for|with)/);
```

**Turns the second capture group to a**
**noncapturing group**

The bridge words are now required in order for a request to successfully match, but the expression will not return the bridge as part of the match. Matching this regular expression to what the user said will return `null` if the pattern doesn't match or an array with the functionality name as the second value (the entire request string will be the first item). This is a useful way to test whether the inbound request is something that the fulfillment can handle, and to figure out what functionality the user wants. It's also enough to start building the intent handler.

**Listing 12.12  Matching the functionality name (./functions/index.js)**

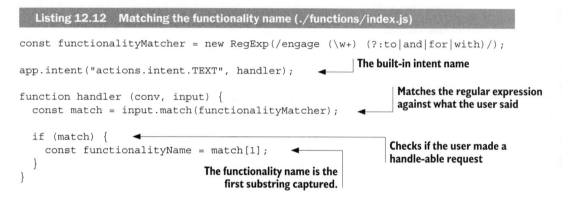

```
const functionalityMatcher = new RegExp(/engage (\w+) (?:to|and|for|with)/);

app.intent("actions.intent.TEXT", handler);          ◀── The built-in intent name

function handler (conv, input) {                          Matches the regular expression
  const match = input.match(functionalityMatcher);    ◀── against what the user said

  if (match) {                                         ◀──
    const functionalityName = match[1];                ◀──   Checks if the user made a
  }                                                           handle-able request
}                        The functionality name is the
                         first substring captured.
```

The matched intent here—`actions.intent.TEXT`—represents the user's request and provides the entire string created from the spoken utterance. When using the Actions SDK, all but the first request in a user–agent conversation will come through a built-in intent, and that's usually going to be `actions.intent.TEXT`. This behavior is confusing for many developers and shows that the Actions SDK is not a good tool for a quickly created app without external NLU. The lack of a robust intent flow, such as we saw with Dialogflow, does not lend itself to fast up-and-go. On the axis of development, with speed on one end and flexibility on the other, we're seeing here a strong bias toward flexibility.

> **NOTE** We aren't using an anonymous function for the handler in listing 12.12, so we can easily reuse the handler for other intents if we desire.

Inside the intent handler in listing 12.12, a couple of things are already happening. The handler checks what the user said against the regular expression to make sure there is a valid request. If the request is valid, the functionality name is pulled from the speech, using the capturing group that matches any word between "engage" and the bridge words. The regular expression, as it is constituted, only allows for single-word functionality names, such as "echo" or "calculator." That's alright. A voice UI needs to be flexible in what it accepts where possible, but sometimes the constraints are such that the conversation must or can be more rigid. This situation fits that. Users will ask for specific functionalities, which are tied to a specific name. The application should train the user in what's possible, and provide a help intent, but it can also expect a higher level of specificity. This is true of other interactions that rely on proper names, too. A baseball fan interacting with a sports application can ask for "Houston" or "the Astros" or even "the 'Stros," but the overall number of options is limited. The application isn't expected to support every nickname ever given a team.

Once the handler has determined that the user is requesting a functionality in the expected manner, and has figured out the name of the functionality, it needs to hand control over to that functionality.

**Listing 12.13   Finding the requested functionality (./functions/index.js)**

**The different functionalities a
user will ask to "engage"**

```
const functionalities = {
  echo: {},          ◄──────    Repeats back what a user asks for
  calculator: {}     ◄────┐
};                        └──  Calculates a numeric value

function handler (conv, input) {
  const match = input.match(functionalityMatcher);

  if (match) {
    const functionalityName = match[1];
    const functionality = functionalities[functionalityName];

    if (functionality) {            Grabs the requested functionality
      //                            object based on its name
    }
  }
}
```

The `functionalities` object exists, essentially, as a store that holds all the information about the functionalities. This is simple, as there are only two functionalities. If the number of functionalities grew significantly, you might want to set up a central repository of functionalities, each with a different name that users could enable and disable, with configuration determining how to handle any requests a user wants from them.

The handler needs to confirm that there's a functionality with the name the user has requested. If there is, it needs to find out what the user wants the functionality to do.

**Listing 12.14   Building the capabilities (./functions/index.js)**

```
const functionalities = {
  echo: {
    matchers: [
      {
        matcher: new RegExp(/(?:repeat|say)(?:ing)? (.+)/),
        name: "RepeaterCapability"
      },
      {
        matcher: new RegExp(/(?:count)(?:ing)?(?: )?(?:up)? to (\d+)/),
        name: "CounterCapability"
      }
    ],
    handlers: {
      RepeaterCapability (conv, slots) {},
      CounterCapability (conv, slots) {}
    }
  },
  calculator: {
    matchers: [
      {
        matcher: new RegExp(/(add|subtract|divide|multiply)(?:ing)? (\d+)
(?:\D+) (\d+)/),
        name: "TwoNumberCapability"
      }
    ],
    handlers: {
      TwoNumberCapability (conv, slots) {}
    }
  }
};
```

Repeats what the users said if they ask for "repeating" or "saying"

Counts up to the requested number

Handles "echo" requests

Performs an operation on two numbers

Handles the two-number capability request

The filled-out `functionalities` object houses the different *capabilities*— what each functionality can do, and the regular expressions corresponding to how a user might ask for them. Remember, regular expressions match patterns, so `(?:count)` `(?:ing)? (?:up)? to (\d+)` will match a number of different utterances. It's once again useful to think of this as collapsing query patterns or sample utterances into a less readable, but more compact, syntax. Each capability has a regular expression to match against, paired with a name, so users can trigger each capability with a range of utterances.

> **NOTE**  Try to write out what each regular expression could match. Do they cover all of the ways a user could make the request?

Each functionality will house one or more capabilities. For example, the "echo" functionality has a "repeater" capability that parrots back what the user says, and a "counter" capability that will count up to a given number. The "calculator" functionality, meanwhile, has a capability that takes two numbers and performs an operation on them.

We can think of these functionalities as a way to organize the capabilities, which is what users ultimately want to do. The capabilities will then *handle* the users' requests through handler functions, which our code calls once it figures out the desired capability's name and matches it to a handler.

**Listing 12.15    Call capability handler (./functions/index.js)**

```
function handler (conv, input) {
  ...

  if (match) {
    ...

    if (functionality) {
      const capability = functionality.matchers.find(capabilityObj => {
        return input.match(capabilityObj.matcher);
      });

      if (capability) {
        const capabilityName = capability.name;

        const handler = functionality.handlers[capabilityName];
        const slotValues = input.match(capability.matcher).slice;

        return handler(conv, slotValues);
      }
    }
  }
};
```

Cycles through all of the matchers for the desired capability based on the user's utterance

If there's a matching capability, grabs the name

Grabs all matched values beyond the first (the entire matched string)

Provides conv and the captured substrings to the handler

Uses the name to find the method that handles it

We're finally getting closer to handling what users want to do. First we're looking through all of the matchers on the functionality to find the first one where what the user said matches what the capability says it will handle. After we find the capability, we take the paired name and use that to find a handler, to which we provide both the conversation object (conv) and the captured substrings.

You can think of these captured substrings as arguments, or slot values. They are the variable pieces of information that can either be constrained, such as the mathematical operation, or entirely open, such as the phrase the user wants repeated. Meanwhile, we provide the conv object so the handler can build and send the response back to the user.

**NOTE** Unlike "normal" Actions SDK arguments, the slot values here aren't named. JavaScript has recently acquired support for named regular expression capture groups, but they are not supported in the current version of Node.js on Firebase Cloud Functions.

All that's left is to fulfill the requests.

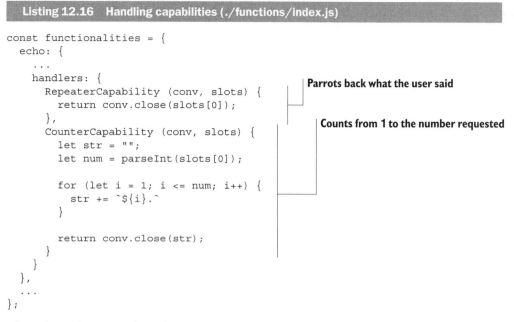

```
const functionalities = {
  echo: {
    ...
    handlers: {
      RepeaterCapability (conv, slots) {
        return conv.close(slots[0]);
      },
      CounterCapability (conv, slots) {
        let str = "";
        let num = parseInt(slots[0]);

        for (let i = 1; i <= num; i++) {
          str += `${i}.`;
        }

        return conv.close(str);
      }
    }
  },
  ...
};
```

**Listing 12.16  Handling capabilities (./functions/index.js)**

Parrots back what the user said

Counts from 1 to the number requested

There is nothing new here in terms of what the SDK can do. The repeater says exactly what the user asked for, and the counter capability takes each number from one to the requested number and counts one by one.

On the VUI side, all three responses end the conversation, because there is no reasonable follow-up expected. All three are taciturn, as well. You will often have to decide between "personality" and efficiency. (Being quiet is a personality trait, but people often mean "outgoing" when they say "personality.") In these situations, efficiency generally wins out. Repeating a phrase, or counting up to a number calls for the action and nothing else. Adding more to the response would be a detriment—the user didn't ask for a conversation here.

> **NOTE**  I'll leave it to you to build the handler for the `TwoNumberCapability`. If you want to compare your result to mine, the code is available on the book's repository.

Now that the code is fully handling the user's request, let's pause and consider what we've built. There are functionalities that contain multiple capabilities, and users invoke them through matchers we've specified. By using the terms "functionalities" and "capabilities," I've been a bit coy, both not to distract from the overall app and to let you come to a conclusion yourself: this is not dissimilar to an application or a skill in its composition. Certainly Google and Amazon are performing NLU that's more complex than simple regular expression matching, but it's a useful mental model to consider. "Apps" or "skills" are our "functionalities," and "actions" are our "capabilities." Query patterns are patterns to match. Slots are like powered-up capture groups. And it all comes together through handlers that build the response.

## 12.4.2 *Handling the unexpected*

What happens when a user wants to "Engage music" or "Engage Echo to sing a song"? Neither of these, and potentially thousands of other unconsidered actions, are supported by the mini-assistant we're building. If you ask Google Home for something unsupported, you'll hear, "I don't know how to answer that." That seems like a good approach for our action, too.

> **Listing 12.17    Handling unexpected requests (./functions/index.js)**

```
function handler (conv, input) {
  ...

  if (match) {
    ...

    if (functionality) {
      ...

      if (capability) {
        ...
      }
    }

    return conv.close("Well, this is awkward. I can't engage that one.");  ◄──  If the user used the expected phrasing
  } else {                                                                       but asked for unsupported behavior
    const response = "Hey, I don't understand. Quick tip. " +
                     "You need to say 'engage' and then what you want. " +
                     "What'll it be?";
    return conv.ask(response);                                                 If the user didn't use the
  }                                                                              expected phrasing
};
```

The responses are different depending on where the failure lies, because the feedback that's most useful to the user is different in each situation.

If there is no match on the initial regular expression, it means the user hasn't formulated the request in the expected way. This calls for a more explicit response that is longer, but that will save the user time in the long term, because it fixes the problem early.

If the user has instead asked for a functionality or a capability that doesn't exist, the response can be shorter, but also notice the language: "I can't *engage* that one." The way an app responds trains the user to use certain language, in short saying, "This is how we speak around here."[1]

> **TIP**  If you truly wanted to be thorough, each functionality could have its own response when a user asks for the correct functionality but a capability doesn't exist. This further highlights to the user what went wrong.

---

[1]  Randy Allen Harris, *Voice Interaction Design: Crafting the New Conversational Speech Systems* (Morgan Kaufmann, 2004).

**NOTE** We've relied on the `actions.intent.TEXT` intent for most of this application. This works just fine for user interaction, but it doesn't allow for the implicit invocation that we saw in previous chapters. For that, you'll need to specify each of the intents inside of the action package. You can handle them the same way through the `actions.intent.TEXT` handler, but users can invoke the action without going through the application if Assistant feels that it's the best action to handle the request.

At this point, you might look back and wonder why someone would use the Actions SDK instead of building an action with Dialogflow. These regular expressions seem constricting, and Dialogflow is much more powerful. The truth is, I used regular expressions for two reasons. The first was to limit the scope of what we examined in this chapter. The second was to understand basic natural language processing. When we built our mini-assistant, we were looking at what the Assistant platform does in another way. There are, though, people who prefer to use the Actions SDK. Generally, they will go this route when they have an NLU tool that they feel works better than Dialogflow. Perhaps it's faster, or they feel that they have more control, or they've tuned it better for their specific situation. Maybe they already had the tool for an existing application with Alexa, Messenger, or elsewhere. If you're happy with Dialogflow, use it. Google is nice for giving us options.

Throughout this chapter, you've not only built an application using the Actions SDK, but you've built a miniature assistant within the application, using regular expressions to parse user intents. Through this, you've seen basic natural language processing. Although regular expressions are not how the NLUs inside Alexa or Dialogflow work exactly, it should give you an insight into how they could match myriad user requests.

## Summary

- The Actions SDK is available for developers who want to build applications with their own NLU.
- The action package establishes the application configuration.
- Regular expressions can parse user requests to find entities and match intents.

# appendix A
# *Adding an AWS IAM profile*

AWS keeps permissions fairly separate, so you will need to add IAM roles to enable the ASK CLI to access other services. This will give the CLI the correct permissions to create the skill fulfillment.

Head to AWS and use the search bar on the console welcome page to find Identity and Access Management (IAM). In the left-hand navigation, select Users, as in figure A.1. On the next page, click Add User, like in figure A.2. As you can see in figure A.3, you will choose any user name you like (such as the name of your local machine) and select both Programmatic Access as well as AWS Management Console Access. You can leave the password as autogenerated and uncheck the box that requires a reset of the password on next login. Finish up on this page by clicking Next.

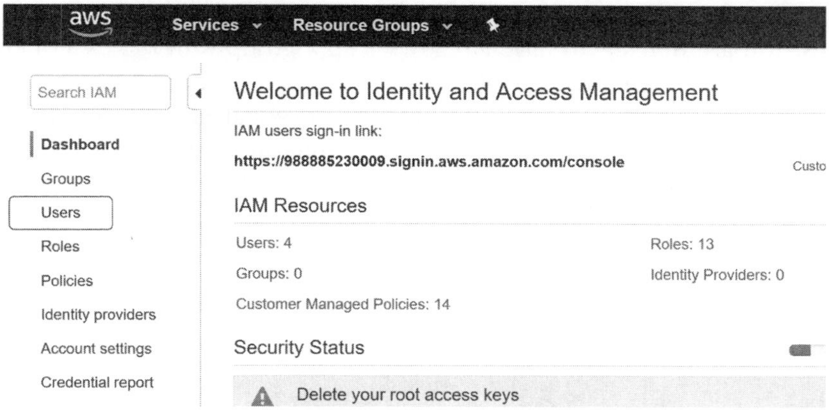

Figure A.1   Click the Users link in the sidebar.

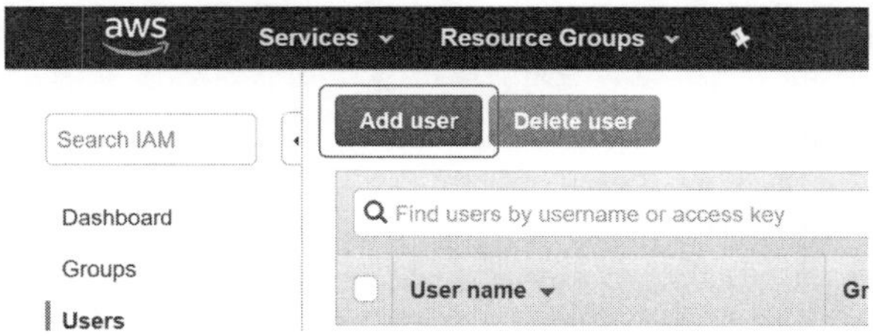

Figure A.2   Click Add User next.

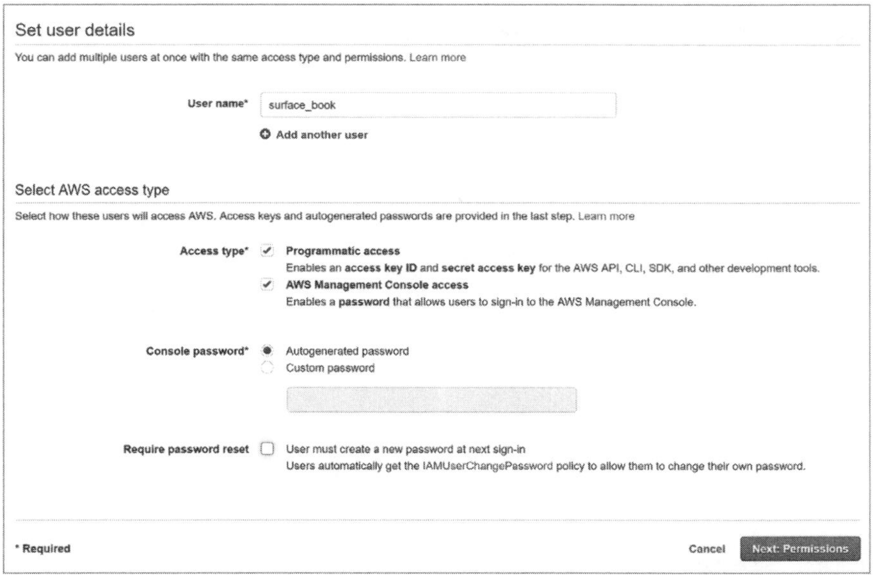

Figure A.3   Provide a name and select both access types.

As you saw when setting up a lambda function, permissions are granted on a granular basis. You are unlikely to have already set up a group with the exact permissions needed, so choose Attach Existing Policies Directly before clicking Create Policy, as in figure A.4. In the next screen, you can either use the visual editor to select permissions one by one, as you see in figures A.5 and A.6, or you can create a policy by providing a JSON object. Do not close the previous tab.

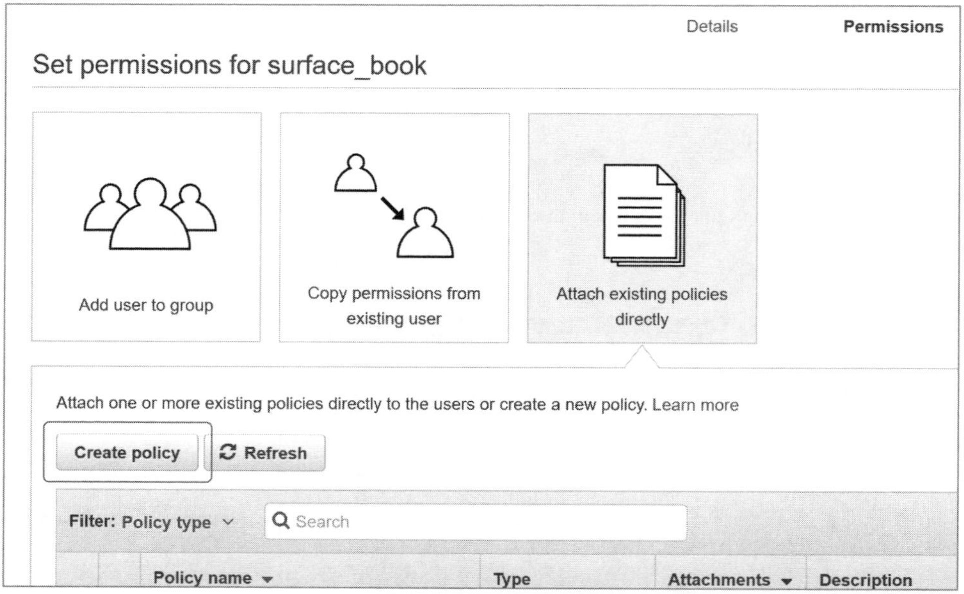

Details    **Permissions**

Set permissions for surface_book

Add user to group

Copy permissions from existing user

Attach existing policies directly

Attach one or more existing policies directly to the users or create a new policy. Learn more

**Create policy**    ⟳ Refresh

Filter: Policy type ⌄    🔍 Search

| Policy name ⌄ | Type | Attachments ⌄ | Description |
|---|---|---|---|

**Figure A.4   Create a policy for the new IAM user.**

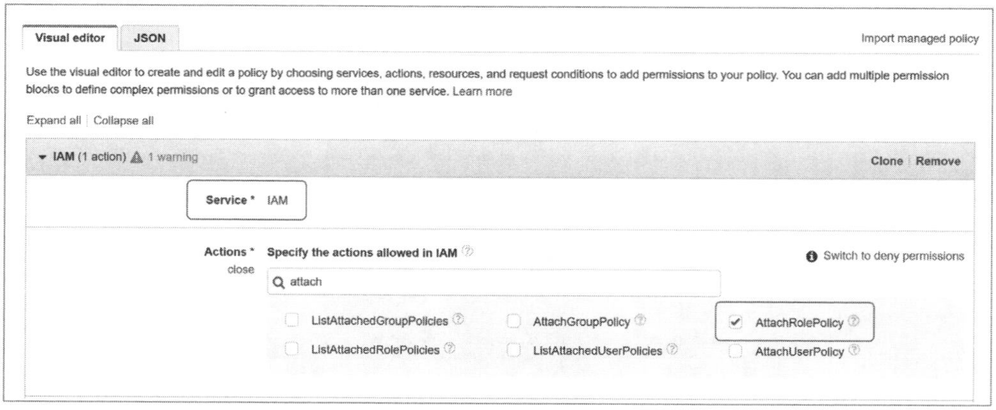

**Visual editor**   JSON                                            Import managed policy

Use the visual editor to create and edit a policy by choosing services, actions, resources, and request conditions to add permissions to your policy. You can add multiple permission blocks to define complex permissions or to grant access to more than one service. Learn more

Expand all | Collapse all

▾ IAM (1 action) ⚠ 1 warning                                      Clone | Remove

Service * IAM

Actions *   Specify the actions allowed in IAM ⑦                      ⓘ Switch to deny permissions
close
🔍 attach

☐ ListAttachedGroupPolicies ⑦    ☐ AttachGroupPolicy ⑦    ☑ AttachRolePolicy ⑦
☐ ListAttachedRolePolicies ⑦     ☐ ListAttachedUserPolicies ⑦   ☐ AttachUserPolicy ⑦

**Figure A.5   Select the service and actions.**

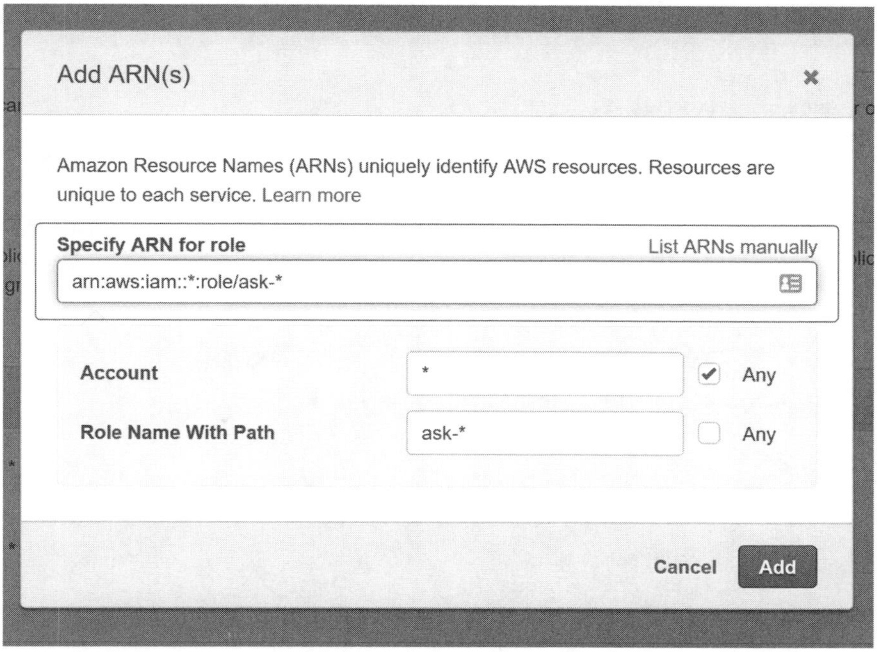

**Figure A.6    Specify the ARN for each role.**

If you choose to use the visual editor, you need to apply each of the permissions in table A.1, all with the Allow effect.

**Table A.1    ASK CLI policy**

| AWS service | Actions | ARN |
|---|---|---|
| IAM (Identity and Access Management) | AttachRolePolicy, CreateRole, GetRole, PassRole | arn:aws:iam::*:role/ask-* |
| Lambda | AddPermission, CreateFunction, GetFunction, ListFunctions, UpdateFunctionCode | arn:aws:lambda:*:*:function:ask-* |
| CloudWatch Logs | DescribeLogStream, FilterLogEvents, GetLogEvents | arn:aws:logs:*:*:log-group:/aws/lambda/ask-* |

Alternatively, you can create your own policy with the following JSON object, providing IAM with a policy name and an optional description.

**Listing A.1    ASK CLI policy JSON**

```
{
  "Version": "2012-10-17",
  "Statement": [
    {
      "Effect": "Allow",            ◄────┐  The permissions in this object are all allowed.
      "Action": [
        "iam:AttachRolePolicy",
        "iam:CreateRole",
        "iam:GetRole",
        "iam:PassRole"
      ],
      "Resource": [                        ┌── For AWS IAM
        "arn:aws:iam::*:role/ask-*"  ◄─────┘
      ]
    },
    {
      "Effect": "Allow",
      "Action": [
        "lambda:AddPermission",
        "lambda:CreateFunction",
        "lambda:GetFunction",
        "lambda:ListFunctions",
        "lambda:UpdateFunctionCode"
      ],
      "Resource": [                              ┌── For AWS Lambda
        "arn:aws:lambda:*:*:function:ask-*"  ◄───┘
      ]
    },
    {
      "Effect": "Allow",
      "Action": [
        "logs:DescribeLogStreams",
        "logs:FilterLogEvents",
        "logs:GetLogEvents"
      ],
      "Resource": [                                         ┌── For Amazon
        "arn:aws:logs:*:*:log-group:/aws/lambda/ask-*"  ◄───┘   Cloudwatch Logs
      ]
    }
  ]
}
```

When you create the new policy, give it a memorable name or note the name that has been generated for you. Go back to the page where you are setting permissions for the new IAM user (this is likely in another tab if you haven't already closed it), click Refresh (see figure A.7), and search for the fresh policy (see figure A.8). Check the box and click Next.

**Figure A.7   After creating the user, you'll need to refresh before finding it.**

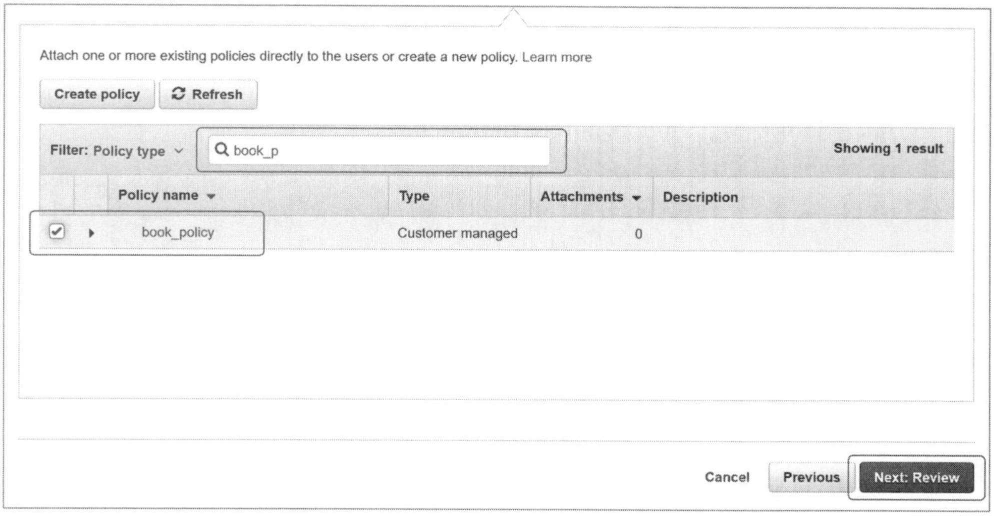

**Figure A.8   Search for and then select the new user.**

If you followed the preceding steps, everything should look good on the next page. Specifically, you'll see the username you created, the Programmatic and AWS Management Console access types, the autogenerated password, no password reset, and the newly created and attached policy.

If it all checks out, confirm and create the user by clicking the button at the bottom. The next page will show you the new user, with access key ID, secret access key, and password. You'll need the first two, as you'll be saving it to a file on your computer.

> **WARNING**   Complete the following steps immediately. The secret access keys must be downloaded or viewed when they are created—if you walk away for dinner and come back to a logged-out account, you will no longer have access to them.

Which file you open next depends on your system. You will likely need to create the .aws directory first.

- On Linux, Mac, or Windows Subsystem for Linux (Bash on Windows): ~/.aws/credentials
- On Windows: %USERPROFILE%\.aws\credentials

Inside the file, add the following while replacing your own values for the access key ID and secret access key:

```
[default]
aws_access_key_id = <YOUR KEY ID HERE>
aws_secret_access_key = <YOUR SECRET ACESS KEY HERE>
```

The [default] syntax notes that this is the default AWS profile for this machine. If you use multiple AWS credentials on a single machine, you can specify these below, separated by a new line with the same syntax, but with the names in place of default.

After setting up all of this, you can go back to skill development with the CLI connected for IAM, Lambda, and Cloudwatch.

# appendix B
# Connecting DynamoDB
# to a Lambda function

Due to the permissions and security model of AWS and Lambda, a function does not automatically have access to DynamoDB. To set that up, you'll need to head back to IAM. (Remember, you can get to any AWS service through the AWS console's search bar.)

From the IAM welcome page, click through to view all of the roles. The ASK CLI created a role specifically for your skill with the name "ask-lambda-" plus the skill name. If you called your skill "super-sleeper," the full role name will be "ask-lambda-super-sleeper."

Not everyone uses DynamoDB in their skill, and security best practices would say not to add permissions until you need them, so the ASK CLI adds only what you always need to run a skill and leaves it up to you to set the DynamoDB permissions yourself. Click through to your skill's role and, from there, follow to Add Inline Policy.

Like you did for the ASK CLI, you can use the policy generator or create a custom policy (through JSON). I'll provide you with the JSON for the custom policy, and if you decide to the use the policy generator, you can use the information in the object to add it manually:

```
{
  "Version": "2012-10-17",
  "Statement": [
    {
      "Effect": "Allow",
```

```
      "Action": [
        "dynamodb:CreateTable",
        "dynamodb:DeleteItem",
        "dynamodb:GetItem",
        "dynamodb:PutItem",
        "dynamodb:UpdateItem"
      ],
      "Resource": [
        "arn:aws:dynamodb:*:*:*"
      ]
    }
  ]
}
```

Add and save that, and the function will now have the ability to create tables and work with items in the table.

# *glossary*

**Action**   For applications on Google Assistant, the combination of intent and fulfillment.

**Dialogflow**   The NLU platform that is most often used with applications on Google Assistant.

**Dialog management**   The interaction in which either the fulfillment or the voice platform requests and confirms slot values, or confirms an overall intent.

**Discourse markers**   Words and short phrases that connect thoughts together. Used when speaking to express such concepts as clarifying, elaborating, or reinforcing. Examples include "well," "as I was saying," and "in conclusion."

**Entity**   A piece of information embedded within a natural language request. These can also be thought of as *on what* or *with what* a user wants to perform an action. In the request "What is the time of the baseball game in Houston today?" we might find the entities "baseball" and "Houston" denoting entities for sport and city, respectively.

**Entity resolution**   A way to resolve ambiguous entity values. On the Alexa platform, entity resolution is used to match synonyms and match common misunderstandings.

**Fulfillment**   The code that handles a user's request in voice applications.

**Implicit invocation**   When a user invokes a Google Assistant action without specifying an invocation name. Assistant determines which action can handle the request best and sends the request along.

**Intent**   What a user wants to do in a request. An application will have multiple intents, and each intent can have multiple entities but doesn't need to have any.

**Interaction model**   Where the developer defines how the user will interact with a voice application, including intents, training phrases, and entity values.

**Invocation name**   The name with which users invoke a skill or action. "Alexa, ask Baseball Scores how the Astros did last night" has an invocation name of "Baseball Scores." Similar to domain names, invocation names are unique for applications on Google Assistant but not on Alexa.

**Natural language processing (NLP)**   When a computer can interact with natural languages, such as English, Hindi, or Latin.

**Natural language understanding (NLU)**   When software takes natural language and extracts meaning from it, such as entities or intents.

**NLP**   See *natural language processing.*

**NLU**   See *natural language understanding.*

**Parameters**   How Dialogflow refers to slots. See *slot.*

**Sample utterances**   The developer-defined phrases that map to an intent on the Alexa platform. See *training phrases.*

**Skill**   A voice application on the Alexa platform.

**Slot**   The specific place within a sample utterance where the NLU should expect an entity value. The fulfillment receives the values extracted as *slot values.*

**Slot filling**   See *dialog management.*

**Speech Synthesis Markup Language (SSML)**   XML to mark up speech and adjust the pitch, rate, volume, or pronunciation.

**Training phrases**   Phrases that application developers expect users to use when interacting with a voice application. The training phrases are used to improve the speech recognition and train the natural language understanding.

**Voice added**   Voice interactions where voice is additive, and users can use other input or output just as easily. The primary example of situations where voice-added interactions occur is on smart phones. Voice-added interactions give the most precise input and the most expansive output.

**Voice first**   Voice interactions where voice is the primary input and output, but is paired with other media. Example devices that rely on this interaction type range from an Amazon Echo or Google Home (with the lights on the top of the device) to the Echo Show or Google Home Hub. Voice-first interactions can provide or accept more information than voice-only interactions, but not as much as with voice added.

**Voice only**   Voice interactions where voice is the only input and output. An example voice-only interaction is on headphones with voice controls. Voice-only interactions are less precise in both input and output than other interactions.

# *index*